WILLIAM L. BULKLEY
1861-1933

WILLIAM L.BULKLEY
1861-1933

AFRICAN AMERICAN
EDUCATOR AND REFORMER

Peggy W. Norris

New Elmwood Press

New Elmwood Press
Elmwood Park, NJ 07407
newelmwoodpress@gmail.com
© 2022 Peggy W. Norris

ISBN: 979-8-9858424-0-1 (paper)
ISBN: 979-8-9858424-1-8 (ebook)

Publisher's Cataloging-in-Publication Data
provided by Five Rainbows Cataloging Services

Names: Norris, Peggy W., 1949- author.
Title: William L. Bulkley, 1861-1933 : African American educator and reformer / Peggy W. Norris.
Description: Elmwood Park, NJ : New Elmwood Press, 2022. | Includes bibliographical references and index.
Identifiers: LCCN 2022904494 (print) | ISBN 979-8-9858424-0-1 (paperback) | ISBN 979-8-9858424-1-8 (ebook)
Subjects: LCSH: African Americans--Biography. | African American teachers--Biography. | African American teachers and the community. | National Association for the Advancement of Colored People--Biography. | National Urban League--Biography. | African Americans--Civil rights—History. | Educational change. | BISAC: BIOGRAPHY & AUTOBIOGRAPHY / Cultural, Ethnic & Regional / African American & Black. | BIOGRAPHY & AUTOBIOGRAPHY / Educators.
Classification: LCC LC2803.W3 N67 2022 (print) | LCC LC2803.W3 (ebook) | DDC 371.1/04--dc23.

CONTENTS

William L. Bulkley

NUL: 40th Anniversary Year Book, 1950

ILLUSTRATIONS

FOREWARD

It was a hot, sunny day several years ago when Peggy W. Norris, her husband, Joe, and I walked on a sandy path into Cedars Cemetery in Camden, South Carolina. We were on a quest to find the grave of Reverend Vincent Henry Bulkley (1835-1886). Bulkley, who had served in the Methodist Episcopal Church in South Carolina since 1867, had moved to Camden in 1884 to continue his church work. He had already reached several of life's milestones. His wife, Madora, had given him a son, William Lewis, and he had made it his mission to help his son and other young African Americans in the state get an education through his work as a trustee of Claflin University in Orangeburg, South Carolina. Reverend Bulkley's life ended in 1886, but by the time of his death his son William Lewis had already begun his own unique trajectory, one that would lead him not only to become the first person of African origin in the United States to earn a doctorate in a classical language, but also to help found the National Urban League and the NAACP.

With the tenacity of a skillful and determined sleuth, Peggy Norris has given us a detailed account of the life of Reverend Bulkley's remarkable son, Dr. William Lewis Bulkley. Dr. Bulkley took his first breath on March 23, 1861 and after a lifetime of work dedicated to racial uplift in the United States died in Nice, France, on August 5, 1933. And so since I cannot go to the coast of France, it seems fitting to return to Cedars Cemetery on the 161st anniversary of Dr. Bulkley's birth and pay my respects to the father who in so many ways paved the way for his son.

Michele Valerie Ronnick
March 23, 2022
Camden, South Carolina

ACKNOWLEDGEMENTS

Many people have encouraged me, provided insights, and contributed special knowledge, skills, and understanding. Thanks are due to Neal Brunson, who first asked me about Bulkley, the only signer of the NAACP call from New Jersey. Professor Michele Valerie Ronnick of Wayne State University supported my work from the beginning. Her insights into his classical education and its importance were invaluable. Librarians and archivists have always been and remain invaluable in providing resources and guidance. I thank them all. I would particularly like to thank David Ment at the New York Municipal Archives, Debbie Bloom, Richland Public Library, Columbia, SC, Mark Shenise of the General Commission on Archives and History of the United Methodist Church, and the staffs of the archives at Columbia University, New York University, the Schomburg Library, Wesleyan University, and Syracuse University. I also owe a debt of gratitude to the librarians at the Ridgewood Public Library who ordered innumerable articles and books from other libraries for me. I would like to acknowledge the Bulkley descendants and relatives who supported my research and enriched my life: Melvin Bulkley, Denise de Murcie, Rovena Owens, and John Bulkley Ross. I also owe a debt of gratitude to all my friends who supported me over these twenty years but most especially to my husband, Joe Suplicki, who supported my research and, without complaint, made photocopies, read microfilms, traveled with me, and read numerous drafts. Thank you to Marion T. Brown for preparation of the images and Libby Norris for the cover design.

INTRODUCTION

William L. Bulkley was born in South Carolina in 1861, weeks before the start of the Civil War. He lived the American dream, rising from poverty to become a cosmopolitan, educated, contributing citizen. He lived through huge changes in life for African Americans. In his youth slavery ended and Reconstruction brought civic and political opportunities to African Americans. However, as he came to adulthood, Reconstruction ended, violence against Black people increased, opportunities were limited, and "Black codes" restricting African Americans were enacted. How did he go on to excel and make contributions? How did he make choices about his family, about how and where his children should be raised and educated? What really happened in his life? Gradually I pieced together the story of this man who, despite being very capable and accomplished, has been nearly lost to history.

Bulkley achieved what few others of his generation did. He was the fourth African American to earn a PhD, an educational leader, and the first African American high school principal of a predominantly white school in the New York City school system. He founded the Committee for Improving the Industrial Condition of the Negro in New York, an organization that preceded both the NAACP and the National Urban League. He was a critical early leader of all three organizations. Bulkley was an eloquent speaker and writer. William Edward Burghardt (W. E. B.) Du Bois called him "a fine man" in 1906.[1] Seven decades later Parris and Brooks characterized him as "a giant in his time."[2] In 2001 David Levering Lewis described him as "awesomely capable."[3] In 2013 Susan Carle wrote, "The long-forgotten activist William Lewis Bulkley, like many others, deserves renewed historical attention."[4] More than a century after he was recognized as a pioneer and leader, it is time to tell William Lewis Bulkley's story and to begin to incorporate that story into the narrative of American history.

Unfortunately, Bulkley left only a few letters in collections of some of the people he wrote to. There are no personal papers. On the other hand, over a period of thirty years he wrote a number of articles and speeches that were published in journals and newspapers. His activities are also reflected in minutes, letters, and documents of the organizations he worked for. These documents portray a man who was dedicated, passionate, thoughtful, and earnest. He railed against injustice and worked hard to support education and jobs for African Americans.

Bulkley's biography is based on research in archives from Syracuse, New York, to Greenville, South Carolina, and on newspapers, public records, published articles, and a knowledge of the places and times he lived in. The book opens with a discussion of his early years in South Carolina. The next two chapters cover pivotal events in 1890: a lynching, a speech, and an assault against a professor. Chapter IV describes his last decade in South Carolina and his voyage to Europe for a year's post-doctoral education. His educational and civil rights activities in his New York years are discussed separately in Chapters V and VI. Chapter VII considers the latter part of his career as educator and reformer. Chapter VIII looks at his withdrawal from activism and his intellectual and family life. Chapter IX examines his personal values, the movements that influenced him, and his legacy. Extensive endnotes are provided for the researcher interested in pursuing more information or constructing a different interpretation.

Bulkley not only played a major role in the early civil rights movement but also led a life that illuminates the opportunities and struggles of an African American man during some very difficult decades. This portrait rescues him from obscurity and opens the opportunity to examine his contributions to the early twentieth-century civil rights movement and to follow the life of a man whose photograph could hang on the wall for decades and never be recognized by his descendants as that of a Black man.

ABBREVIATIONS

AME	African Methodist Episcopal
CIICNNY	Committee for Improving the Industrial Condition of the Negro in New York
CUCAN	Committee on Urban Conditions Among Negroes
NAACP	National Association for the Advancement of Colored People
NYAPCW	New York Association for the Protection of Colored Women
NLPCW	National League for the Protection of Colored Women
NLUCAN	National League on Urban Conditions Among Negroes
NUL	National Urban League
YMCA	Young Men's Christian Association
YWCA	Young Women's Christian Association

William L. Bulkley
Fifty Years in Brooklyn, 1903

William L. Bulkley
Carlton Avenue Branch

Mary Fisher Carroll Bulkley
Private collection

I

THE TRIUMPH OF
PERSEVERANCE

W. L. Bulkley: A noble example of the triumph of perseverance [5]

William Lewis Bulkley was born in 1861, in Greenville, South Carolina. From very humble beginnings he achieved what few other African Americans of his generation did—a PhD, a career as a teacher and school principal, and a role in moving the civil rights agenda forward. This was not by accident.

> The parents of William Lewis, having "tasted of the Pierian spring," had a consuming desire that at least their eldest son should "drink deep," and began by sending him to school at a very early age. [6]

The family had a legacy of education. They were a free family, but for much of the nineteenth century, education for Black people was severely controlled or forbidden. In 1834 a law banned free people of color from educating enslaved or free persons. [7] However, education took place in homes, churches, and hidden schools; in 1850, 99 percent of free African Americans in Charleston could read. [8]

The Bulkley family also had a legacy of freedom. William's grandfather, Henry Bulkley, was on the tax rolls in 1832 paying the capitation tax required of all free people of color. He and his family lived with several other free African American families on Sullivan's Island, situated at the mouth of Charleston harbor, where Henry was a carpenter.

Free People of Color

In South Carolina there was a small population of free people of color, most of whom lived in the Charleston area. In 1840, of the 594,398 people living in South Carolina, 43 percent were free white people, 55 percent were enslaved Africans, and 1.4 percent were free people of color. [9]

The relationships between white southerners and free people of color were complex. [10] Social class was based on economic status, "condition" (slave or free), and color (Black, mixed race, or white). People with varying degrees of freedom and economic success occupied the space between people enslaved on plantations and the wealthy plantation owners. Some slaves were hired out by their owners and had some freedom of movement within the city. There were free African Americans who were barely surviving. A few of the most desperate actually petitioned to be returned to slavery for their own survival or to be reunited with family members. There was a free African American elite, some of whom were the wealthiest of any color in the city of Charleston. Some free Black people enslaved others, who may have been family members who could not be freed, but they also enslaved people to enrich their own economic status. William Ellison, a cotton gin maker, [11] Betsey Walker, a pastry cook, [12] and Samuel Weston, a tailor, [13] owned enslaved people who were not family members. The wealthy elite were businessmen who owned property and interacted with the white elite of the city and in many ways identified with them. In 1792 members of the wealthy multiracial elite formed the Brown Fellowship Society, a burial and benevolent society, to provide a social safety net and a decent burial for their members, who were required to be "brown" (light-skinned). [14] Most free people of color were laborers or made their living at a trade. Henry and V. H. Bulkley, William's grandfather and father, were carpenters.

From colonial times "Black codes" were enacted to control free people of color and limit the growth of the community. In 1792 a capitation tax of two dollars was imposed on every adult person of color between the ages of sixteen and fifty. It was in effect for the next seventy years.[15] In 1820 the South Carolina legislature enacted legislation that banned manumissions (except as an act of the legislature), barred immigration of free Black people from other states, and denied South Carolina African Americans the right of return if they left the state. Despite these laws there were opportunities for freedom across color, condition, and status, particularly in the short period between 1815 and 1822, when the African Methodist Episcopal (AME) Church existed in Charleston.

In 1822 Denmark Vesey planned a rebellion of free Black and enslaved people in Charleston. After the aborted plot, laws were passed that outlawed African American churches and banned slaves from hiring out their own time. In Charleston slaves hired out by their owners were required to wear tags when they were not on their owner's premises. All free African American men over fifteen were required to have a white guardian. Some of these laws were enforced capriciously. For example, free Black people routinely chose not to have white guardians.[16]

As America moved toward the crisis of the Civil War, southern states grappled with the rights and role of free African Americans. In the Dred Scott decision of 1857, the Supreme Court ruled that African Americans were not citizens and did not enjoy the protection of the Constitution but were property. In October 1859 John Brown's raid on Harper's Ferry, Virginia, increased Southern white fears of a slave rebellion. That year a bill was introduced into the South Carolina legislature to enslave all free African Americans as of March 1860. Although the bill did not pass the legislature, the threat was clear. In October 1858 and again in December 1859 Charleston police arrested free persons of color for failure to pay the capitation tax. They also made arrests for violation of slave badge laws. Free persons of color were swept up in this crackdown because they could not prove their free status.[17] Today the state maintains the records with which people can prove their identity. In nineteenth-century South Carolina birth and marriage were not officially documented. Manumission by will (before 1820) may have been otherwise undocumented. Some slaves took or were granted their free status with no paperwork or legal structure at all. Children of free women were born free, but that status, too, was undocumented. Free people had difficulty proving they were free.

It is not known how the Bulkleys attained their freedom. The only documentation they may have had was their enrolment on the tax lists for the capitation tax. If the Bulkleys had no proof of their freedom, they were vulnerable to being captured and enslaved.

Vincent Henry Bulkley

William's father, Vincent Henry (V. H.), was born on Sullivan's Island in 1835 to Henry Bulkley and Mary Peters. He learned carpentry and to read and write, but likely had no documents to prove his freedom. In 1859, at the age of twenty-four, he moved to Greenville, South Carolina. Maybe his freedom would be safer there.

Greenville is in the hilly piedmont of South Carolina, on the falls of the Reedy River and 200 miles northwest of Charleston. Early industries included grist, textile and paper mills, and a large carriage factory. The Greenville and Columbia railroad was completed in 1853,[18] connecting the city to Charleston and setting the stage for economic and cultural growth. The railroad brought banking services to Greenville and a new courthouse, three churches, and two colleges. The population of Greenville was far different than that of Charleston. It was a small town of 1,500, about seventy of whom were free African Americans.[19] Countywide there was a smaller proportion of slaves in Greenville than in Charleston, and each slaveholder owned fewer slaves. The economy was based on both farming and manufacturing. Greenville also was a popular summering place for people from the Low Country. In addition to its distance from

Charleston's racial tensions, Greenville may have been attractive to Vincent for its opportunities for carpentry work. On December 24, 1859, he married Madora Wilson, a seamstress who had been raised in Greenville.[20] Her adoptive mother was Margaret Walker, a free African American seamstress who owned her own home and had come to Greenville from Charleston in 1848. Her mother was Betsey Walker, free African American pastry cook mentioned above.[21]

The following year, 1860, brought increased tensions throughout the country. On December 20, 1860, after Abraham Lincoln was elected president, South Carolina seceded from the Union. Lincoln was inaugurated on March 4, 1861. On March 23 William Lewis Bulkley was born in Greenville in "a humble but neat cabin" heated with an open fireplace.[22] On April 12 troops in Charleston fired on the federal forces at Fort Sumter in Charleston Harbor, and the Civil War began.

The men of Greenville, traditionally a Unionist stronghold, were slow to join the Confederate forces but eventually mustered fifteen companies. The textile mills and carriage factory were used to produce shirting and wagons for the Confederacy. In 1862 South Carolina established the State Military Works at Greenville to manufacture and repair small arms. It operated until the end of the war.[23] As the need for labor in the war industries increased, free African Americans became the target of both state and Confederate laws conscripting them into service on the home front. They were not wanted in the army. Although Vincent was a carpenter, he was impressed into service, stocking guns and manufacturing shoes for the war effort.[24]

With the Union victory, previously unimaginable opportunities opened for V. H. Bulkley.

> Having felt for years the call of God to the work of the
> ministry, and being a daily witness of the barbarisms of slavery
> and the degradation of the slaves, his heart often yearned to
> mitigate their bondage and relieve the tedium of the tread-mill

by administering to the famishing multitudes of our people the word of eternal life.[25]

In 1865 Vincent returned to Charleston to enroll in the newly established Baker Theological Institute. He studied there for six terms; thus began a long career in the ministry serving congregations all across upper South Carolina.

Vincent's religious life had begun in 1852 when he was converted in Charleston's Old Trinity Methodist Church. Both enslaved and free Black people were members of churches organized and run by white people. African Americans had their own services or joined the white people for service, forced to sit in the back and in the galleries. African American evangelists Samuel Weston and Henry Cardozo, both tailors, conducted services and classes in the "Old Trinity Basement," a Methodist Episcopal church. Weston, Cardozo, and Bulkley labored their whole lives in the Methodist Church in service of their people and remained lifelong friends. Vincent may have received some of his early education through the church.[26]

The Methodist Episcopal Church played such an important role in both Vincent's and William's stories that it is worth taking a brief look at its history. Slavery was an issue from the beginning. In 1796 the Methodist Episcopal Church noted "the great evil of the African slavery which still exists in these United States" and promulgated rules to prohibit slave-owners from membership. [27] However, General Conferences (the governing body of the Methodist church, which convened every four years) struggled with the issue of slavery for the next four decades. In 1844 the General Conference ruled that a slave-holding bishop must "desist from the exercise of his office so long as this impediment [slave ownership] remains."[28] Methodist churches in slaveholding states (except Maryland and Delaware) withdrew and formed the Methodist Episcopal Church, South. The Methodist churches in the South continued to have Black members who had subordinate roles and/or separate services and meetings, and the Methodist Episcopal Church had no presence in South Carolina until the Civil War. Northern Methodist missionaries and the Freedmen's Aid Society of the Methodist Episcopal Church followed the Union troops as they moved into southern towns.

The mandate of the General Conference of 1864 was to organize mission conferences, include newly freed people in the church, and encourage "Colored pastorates for Colored people." [29] The Baker Theological Institute, the first theological institution for African Americans in America, was formed in Charleston at the first meeting of the new South Carolina Methodist Conference in April 1866.[30] It was here that V. H. Bulkley took up his calling, leaving his wife and child in Greenville, to start a career in the Church. In 1867 he was appointed by the South Carolina Methodist Episcopal Mission Conference to the church in Greenville. His ministry was itinerant, so he preached to congregations throughout the county. It was into this family committed to God, to education, and to service among the African Americans of South Carolina that William Lewis was born.

Two of his great-grandparents were a white man from France, Vincent Peter,[i] and an enslaved woman, Betsy, born in Africa. They lived as a married couple on Sullivan's Island. Since Betsy was enslaved, her children were also legally enslaved. Vincent manumitted them each as they were born. He also provided in his will that Betsy should never be sold and "should be treated by them [the children] with every attention and care in their power."[31] Mary Peters, the daughter of Vincent and Betsy, married Henry Bulkley. Henry. is described in census reports as "Mulatto" (mixed-race), but nothing is known of his parentage. Henry and Mary are William Bulkley's paternal grandparents. Bulkley's maternal grandparents are unknown, but his mother is also described as "Mulatto" in the censuses. Thus, Bulkley is a man of mixed race. When looking at William Bulkley's

---

[i] Vincent went by the surname Peter, and his descendants all went by Peters.

photograph, it is not necessarily apparent he is a Black man. He was of indeterminate race. Yet he lived his life as a Black man.

Early Education

William's education had inauspicious beginnings. After the war schools for African Americans labored under tremendous difficulties. South Carolina did not have free public schooling, and what public moneys were allocated usually went to white schools. Northern religious and philanthropic organizations and the federal Freedmen's Bureau provided some teachers and money for buildings, but there was not enough to meet reasonable standards.

However, the freedmen saw education as the way forward out of poverty and into acceptance in society. Horace Mann Bond described this era:

> At no time or place in America has there been exemplified so pathetic a faith in education as the lever of racial progress. Grown men studied their alphabets in the fields. . . . Mothers tramped scores of miles to towns where they could place their children in school. . . . No mass movement has been more in the American tradition than the urge which drove Negroes toward education soon after the Civil War.[32]

In 1866, without support from the church or the government, Charles Hopkins, a former slave from Charleston and a lay preacher, established a school in Greenville. The school was first held in a room in an abandoned hotel. To create a permanent school, Hopkins raised money from the local community, bought a building from the defunct State Military Works, dismantled it, and rebuilt it on a leased lot with the labor of a large group of freedmen. In fall 1866, 106 pupils were registered.[33] This was the school where William learned to read and cipher.

> [Bulkley's] earliest recollections of school life are a poor frame building, with an old, gray-haired Negro schoolmaster, who had picked up a little "larnin' 'fo' de wah." The curriculum in

this institution was a Webster's blue-back speller (a species fast becoming extinct). The magic wand that made the pupils look studious and "wondrous wise" was a well-grown hickory switch, an article that was neither an ornament or a mere scarecrow, as the back of more than one dullard can testify. In fact, that period of life was to William "the reign of terror."[34]

The Freedmen's Bureau, established by the United States Congress in 1865, was charged with aiding the freed slaves in establishing new lives. The Bureau supported education, supervised labor contracts, and provided food and transportation to those with no resources. Between 1865 and 1870 the Freedmen's Bureau established 4,239 schools, employed 9,307 teachers, and instructed 247,333 students.[35]

The Freedmen's Bureau assigned John William De Forest, formerly an adjutant-general of the Veteran Reserve Corps and a professor of chemistry, as its agent for the three upper counties of South Carolina, including Greenville. He arrived in Greenville in fall 1866 and described the town:

> In population and wealth Greenville was then the third town in South Carolina, ranking next after Charleston and Columbia. It boasted an old and a new courthouse, four churches and several chapels, a university (not the largest in the world), a female college (also not unparalleled), two or three blocks of stores, one of the best country hotels then in the South, quite a number of comfortable private residences, fifteen hundred whites and a thousand or so of other colors.[36]

In 1874 the educational opportunities in Greenville improved. The South Carolina Conference of the Methodist Episcopal Church appointed Rev. Lewis M. Dunton, a white New Yorker who had moved south for his health, as pastor of the church in Greenville. (V. H. Bulkley was now presiding elder for the district.) Dunton also took charge of the school and increased the enrollment to 500 pupils. The educational horizons for thirteen-year-old William began to broaden. He later wrote about his introduction to the learning that Dunton brought to the school:

> I remember when this boy [himself] began the study of Latin and algebra 17 years ago, what a stir there was in the town. . . . Well; when the teacher put that boy into algebra and Latin they all said, "Humph! Jes think of it." They declared it "no use! No use. He'll never learn it." . . . I remember that boy as ambitious to learn, yet always feeling the effects of poverty. I remember how he said, "If others can, I can. Yes, I will."[37]

Determination and ambition propelled Bulkley forward through these years, which also provided a foundation in the piety and devotion in the Methodist tradition:

> When he [Martin Luther in a play] was gathered with his beautiful little family at evening prayer and together they sang so softly, so sweetly, so innocently, so trustfully, my mind was carried back over the years to my boyhood. I could see myself with the others gathered about our family altar and hear the voice of my sainted father singing with the rest of us: "If swift death this night o'ertake us, And our couch become our tomb, May the morn in heaven awake us, Clad in light and deathless bloom."[38]

In January 1877 William's father was assigned as presiding elder for the Columbia District and moved his family to Columbia, capital of South Carolina. Bulkley, now sixteen, enrolled in the University of South Carolina for the spring term.[39] The university had been teaching Black students since 1873 and was the only state-supported southern university to fully integrate in the nineteenth century. His first-term grades were a sixty-five in Natural and Mechanical Philosophy and an eighty-one in Evidences of Christianity. In July 1877, after Bulkley's first term, the white-dominated legislature closed the university. When it reopened in 1880, African Americans were barred from attending. The University of South Carolina finally desegregated in 1963.[40] Bulkley needed another university where he could pursue his advanced education. "If others can, I can. Yes, I will."[41] Nothing was holding him back.

Classical Studies

Higher education in America in the nineteenth century bore little resemblance to our system of education today. Before the Civil War a college degree was a preliminary step for a man to take his place in the upper levels of America's economic and cultural life. Study of classical languages, literature, and history was part of the best degrees. Schools that had traditionally been places to get a classical education based on the study of ancient languages and texts had already begun to become multipurpose institutions that followed a classical course but added preparatory departments and alternate bachelor's degrees (science, philosophy). Many functioned at the level of the high schools and community colleges of today. [42] In both the Southern and New England traditions, higher education produced gentlemen with "solid American values: honesty, morality, responsibility, industry, thrift, ingenuity, and, of course, religiosity."[43]

Claflin University in Orangeburg, South Carolina, was founded as one of these multipurpose institutions. It attempted to address the needs of the freedmen with the academic model at hand. Although a classical education might seem ill-suited from our twenty-first century perspective, it provided a solid foundation that not only challenged and broadened the intellect but also put the graduate on an equal footing with their white peers. Claflin University's catalog described its classical studies as suited to the development of "proper and effective expression of thought."[44] Bulkley's education contributed to his ability to speak eloquently, write with precision and passion, think in the context of history, and continue to explore the world with an intellectual curiosity that informed his action, speaking, and writing.

In the nineteenth century many people felt that people of African descent were not human. Others might have acknowledged their humanity but felt that they did not have the intellectual capability to function as full citizens. Alexander Crummell, at the end of his life, spoke about an experience he had as a young man.

A distinguished illustration of this ignoble sentiment can be given. In the year 1833 or 4 the speaker [Crummell] was an errand boy in the Anti-slavery office in New York City. On a certain occasion he heard a conversation between the Secretary and two eminent lawyers from Boston,—Samuel E. Sewell and David Lee Child. They had been to Washington on some legal business. While at the Capitol they happened to dine in the company of the great John C. Calhoun, then senator from South Carolina. It was a period of great ferment upon the question of Slavery, States' Rights, and Nullification; and consequently the Negro was the topic of conversation at the table. One of the utterances of Mr. Calhoun was to this effect—"That if he could find a Negro who knew the Greek syntax, he would then believe that the Negro was a human being and should be treated as a man." [45]

Learning Greek and Latin was a hallmark of an educated man—of men with power. To gain respect and an equal footing, African Americans needed the same education. They took it wherever they could: Harvard, Oberlin, Claflin, Wilberforce, Atlanta. Many of the early Black classicists became the Latin and Greek teachers of the next generation. Bulkley was a member of the American Philological Association (now the Society for Classical Studies) from 1895 to 1900, taking his place among other African American classical scholars such as Richard T. Greener and William Sanders Scarborough. [46]

Many of Bulkley's associates in education and activism were classical scholars. William H. Crogman (1841–1931) taught at Claflin from 1870 to 1873 and profiled Bulkley in his book, *Progress of a Race*. He later taught Greek for forty years at Clark University. [47] Richard T. Greener (1844–1922), a graduate of Harvard University, was a professor at the University of South Carolina when Bulkley was there. Greener was a professor, lawyer, public servant, and diplomat. [48] William S. Scarborough (1852–1926) had a master's degree from Oberlin and was a professor in the classical department at Wilberforce University and its president.[49] Bulkley and he shared speaking platforms and committee memberships. W. E. B. Du Bois (1868–1963) studied classics at Fisk, Harvard, and the University of Berlin. He was an author, activist, intellectual, and the editor of the NAACP's *Crisis*.[50] He and Bulkley were close associates during the early days of the NAACP. After many years in the fight for civil rights, Du Bois still saw the power of the classics. He wrote, "Fill the heads of these children with Latin and Greek and highfalutin' notions of rights and political power, and hell will be to pay."[51]

Claflin University

Claflin University was founded in 1869 under the auspices of the Freedmen's Aid Society of the Methodist Episcopal Church, with the assistance of Lee Claflin and his son William of Massachusetts. Lee Claflin was an abolitionist who was concerned about the social and religious welfare of the freedmen and provided the money to T. Willard Lewis to found the Baker Theological Institute. William Claflin continued his support of Baker and of Claflin University, which was named after the father. The University's mission was to provide schooling for African Americans, including many newly freed slaves, from primary through university level. A student, adult or child, could learn to read, learn a trade, or obtain a classical college education. At one time it was the only high school for Black people in South Carolina, and it remained the outstanding African American educational institution in South Carolina for many years. The administration and faculty were primarily white, although those paid by the Methodist Freedmen's Aid Society were often African Americans. Claflin has been described as "an oasis of white and Black social equality,"[52] but Gore writes that the hiring of Caucasian teachers and administrators "sowed the seed of a problem which in time would germinate, take root, and grow large enough to demand recognition and a remedy."[53] This set the stage for the explosive events of spring 1890. (See Chapters III.) Eventually the racial tensions resulted in the split of Claflin University and Claflin College of Agriculture (formed as the South

Carolina Agricultural College and Mechanics Institute[ii]). It wasn't until 1922 that the first Black president, Joseph B. Randolph, was appointed.

When the charter of the University was approved by the state of South Carolina on December 18, 1869, the size of the board was increased by seven members nominated by the South Carolina Mission Conference of the Methodist Episcopal Church. V. H. Bulkley was elected a trustee in June 1870 and remained a trustee until his death in 1886.[54] The charter mandated that no instructor "shall ever be required by the Trustees to have any particular complexion or to profess any particular religious opinions as a test of office and no student shall be refused admission to or denied on account of race, complexion, or religious opinions."[55]

At its founding Claflin consisted of the Preparatory Department (elementary education), the Normal Department (for the training of teachers), the Baker Theological Department (for the training of ministers), and the College Proper, the classical course of study. It was ten years before there was a graduate of the Normal Department (S. Eugenie Middleton in 1879) and thirteen years before the first students graduated from the College Proper (Bulkley and Nathaniel H. Middleton in 1882).

The federal Morrill Land-Grant Act of 1862 provided land grants to states to establish institutions to teach agricultural and mechanical arts along with the traditional curriculum of the multipurpose college. In 1872 the legislature established the South Carolina Agricultural College and Mechanics Institute "in connection with" Claflin University, adding these practical arts to the curriculum.[56] The land-grant colleges were established for working-class students to have practical learning along with scientific and classical studies. The classical model was waning, and the colleges began to incorporate scientific subjects.[57]

[ii] The college originally called South Carolina Agricultural College and Mechanics Institute was renamed Claflin College in 1878. To facilitate the discussion of the two schools, I have used Claflin College of Agriculture for Claflin College and Claflin University for the university.

Emphasis on industrial education for African Americans was also increasing throughout the country. Claflin reflected this trend. By 1890 every student, elementary through college, received industrial training in such trades as printing, blacksmithing, and bricklaying. This satisfied several needs: expectations of white benefactors, provision of services to the school (particularly in building and growing food), and providing some students with training for economic self-sufficiency. However, the trend toward increasing normal and industrial education affected Black people disproportionately. Around 1890 less than half of white college students were in normal and industrial schools. Over three-quarters of Black people were in these schools, and at Claflin the total approached 90 percent of college students. The 10 percent of students in nonindustrial majors also received industrial training.[58] The emphasis on industrial training was evidence of white people's expectations about the place of African Americans in Jim Crow America.[59]

Black people who had been free before the war were critical to Claflin University's early success. In fact, families such as the Bulkleys and the Middletons had students at the University over multiple generations. E. Horace Fitchett writes:

> It was these families [those who had freedom and educational opportunity before emancipation] that persisted at Claflin College. It was they who used the school as a means of giving expression to the desires to develop their abilities for the attainment of full manhood rights.[60] The Northern missionaries, the southern sympathizers, and the Negroes themselves who had in spite of the vicissitudes of the system received some advantages, envisaged a plan of formal education as a panacea for a disintegrated social order.[61]

After the University of South Carolina closed, William enrolled in Claflin University. In 1878 the classical college course included mathematics (through trigonometry, surveying, and mechanics); study of

Latin, Greek, and English (including Livy, Tacitus, composition and declamation, history and literature); and in the senior year science, metaphysics, polity, and ethics.[62] Tuition was free, but the student had to pay room (one dollar per month) and board (ten dollars per month)[iii] and fees of one dollar and fifty cents per term. All classes were small. In the school year 1883–1884 eighteen students were enrolled in the college course, six in college prep, ninety-two in the normal course, and about 270 in the grammar school.

Extracurricular activities included literary societies: Alpha Alpha for the Normal Department course and Belles Lettres Society for the students of the College Proper course. These societies provided opportunities for reading, debates, and other literary pursuits. Religious instruction included required devotional services in the college chapel every morning. Rules required observance of study hours, required attendance at examinations, and prohibited gambling, intoxicating drinks, profane language, and smoking or chewing tobacco.[63]

In the academic year 1881–1882 Claflin University celebrated as N. H. Middleton and W. L. Bulkley became the first two graduates of the College Proper. Bulkley received an AB for completion of the four-year college course, and N. H. Middleton received an SB for completing the three-year course.[64] Graduation was always an important and festive occasion that demonstrated and celebrated the achievements of students at all levels. In 1882 the closing activities for the school year were spread over four days. On Sunday President Edward Cooke delivered the baccalaureate sermon in the chapel. On Monday faculty conducted oral examinations in front of the gathered family, friends, and spectators. The teachers asked questions of their students in their respective disciplines, even requiring math problems

---

[iii] Board was a high-carbohydrate diet of oatmeal, hominy, rice, potatoes, and white bread, leavened with a bit of bacon or cabbage. "A Model Boarding Hall," *The Christian Educator: A Quarterly Magazine of Facts*, (October, 1890): 30-31.

to be worked at the blackboard. "Prof. De Treville's examination of W. L. Bulkley, who graduates, was a very pleasing exhibition. The students went through problems of trigonometry and mechanics [a branch of classical physics] readily."[65]

Tuesday was Class Day under the auspices of the Belles Lettres Society. There was a debate on the question of "Whether the Persian invasion of Greece was of greater importance in history than the Grecian invasion of Persia?"[66] During the planting of the ivy, W. L. Bulkley gave an oration. "It was graceful, to the point and effective." [iv] Ten Normal Department students sat for a written examination for the Peabody Prize, sponsored by the national Peabody Education Fund to provide funds for "worthy, promising, struggling" students. [67] The day concluded with fourteen students competing for a prize in declamation and an evening lecture by Rev. Dr. Willard F. Mallalieu, "Christian Scholarship the Imperative Demand of the Present Age."

On commencement day "a gay and holiday appearance enlivened the [chapel]."[68] At 4:00 p.m. the exercises commenced with music provided by the students. Jennie A. Thompson opened the program with a speech in Latin, which was followed by many more speeches (in English) on such topics as Pericles, the character and ambition of President Garfield, the blessings of trials, and the Liberty Bell. Each student's standing was read before the large audience. Diplomas and prizes were awarded and the degrees conferred. Bulkley provided the valedictory address, which was "very fine." [69] Reporters took the occasion to comment on Claflin. "President Cooke and his corps of professors, both in the Claflin and State Agricultural departments of the institution, should feel gratified at the growth and progress of their work, and we feel assured they have the support and encouragement of our people in their efforts in the cause of education."[70]

[iv] The planting of ivy and the "ivy oration" were nineteenth-century traditions at many colleges. The ivy commemorated the senior class.

From humble beginnings in a difficult political and social climate, William L. Bulkley grew up to be a well-educated young man with ambition and a deep faith that propelled him into service of his people.

Wesleyan University, 1884–1886

After graduation from Claflin University, Bulkley immediately joined Claflin's faculty as a tutor in Latin and Greek and as librarian in the grammar school. The following school year he was adjunct professor of Latin and Greek and English literature and librarian in the grammar school.[71] But he clearly wanted more. Established northern schools could offer an education more advanced than the one he had received at Claflin. Wesleyan University, a Methodist school in Middletown, Connecticut, was one such school. Wesleyan was established in 1831 by the Methodist Episcopal Church and offered a classical education with the addition of modern languages, literature, and natural sciences, a forward-looking model at the time.[72] It was regarded as the best of the Methodist colleges and universities.[73] Edward Cooke, the president of Claflin University, was a graduate of Wesleyan (BA 1838, MA 1841) and may have encouraged the young Bulkley to pursue more education there.

Potts describes the educational philosophy of the college. The faculty was called to

> educate "the whole man"—intellect, imagination, and heart—
> for careers of Christian service. With characters thus
> cultivated, students were expected to engage energetically "the
> duties you must do . . . as citizens, legislators, leaders of the
> thought and life of communities, states, nations perhaps."[74]

In 1884 Bulkley was admitted to Wesleyan University as a freshman in the classics program. The entrance exam required him to know, among other things, Caesar, Virgil, Homer, Xenophon, history, geography, and the first seven books of Newcomb's *Algebra*. The exam required him to write a one-hour composition on one of seven listed books. His course of study at

Wesleyan included Latin, Greek, math, English, analytic geometry, mechanics, and physics.

For a young African American man from the South, Wesleyan and Middletown would have been a radical change. For the first time he was a minority in his school (in fact a minority of one). The town itself was overwhelmingly white. The imposing stone buildings in a row on a hilltop and the stone chapel with its well-appointed interior and comfortable pews contrasted sharply with the modest hilltop buildings in Orangeburg.

Bulkley worked to support himself, as surely others of the ministers' and farmers' sons did. Most of the students received financial assistance. Bulkley received a Seney scholarship in fall 1885.[75] Bulkley reports, "I was able to get through Wesleyan by the strictest economy only." During the school year he had jobs caring for the museum (100,000 specimens—"animals, plants, minerals, fossils, and ethnographic objects"), lighting the campus gas lights, and working as a steward at the Dirigo Club (a dining association). During the summers he peddled steam cookers, fruit trees, and pictures from door to door. He saved money by cooking oatmeal, mending his clothes, and ironing his handkerchiefs between the pages of a book.[76] He had little time for, and no access to, the social life that centered around the fraternities on the campus. Fraternities did not admit women, non-white students, or non-Protestants.[77] However, he had roommates and was elected second vice president of his class in 1885 and secretary in 1886.[78]

Bulkley completed two years at Wesleyan and was in first semester junior year when his father died suddenly on October 18, 1886, in Camden, South Carolina. He returned home immediately. He never returned to Wesleyan but considered himself an alumnus. He maintained ties with the school throughout his life—sending reports for the *Alumni Directory*, staying with a former classmate when he was on a speaking engagement for Claflin in 1898,[79] and writing to the *Argus*, the student publication.

Claflin University, 1886–1890

With the death of his father, Bulkley now had the responsibility of supporting his mother and four brothers and sisters, aged eleven to eighteen. The family moved from Camden to Orangeburg, and William rejoined the faculty of Claflin University as a professor of Latin and Greek. His mother, Madora Wilson Bulkley, took a job in the sewing department. On March 8, 1888, William married Mary Fisher Carroll of Columbia.[80] Mary was an 1885 graduate of Claflin's Normal Department and worked at Claflin as a student assistant in the grammar school from 1884 to 1885 and as an associate teacher from 1887 to 1888.[81] She had four siblings who also earned degrees from Claflin. The Carrolls were from Columbia and, unlike Bulkley's family, Mary's father, Captain James (C. J.) Carroll, had been a slave and was freed only at the end of the war. He was a barber and real estate investor in Columbia. He built the house at 999 Lady, which still stands today (now 1416 Park). It is one of only two buildings that remains in what was once the heart of the Black community in downtown Columbia.[82]

Bulkley followed current events closely and commented on them from time to time. In a long letter to the *Charleston News and Courier*, he responded to discussions about disfranchisement during the presidential election of 1888. In elegant words he said that actions, not the party, matter.

> Let the party be Prohibitionist, Democratic, Republican or Mugwump, it matters but little. "What's in a name?" Let that party have good men at its head.
>
> We want no more reconstruction, if reconstruction means a holiday for illiteracy, a carnival for vice. We do not want negro supremacy. Such a thing this State has never seen, even in the years from '68 to '76. We want an honest Government, a Government based on no race or class lines . . . a Government of the people, for the people and by the people. . . . My duty is only to work in my feeble way for the development of the mind, for the inculcation of moral principles in the youth of

to-day, the men of tomorrow. It must come or civilization is a failure, Christianity a farce, the Bible a lie.[83]

The young Bulkley, now twenty-seven years old, had found his voice.

World's Sunday School Convention, 1889

In 1889 Bulkley had a life-changing opportunity. He was elected as a delegate to the World's Sunday School Convention in London, England, held July 1–6, 1889. This was a meeting of almost a thousand lay and ministerial delegates from England, North America, Europe, Asia, and Africa. Conventions were a "means of quickening the zeal of Sunday-School Teachers, and exciting a greater and more general interest among Christians in the religious education of the young."[84] There were three delegates from South Carolina, another Methodist and a Baptist. The International Executive Sunday School Committee chartered the *Bothnia* to take some of the delegates. On the voyage to London, the convention got an early start as the passengers participated in singing, prayer services, lectures, and socializing.

The first evening of the convention, Right Hon. Sir Henry Isaacs, the lord mayor of London, received over 700 delegates at the Mansion House, an eighteenth-century Palladian building featuring a portico with six Corinthian columns. The rooms used for the reception, the Long Parlour, the Saloon, and the Egyptian Hall, are sumptuous and elegant. As different as Wesleyan's collegiate buildings were from Claflin's, this was another level of elegance that Bulkley would not have experienced before.[85] Imagine, if you will, the young man who had spent most of his life in small-town South Carolina arriving before this majestic building and being one of the people to enter and enjoy it. This is a man who could not legally ride in a first-class train car in his home state. The convention itself was serious business. Topics included "Work Reported," "Work Improved," "The Best Methods of Bible Study," "Among Coloured People," and management of Sunday Schools. Sunday Schools were no small matter—they were a venue for not only religious indoctrination but also school learning. At this time South Carolina had 1667 Sunday schools with 103,315 scholars.

Bulkley also traveled on the continent. He visited Paris and completed a tour through southern Europe,[86] where he may also have visited the places whose languages he had been studying. In Paris he surely visited the Exposition Universelle, a world's fair that featured palaces of machines, fine arts, and liberal arts. There were gardens and horticultural exhibits. The Eiffel Tower, as yet unfinished, served as the gate to the fairgrounds. The fair covered almost a square kilometer and had three kilometers of railway to carry the fairgoers who visited the "Negro village," locomotives, a "Wild West Show," and an Aztec Temple. [87]

Bulkley returned home in July and resumed his life in Orangeburg. He was also preparing his speech for Emancipation Day, January 1, 1890. Bulkley, not yet thirty years old, had become a well-educated, devout man, a world traveler, and a professor of Latin and Greek.

GENERAL VIEW OF WESLEYAN UNIVERSITY.

Wesleyan University   *Scribner's Monthly*, 1876

VIEW IN THE MUSEUM, WESLEYAN UNIVERSITY.

Museum, Wesleyan University   *Scribner's Monthly*, 1876

Mansion House, London, England   Collection of the author

Le Palais de Beaux-Arts, Exposition Universelle, Paris   Library of Congress

II

TROUBLOUS TIMES, 1890

We live in troublous times.[88]

From the time William Lewis Bulkley was born in 1861, African Americans had been on a roller-coaster of political and social change. They had experienced the terror and confusion of the Civil War and the joy of emancipation. Following the war whites wrote the South Carolina State Constitution of 1865, denying the new citizens the right to vote and attempting to create a new slavery. This was quickly overturned by the US Congress, which passed laws in 1866 and 1867 establishing a federal presence to guarantee civil rights in the former Confederacy and mandating that southern states ratify the Fourteenth Amendment, which guaranteed equal protection of the law, before being readmitted to the Union.

In 1868 Black people participated in writing a new state constitution that gave equal protection and equal standing to all citizens, regardless of race. It mandated public education for the first time and abolished property requirements to vote. Education was important; less than 10 percent of African Americans in the South, immediately following the war, could read. [89] Schools from elementary through college were established, and people of all ages attended to learn to read and cipher. African Americans participated in the government in both elected and appointed office and were legally considered equal citizens with white people. Their status was protected by the presence of federal troops. South Carolina elected a majority of African Americans to the lower house of the state legislature and elected eight African Americans to Congress. Two Black men were lieutenant governors and one was appointed a justice of the state Supreme Court. Numerous African Americans were appointed to civil service positions, and African American teachers taught in the African American schools. In 1870 the Fifteenth Amendment to the US Constitution was ratified, and all men became qualified to vote in federal as well as state elections. The period from 1867 to 1877, called the Radical Reconstruction, was the federal effort, led by both radical and moderate Republicans in Congress, to incorporate Black people into Southern culture. However, it was doomed to failure.

Throughout this time there was resistance from Southern white people. In 1877 Rutherford B. Hayes, in a political compromise to win the presidency, removed federal troops from the South, ending Reconstruction and setting the stage for the southern states to strip away the hard-won civil rights for African Americans and their right to civic participation. The years from 1877 until the new state constitution of 1895 were ones of gradual erosion of rights and of resistance to that erosion. Violence perpetuated by white people against African Americans increased. In the years following 1877, South Carolina (and other southern states) instituted new laws and practices that were to become known as Jim Crow—laws relegating African Americans to second-class citizenship, denying them the vote, and segregating every aspect of life. In 1890, five years short of the 1895 constitution and six years short of the 1896 Supreme Court decision legalizing segregation, it was still possible to hope that the political and social situation could be improved.

Bulkley was six when Reconstruction began and sixteen when it ended. It seems the child growing to a young man was powerfully affected by the optimism and freedom of those years. In 1890, after thirteen years of violence, loss of rights, and legislation of segregation in South Carolina, he remained positive and hopeful about the future. However, within the space of six months William Lewis Bulkley's world brought into high relief the brutal repression of Black people in the South and the stark divisions of society that accepted, without punishment, the lynching of eight African Americans and an assault on an African American professor by a white one.

Emancipation Day

Emancipation Day was observed on January 1, in commemoration of the day in 1863 that Abraham Lincoln issued the Emancipation Proclamation. In 1890 African Americans throughout the South marked the day with celebrations. In Orangeburg, South Carolina, Black people from throughout the county formed a parade as they came into town. Three brass bands were drawn in wagons. The people came on foot, on horseback, and in carriages, buggies, and carts. The noisy procession arrived at Claflin University and proceeded into the low wooden chapel. The group was hushed as the Rev. Richard Carroll,[v] of Columbia, opened with prayer. Rev. A. G. Townsend, professor at the university, read the Emancipation Proclamation reminding all of the historical context of the occasion. Then young Professor William L. Bulkley rose to the podium.[90]

> Dear Friends, Fellow-Citizens, Brethren of the Africo-American race, . . . We are gathered here to-day from near and from far to celebrate a great day, a great act in the history of a remarkable people. Old men and old women are here who have lived on both sides of a great conflict. Young men and young women are here, who were born while the battle waged hot and the earth was drenched in blood. Children are here whose eyes opened in a land where blood-bought laws pronounce all men equal and free. Wonderful is this picture![91]

In the course of the speech, he named and honored abolitionists and Union heroes of the Civil War (including the US Colored Troops) and reminded the audience of the famous of their own race. Some of the names

[v]no relationship to the C. J. Carroll family

he mentioned we would all recognize today: astronomer Benjamin Banneker, poet Phillis Wheatley, and activist, author, and orator Frederick Douglass. Others were heroes whose names are not as familiar to us: John M. Langston, abolitionist and educator; Bishop B. W. Arnett, minister and Ohio legislator; Richard T. Greener, Harvard graduate, professor at University of South Carolina and Howard University, and diplomat; James M. Townsend, minister and recorder of the U. S. General Land Office; Blanche K. Bruce, register of the US Treasury and US senator from Mississippi; and Dr. J. C. Price, scholar minister and civil rights leader.[92]

After paying homage to the past, he turned to the present and the future—the "Negro problem," as he referred to it, that, "like Banquo's ghost,[vi] will not down."[93] He reviewed the current "solutions" and then provided his own: uplift of the people by education, civilization, and Christianization.

Bulkley examined and refuted all the reasons given by white people for getting rid of African Americans. The Black man cannot be educated, is dishonest, fond of drink, and will not work. He is not as well off now as he was in slavery.[94] Bulkley showed with examples and statistics and passion that each of these statements was false. He lauded and defended his people and then addressed the present solutions being offered to the "Negro problem:" amalgamation, extirpation, and emigration.[95]

He commented briefly on amalgamation: "Even if amalgamation [intermarrying of white and Black people] were agreeable to both races, it would take a long time, as Dr. Price showed last year, to make six million Black men [into] white men. The millennium would get here first."[96]

He dismissed extirpation, saying, "Surely no sane man in Christian America would cherish a thought of settling the difficulty by exterminating

---

[vi] In Shakespeare's Macbeth, Act III, Scene IV, the ghost of the recently murdered Banquo sits in Macbeth's chair at the feast.

the race by the sword, the bullet, and the bayonet. Both races would suffer thus in an incalculable degree."[97]

He then turned to emigration, an issue of high current interest. At Claflin's commencement the previous year, Bishop B. W. Arnett of the AME Church said, "Get up and Go? Go, take your family with you. Go as one of the pioneers and you will have a pioneer's reward."[98] Later in 1890, Matthew Butler would introduce a bill into the US Senate proposing to spend $5 million to relocate African Americans who would like to emigrate to Liberia. Bulkley considered the concept under the following topics:

> (1.) What is emigration?
> (2.) Why should we emigrate?
> (3.) Where should we emigrate?
> (4.) What would be the result upon this country if we were to leave?[99]

Bulkley contrasted the voluntary emigration of the Jews, Helvetians, and settlers of the Americas, with involuntary emigration of the Israelites to Babylonia, Saxons in slavery to Rome, and Africans in slavery to the Americas.

He then explored the reasons that white people put forth to justify both voluntary and involuntary emigration for African Americans: that he is a burden, that he blocks white immigrants, and that this is a white man's country. In his long discussion demonstrating that the Black man is not a burden, he wrote:

> It has always been a mystery to me why so many hundreds of thousands were killed and so many hundreds of million dollars [were] spent from 1860 to 1865, if the Negroes were such an awful burden to this land. The money thrown away would have bought us all forty acres and a mule and given us a buggy to drive the mule into.[100]

He claimed that it was not the Black population that deterred white immigrants from coming to the South but that they didn't like the agricultural work and the disregard of human life evidenced by lynch law. To demonstrate that this is not a white man's country, he spoke of the Indians who were here first and of the Black men who fought in the Revolution, the War of 1812, and the Civil War.

> I challenge heaven, earth and hell to show me a race that ever lived, who, though suffering the ignominy of ill-treated and despised slaves, performed such a meritorious part in the defense and preservation of the country that welded the shackles for their limbs, and fastened the iron yoke of oppression about their necks![101]

He pointed out that the Black man's labor built this country and that Black people owned five and a half million acres of land. And finally he said, "This is not the white man's land; it is not the red man's land; it is not the black man's land. It is God's land."[102]

Answering his question, "Where shall we emigrate, if any of us want to go?," he said, "Go anywhere you please. That is your privilege."[103] He mentioned Haiti, Cuba, Mexico, and the West. For those who wanted to emigrate to Africa he had cautions, including not to expect a land flowing with milk and plenty. However, he also stated, "The very men we would like to go are the very ones that will be sure to stay. . . . If we could get rid of a million or so of lazy, good-for-nothing, lying, roguish blacks, and a million or so of lazy, good-for-nothing, lying, roguish whites, the South would take a fresh start."[104] If there were a wholesale exodus of Black people, the "Southern States would suffer incalculably,"[105] but in the long run, no one was really indispensable, and it would be needless to take alarm at the "*gradual* emigration from the South of six million human beings."[106] Indeed, six million African Americans did leave the South during the twentieth century.[107] The gradual migration changed both the South and the North but did not leave the South destitute of labor.

The overly optimistic Bulkley predicted that Black and white folks would settle "the whole trouble in the future."

There is no doubt but that it will be settled. . . . The white man and the Black man must join hands to settle these differences. The white man must be patient and liberal in his judgment. The Black man must be diligent and earnest in his efforts to build himself up.[108]

He then admonished his listeners:

Be honest . . . Mind your own business . . . Be industrious and economical . . . Get all the religion you can. Get all the education you can. Get all the property you can. And, even if money should be the root of all evil as we sometimes hear, get as much of that root as you can. . . . Have characters that are blameless. Defend your homes with ceaseless vigilance. Protect your wives, your daughters, your sisters at the risk of your lives. . . . Have your own mind. . . . In politics be conservative.[109]

His Christian faith was an important underpinning of his optimism:

My dear friends, the future of the race is not so dark as we sometimes think. An all-wise God is leading us. There is the pillar of cloud by day and the pillar of fire by night. . . . The white man and the black man shall yet acknowledge each other's worth. They shall yet be inseparably united in the development of the country, in the upbuilding of each other's mental and moral condition, in the glorification of a God, who is "no respecter of persons."[110]

The Robert Burns lines quoted at the end of the speech eloquently stated his plea:

That man to man the warld o'er
Shall brothers be for a' that.[111]

Bulkley's speech reveals him as an optimistic, religious, well-educated, perceptive man. His admonitions to his listeners would be familiar to any churchgoing Christian. He counseled participation in politics and "whenever our legislators do those things that oppress us, let us spare no pains to let them know that we are incensed, that we are aggrieved."[112] He does not call for organizing, or revolution, but puts his faith in progress, individual improvement, and Black and white people working together to settle their differences. At this remove, these expectations seem naïve. It has taken organizing, civil disobedience, political power, and solidarity for rights and opportunities to come for African Americans. Little did Bulkley know that 1890 is now identified as the beginning of the nadir period in civil rights,[113] which lasted the rest of his life. His youthful beliefs were to be sorely challenged.

His hour-long oration was "so instructive, so powerful in the noble defence [*sic*] of our race"[114] that it was published on the petition of the students. His passionate belief in the brotherhood of man, under the Fatherhood of God, and his wide-ranging intellect and knowledge ran throughout the speech. His language was enriched by his classical education, including references to Shakespeare, the Greek philosopher Diogenes, and the Bible; quotes from current newspapers and books; folksy stories in the style of a preacher; and examples from his own life. He bolstered his speech with a widespread knowledge of history—classical, political, African American—and his familiarity with contemporary sources of sociological research and statistics. Bulkley's speech revealed some prejudices that do not sit easily today. He loathed Catholicism; he did not like alcohol (not surprising for a Methodist); and he dismissed the "degraded" lower class, although he believed everyone was redeemable through education and religion.

The published speech does not include the extemporaneous words[115] Bulkley added regarding a terrible event that had taken place days earlier, casting a dark pall over this Emancipation Day celebration and the uplifting oration. On December 28, 1889, eight African American men were lynched—kidnapped from the jail, tied to trees, and riddled with bullets in Barnwell, South Carolina, less than 50 miles away.

Barnwell Lynching

> We live in troublous times. The country knows of the horrible
> butchery of helpless and innocent men at Barnwell, a town
> only a few miles from here. . . . Where are we now? Whither are
> we drifting? Where shall we end? God knows!" . . . What can
> be done? We, the wronged race, can do nothing lawfully; we
> shall do nothing unlawfully. We are waiting in breathless
> anxiety to see what those who have the law and the military
> under their control, will do. . . . But can we be contented when
> we know that our lives are no more precious than the ox with
> which we plow? Can there be peaceful fields when a whole
> family can be shot down and the murderers go free?[116]

Bulkley was not exaggerating when he wrote, "Our lives are no more
precious than the ox." White supremacy was the rule. Benjamin Tillman,
who was to become governor of South Carolina in 1890 and represented
widespread attitudes, was an advocate for white supremacy. His "lynching
pledge" was a cornerstone of his political career.

> We of the South have never recognized the right of the negro
> to govern white men, and we never will. We have never
> believed him to be the equal of the white man, and we will not
> submit to his gratifying his lust on our wives and daughters
> without lynching him.[117]

Lynching was used to terrorize the African American community, to
attempt to reduce their participation in community and political life, and
to try and return Southern life to the rigid caste system that had been
established by slavery. This was the process Bulkley and many others were
fighting against, but nevertheless it moved inexorably forward.

The lynching on December 28, 1889, shocked South Carolina and the
nation. It was widely reported and decried. The eight African American
men were both the accused and the witnesses to two different murders. The
jail at Barnwell Courthouse was on a side street and housed the jailor and
his family on the first level and prisoners in cells on the second. Two Black

prisoners had been charged in the October 30, 1889, murder of John Heffernan, a white merchant. The court case was on hold because the defendant's attorney felt the accused men would be lynched if they were removed from the jail to face the judge at the courthouse. Two other men in the prison were charged with the December 21 murder of Robert Martin, a young white man who ran a small store on his father's station. Four men were also jailed as witnesses to Martin's murder.

Judge Kershaw had ordered the sheriff to keep a guard at the jail, but the county commissioners refused to pay the deputies, and the guard was withdrawn. At two o'clock in the morning, December 28, over a hundred armed and masked men roused the jailor and forced him to hand over the keys. The men kidnapped the four accused murderers and the four witnesses to the Martin murder. They tied the prisoners with ropes and marched them across Turkey Creek and bound them to small trees and a sign post. Then the masked men raised their pistols and fired 150 rounds at the eight prisoners. The murdered men were left slumped grotesquely against their bonds, shot to pieces, and in pools of clotted blood. At the inquest it was reported that forty-seven balls were found in the eight men, any of which could have been fatal. After the shooting the mob dispersed.[118]

An African American cook on her way to work in the early morning came on this gruesome and appalling scene. By sunrise great crowds of African American men and women had come to the site, and the wails could be heard throughout the town. White people gathered, too, and began to fear retaliation or an uprising. They telegraphed South Carolina governor John P. Richardson for troops, who were sent by the next train. No disorder ensued, and the troops withdrew the next day.[119] A large crowd of African Americans buried two of the murdered men in the African American cemetery. The families of the others refused to bury them, leaving the white people to deal with the butchery they had committed.

The murdered men left seven widows and twenty-three young children. Several people, including New Hampshire senator W. E. Chandler, solicited contributions to send to the grieving widows and children. Frances E. W. Harper, abolitionist, journalist, poet, and the well-known president of the Woman's Christian Temperance Union, visited Barnwell "in the interest of the wives and children."[120]

Chandler wrote a letter to the *New York Tribune* in which he detailed the human face of the massacre. Those accused in the murder of J. J. Heffernan were Mitchel Adams, a farm laborer, 35 years old, and Ripley Johnson, who ran a cotton gin and was about 30 years old. Adams left a wife, Dicey, and three children. Dicey had mortgaged her house and cow to raise money to pay the lawyer for her husband's defense. Ripley Johnson was unmarried but caring for his aged mother, Jane Winters.[121]

The witnesses to the Robert Martin murder were Judge Jones, about thirty years old, Rafe Morrall, over sixty years old and a farmer, Robert Phoenix, a thirty-year-old carpenter, and Harrison (also known as Handy and Hudson) Johnson, about thirty-five years old. Accused of murdering Martin were Peter Bell, about sixty years old, and Hugh Furz, about twenty-five. Jones left a wife, Susan, six children, and his aged parents. Morrall was survived by wife Clara and one child. Phoenix had been married to Marie only a few days before he was arrested. Harrison Johnson, a deacon in the Baptist Church, left his wife, Leah, to care for eight children. Bell's wife, Rina, was left with an infant and a toddler. Furz left a wife, Rina, and three children. The same day as the lynching, these six families were evicted from their homes on the Martin plantation. They were now not only grieving but also without a home and a means to earn a living. Some in the town, Black and white, considered all six of these men innocent and the real murderer to be a white man who had threatened Martin "for breaking up the happiness of his family."[122]

The lynching was covered in the media nationwide. Although mass lynching would become more common later, this was the first time eight people had been lynched at the same time. It was also the first (and perhaps only) time that imprisoned witnesses were lynched along with the accused.[123] Among white people there was outrage and justification in about equal proportions. On the morning of December 28, the sheriff formed an advisory committee of five white men to counsel a course of action. There was great fear that a riot or even a race war would ensue. Their report, released the same day, described the crimes and concluded that the lynching was justified:

> These several brutal murders of prominent white men by negroes caused a state of indignant resentment among our people that can be better imagined than described, but cannot be imagined by any one not in our midst.[124]

The *Manning Times* editor, after describing the horror of the case, wrote, "The case is not without some merit. Prominent white citizens had been killed, and less than ten days before two white men had been assassinated. If lynching is ever in such cases justifiable, this was one of the cases."[125] The *New York Tribune* published an editorial that began and ended,

> Surely South Carolina will not expect the great American Nation to be blind to such a fiendish outrage as that perpetrated at Barnwell. . . . This sort of human butchery must be stopped, and if South Carolina has no worthier motive for avenging her honor she should find at least a sufficient one in the universal horror and disgust which the Barnwell atrocity has excited.[126]

The Charleston *News and Courier* editorial was damning. "The lynching of eight defenceless [*sic*] colored men at Barnwell on Friday night was absolutely without justification or excuse. A more infamous, cowardly, inhuman deed has never stained the reputation of the State."[127] These were useless words in a culture that spoke high words on one hand and condoned mayhem and murder on the other.

African Americans responses were outrage, fear, grief, and calls for action. The idea of leaving Barnwell County permanently was put forth immediately. This editorial appeared in the African American newspaper the *Richmond Planet*:

> We are glad to see that the colored people are disposed to tolerate the lawlessness no longer and that trouble is feared. So long as the colored man submits supinely he'll have these outrages to stand. Had we more martyrs and less victims of the shot-gun, the midnight assassins and the lynchers, the race as such would be better off. *Lynch law must go!*[128]

By the *Planet*'s continuing count, published in each paper, 132 African Americans had been lynched in the United States in the last six months of 1889.

Two hundred men in Charleston issued a call for "leading colored men of the State to assemble in the city of Columbia on the 2nd day in January, 1890, at 8 P.M." They called for upholding the law of the state and bringing justice to "those who defame and traduce her fair name."[129] Prominent men from twenty-six of the thirty-four counties gathered at Wesley Methodist Episcopal Church in Columbia. Attendees included Alonzo Gray (A. G.) Townsend, professor of Greek at Claflin University; Wilson Cook of Greenville, Bulkley's uncle by marriage; and Bulkley himself. This may have been one of Bulkley's first experiences with a political gathering of African Americans fighting for their civil rights.[130] In a statement the group reviewed the event and the state of affairs:

> [T]here are no rights for the negro which a white man, whether worthy or unworthy, is bound to respect, when the observance of these rights is judged by the white man as in any way contrary to his personal views or prejudices. . . . The indescribable and inhuman butchery of eight men of our race, taken from the prison cells of Barnwell County, in the presence of the agents of the law, is an unprecedented instance of barbarity, unbecoming a civilized community.[131]

This was followed by a statement that, under the circumstances, was remarkable for its restraint. They condemned the taking of human life except by the state and advised staying calm and allowing "the proper authorities [to] vindicate the law." They defended Black people as loyal to South Carolina, condemned newspapers for agitating separation of the races, denied the danger of insurrection, and advised African Americans to abandon lawless sections of the state such as Barnwell County "and move to a state where the laws are observed." The following day a committee of nine met with the governor.[132]

Despite both Black and white citizens' purported confidence in the law and Governor Richardson offering a two-hundred dollar reward for each lyncher convicted, no one was ever indicted for these murders. The coroner's inquest, held immediately after the crime, found that the victims "came to their death from gunshot wounds at the hands of parties unknown."[133] When the Court of General Session of Barnwell County convened in March, the judge's charge to the jury was forceful, but *The Appeal* noted, "White men in the South can seldom find white men guilty of crimes committed against Colored ones much less subject them to the death penalty."[134] The jury declined to deliberate, since they did not have bill of indictment laid before them, and the judge ordered no further investigation.[135] In the end a *Chicago Tribune* editorial summed up the horrible situation: "No amount of talking is going to check Southern Negro-hating mobs. Something must be done. Fine words butter no parsnips." In the end the fine words of the committee made no difference.[136]

Emigration

In the immediate aftermath of the lynching African Americans spoke of leaving Barnwell County for safer areas. The resolutions of the group of leaders who met on January 2 recommended emigration. On January 21, African Americans of Barnwell County met to discuss emigration to Arkansas and Mississippi. Some had their belongings piled in wagons and were ready to go.[137] This was not without precedent. Between 1870 and 1910, 10 percent of southern Black people moved to other southern states, mostly westward. Arkansas had rich agricultural land, relatively high wages, and a delay in the development of Jim Crow laws.[138] In 1886 fifty-one African Americans had moved from Barnwell County to Arkansas. There was no wholesale exodus after the lynching. However, many of the victims' families must have left the area, as they do not appear in later public records in Barnwell.

The issue of emigration had been one of importance to African Americans throughout the nineteenth century. White people often saw emigration as a way to rid the state or country of African Americans. But their economy was also reliant on Black people as laborers in farms and factories. As Narciso G. Gonzales, editor of the *State* (Columbia, South Carolina), observed, "Politically speaking there are far too many negroes in South Carolina, but from an industrial standpoint there is room for many more."[139] Black people universally fought against mandatory emigration. Voluntary emigration was a different matter. Some saw emigration as a way to establish all-Black communities. At an individual level, emigration or migration was a way to begin a new life in a better place of their own choosing, a way to catch a little of the American dream.

There had long been movements for emigration from the United States (to Liberia or Haiti, for example) or migration from one state to another state or territory in the United States. White people often promoted schemes with motivations ranging from paternalistic to virulently racist. In Bulkley's own extended family, a young couple excitedly moved to Liberia in the 1840s, and an uncle emigrated to Haiti on the eve of the Civil War. In 1883 V. H. Bulkley visited Arkansas to assess the opportunities for African Americans who desired to relocate and published a pamphlet, *The Truth about Arkansas*.[140] The folks from Barnwell County whose goods were packed and ready to move on January 21 were part of this movement, too, trading the tenuous security and prospects of South Carolina for the hope of a better place.

In February 1890 eleven representative leaders of the African American community were invited by the *Charleston News and Courier* to provide "testimony from colored men about the exodus."[141] The men chosen by the editor were a group of accomplished leaders in religion, politics, education, and activism. Bulkley is included among these men, a sign of his rising importance as a national leader. Bishop Henry McNeal Turner, of the AME Church, unequivocally supported emigration. He was "the most vociferous and visible leader of the emigration movement throughout the 1890s."[142] The remainder of the contributors (T. Thomas Fortune, Dr. James T. Still, Rev. J. H. M. Pollard, Bishop B. T. Tanner, Robert Smalls, William L. Bulkley, Jacob W. Powell, D. Augustus Straker, W. S. Scarborough, and John M. Langston) opposed the legislation to varying degrees.[vii] Some also challenged the assumption that money should be used to send African Americans away rather than to enforce their civil rights under the Constitution. Several, including Bulkley, supported voluntary emigration. His remarks were similar to those he made in his address in January. He addressed some of the points made in a recent publication by Carlyle McKinley, *An Appeal to Pharaoh*,[143] which proposed complete segregation of the races by deporting all African Americans from the United States.

> I favor a partial emigration of the laboring classes to any place they may desire, call it Africa, Cuba, Mexico, or the West. . . . May men cease to terrorize on negro deportation and practice on negro education and elevation! May fire-eaters consume less

---

[vii] Fortune was editor of the *New York Age*. Still was a graduate of Harvard Medical School and nephew of abolitionist William Still. Pollard was a minister in the Episcopal Church. Benjamin T. Tanner was bishop in the AME Church. Smalls was a Civil War hero and US representative. Powell was active in religious education in the AME Church. Straker was a lawyer and South Carolina representative. Scarborough was a classics scholar and president of Wilberforce University. Langston was a politician, activist, and founder of the law school at Howard University.

time in teaching the 3,000,000 illiterate whites of the South how to hate and fight and show them to read and write![144]

A challenge to Bulkley's Emancipation Day optimism was only a few months away at Claflin University. Three months after the Barnwell massacre and Bulkley's Emancipation Day speech, Professor William J. DeTreville, Jr. (white) beat Rev. Isaac N. Cardozo (Black) with a cane on the steps of the Main Building. The campus exploded.

Chapel, Claflin University   *Claflin Univerity Catalogue*, 1893

Chapel, Claflin University   *Claflin Univerity Catalogue*, 1898

III

CRISIS AT CLAFLIN, 1890

"Prof. DeTreville's Murderous Assault on Prof. Cardozo at Claflin University, Orangeburg, S.C."[145]

Just two months after Emancipation Day, Claflin was thrown into a crisis that had a direct impact on Bulkley, although his response is obscured by the lack of resources. This pivotal event demonstrates his commitment to multiracial institutions and to Claflin University.

Setting the Stage

In 1890 the institution generally referred to as Claflin University was actually two intermeshed institutions. Claflin University was funded through a number of sources, including the Methodist Episcopal Church's Freedmen's Aid Society. Coexisting with Claflin University was Claflin College of Agriculture, established in 1872 by the South Carolina legislature, funded with money derived from the state received under the Morrill Land-Grant Act of 1862. Claflin University's board was multiracial. The appointees of Claflin College of Agriculture's board were all white and included many ex officio politicians. At the policy and funding level they were two separate institutions. However, the lines between the two institutions were blurred because they shared teachers, students, and facilities, and L. M. Dunton was the president of both . The duality of the university reflected two different models for African American education. The university itself was nominally a mixed-race institution, with Black students (although open to everyone), Black and white faculty, and an administration led by white men and the Freedmen's Aid Society. Claflin College of Agriculture was a segregated school for

African American students run by a white board and faculty. Another segregated model in the sights of some African Americans was an institution for Black people run by Black teachers, board, and administration. Such an institution did not exist in South Carolina. A truly multiracial institution also did not exist. Some African Americans saw the possibility of turning Claflin College of Agriculture into a completely Black institution. There were also resentments that state money at Claflin was being administered by a religious organization. Twenty years after the founding of Claflin University, discontent was in the air. Of the three African American faculty members at Claflin University, William L. Bulkley was firmly committed to a multiracial institution. It is clear from his Emancipation Day speech that he believed the "white man and the black man must join hands." [146]

The other two African Americans on the faculty (I. N. Cardozo and A. G. Townsend) had espoused separatist views through their newspaper *The Plain Speaker*. Townsend stated his position to a *Charleston News and Courier* reporter. He was not opposed to all white people but to the many who felt themselves superior. "The instructor's heart should be in sympathy with the race he instructs. It is the color of the heart, not the hide, we want."[147] In light of Townsend's later resignation and that he had been contemplating resigning for several years, the subtext in his careful remarks was that many professors at Claflin were not in sympathy with the students. Townsend was described in the white press as "one of the most bitter and partisan Republicans on the staff of Claflin College." [148]

White newspapers describe Cardozo as "pronouncedly bitter in his hostility to the white people."[149] Isaac N. (I. N.) Cardozo was born a free African American in 1856 in Charleston, son of Henry Cardozo, a friend of V. H. Bulkley. He was the nephew of Reconstruction-era officeholders Francis Lewis Cardozo and Thomas Cardozo. He grew up in Ohio and South Carolina and attended preparatory school at Oberlin College. He also took classes at the University of South Carolina and Wesleyan University. By 1884 he was principal of the Haven Normal School in

Waynesboro, Georgia, a preparatory school for Clark University, an Atlanta college founded by the Freedmen's Aid Society of the Methodist Episcopal Church. In 1885 he was admitted as pastor to the South Carolina Conference of the Methodist Episcopal Church. He completed the College Course at Claflin in 1886, was reassigned to the Methodist congregation at Trinity in Orangeburg, and was named to a position at Baker Theological Institute (a department of Claflin University) as teacher of historical theology.[150] In 1888 he was transferred from Trinity to Webster Memorial Chapel at Claflin University in Orangeburg, where he continued to teach.

A. G. Townsend, an African American, was born in Charleston on August 28, 1853. He began working at age nine to support his widowed mother. He attended the Avery Normal Institute in Charleston (a leading institution for African American education founded in 1865), took classes at Howard University, and graduated from the University of South Carolina on December 13, 1876, during the short period when African Americans could attend. He began leading prayer meetings at the age of fourteen and became a Methodist Episcopal minister in the South Carolina Conference in 1878. He was master of the grammar school at Claflin from 1882 to 1884 and then was appointed professor in 1886, teaching subjects as varied as ancient languages and military tactics.

William J. DeTreville Jr. was born about 1857 in Beaufort, South Carolina, into a prominent white family. His father, who had served in the Confederate government,[151] was an attorney. During the Civil War the DeTreville's family home in Beaufort, South Carolina, was sold to Robert Smalls, an African American. At that time Smalls was already famous for commandeering a Confederate ship in Charleston Harbor and sailing it to freedom. Later he was a US Representative. When the war ended, the elder DeTreville sued for return of his property. The case went to the US Supreme Court, where in 1878 the sale to Smalls was affirmed and DeTreville was denied compensation.[152] DeTreville Jr. graduated from Union College in Schenectady, New York, in 1877 and joined the Claflin faculty in 1879, [153] teaching, among other things, pure and applied mathematics. He was a member of the Edisto Rifles (Second Palmetto Regiment Infantry), a white militia group.[154]

The Caning of Professor Cardozo

From its founding in 1869 as a Methodist Episcopal school, Claflin University was firmly committed to providing education in a Christian environment. Claflin had a theological school, campus chapel, and chaplain, and sponsored Christian events. In February 1890 the school sponsored a religious revival for the students. A revival, which could last several days or even a week, was characterized by prolonged emotional preaching and singing. An event like this was often held outdoors, and revival leaders urged people to commit their lives to Jesus, confess their sins, and join the church. Rev. Cardozo, as chaplain of Claflin, conducted these revivals, and classes were suspended for several days so the students could attend. The *Southwestern Christian Advocate* reported,

> Claflin University . . . has just closed one of the most successful series of revival meetings they have ever had at that University. Some of the results are sixty conversions; three baptisms; one hundred and seven accessions in the church, many Christian hearts encouraged, [and] joy in many households all over the state. Nearly all of the three hundred boarding students now profess religion.[155]

At a faculty meeting on March 3, 1890, shortly after the revival, a special series of lectures was proposed for the spring. W. J. De Treville Jr., protested that the lectures would be as disruptive as the recent religious revival. I. N. Cardozo claimed the revival was not unduly disruptive and furthermore accused De Treville of opposing all revivals of religion at the university. This he claimed to have heard from De Treville's students. De Treville denied it, and Cardozo basically called him a liar. In the nineteenth century, particularly in the South, this was a serious breach of civility and the Southern code of honor.

The next morning as Cardozo was coming up the steps of the main classroom building, DeTreville stood above, waiting for him, and attacked him with his heavy hickory cane, striking him repeatedly about the head until Cardozo was knocked down senseless to the ground or, as the *Charleston News and Courier* described it, "whaled him terribly with a hickory stick."[156] DeTreville walked away. Cardozo was taken to the parlor and seen by a doctor, and took some time to recover. Cardozo wrote this dramatic account.

> As I began to ascend the lower steps of the main college building, Prof. DeTreville was descending the same. As we approached each other, while he was about two steps above me, I expecting to pass on up to the right, and with eyes upon the steps so attempting, he suddenly without the slightest warning of any kind, dealt in rapid succession three terrific blows upon my head. As I recovered from the shock I looked up and saw him holding the smaller end of a knotted hickory stick (the large end thicker than a policeman's club) with both hands and preparing to strike again. I felt a sickening sensation of giddiness begin to possess me, but I at once endeavored to save another blow by grasping his stick first with one hand then with both, and trying to wrench it out of his hands.
>
> As we pulled back and forth for possession of the weapon, we were both jerked off of the steps to a stand on the level ground. The violence of the jerk enabled him to gain the stick again, and my devoted head at once echoed to the dull thud of the cruel club. Here my dizziness increased, but I once more got hold of the stick with one hand (he retaining similar hold) and at the same time was returning with the other hand the blows he was raining down upon my face. What next occurred I only know from the solitary eye-witness who saw the last part of the assault.

He says I then commenced to swoon; as I did so, DeTreville pulled the stick out of the one hand holding it, struck me with it while falling, and then as I lay prostrate and unconscious, dealt me three more murderous blows upon the bare skull and hurried off the grounds.

During all this time I had been impeded in movement by overcoat, books, and gloves, and had no weapon whatever of my own. The bark from his hickory was found scattered on the ground, and a friend afterwards gathered it up, and presented it to me as a relic of the characteristic cowardice of the Southern dastard![157]

Word of the attack spread quickly, and several hundred outraged students gathered and marched to the nearby railroad depot to escort DeTreville out of town. Two local members of the legislature and the mayor of Orangeburg called on Dr. Dunton to support DeTrevilles's return to the classroom. The mayor warned Dunton that if there were any demonstrations, it would be considered a breach of the peace and he would act accordingly. The town seemed to be headed for a major race conflict before President Dunton established an uneasy peace. Bulkley probably played a part in defusing the situation, as he and Dunton had a long relationship. Bulkley's experience and views, as expressed in his Emancipation Day speech, had undoubtedly earned the students' respect and enabled him to be an effective voice in calming the situation and calling for rule of law, not rule of the mob.

DeTreville declared he was ready to return to duty. However, the students refused to go to his classes. On the advice of the State Board of Claflin College of Agriculture, and to give time for the situation to be resolved, Dunton canceled all classes. The university was at an impasse. The incident threatened to break up the college or create an all-white or all-Black faculty.[158] Personal and institutional issues that had been festering for years came to the fore. Positions hardened as DeTreville "consulted friends in the city," and the Edisto Rifles offered to escort him to class.[159] By March 12, all classes at Claflin had resumed except those of Professor DeTreville. He agreed to wait for the action of the State Board of Trustees, who paid his salary, before resuming his duties.[160] On March 15 Rev. Joseph C. (J.C.) Hartzell, secretary of the Freedmen's Aid Society wrote to Rev. Dunton:

> Our feeling here is that DeTreville cannot under any circumstances remain in the school. I say this to you confidentially, and that there can be no compromise even if it should lead to the breaking off of our relations to the state. Irrespective of the provocation, the fact that he did brutally assault one of our colored men has created such a feeling throughout the church that his retention will be impossible, besides it would make such relations between the institutions and the South Carolina [Methodist] Conference as would make co-operation impossible.[161]

By March 18 Dunton secured a pledge from DeTreville to resign if the state board would accept it.[162] Finally in the middle of April as the situation remained unresolved, J. C. Hartzell wrote to South Carolina governor Richardson to unofficially express his insistence that DeTreville resign. It was a veiled threat couched in polite words:

> We have had full confidence in the gentlemen composing the State Board of South Carolina and felt that when they shall come together they will do the right thing; hence, we have not said anything which might embarrass them or the school.[163]

The state board delayed meeting, but on April 22, seven weeks after the attack, they met and announced "that students in the mathematical department were in a state of insubordination in refusing to report for recitation, which must first be remedied; and second that the difficulty between the professors should be referred to a special committee, to report at a meeting to be held April 30."[164] Insubordination or refusal to attend class was grounds for automatic dismissal. President Dunton, at the behest of the state board, required the students to sign that they were not in rebellion against the board, and when those pledges were made, DeTreville submitted his resignation and it was accepted by the board on April 30. How the students were persuaded to give in and sign the affidavits is untold. Perhaps Bulkley, ever the pragmatist, despite his flamboyant rhetoric, pled with them to secure their future by continuing in school. President Dunton reported the situation was "amicably and fully settled," which seems to be an optimistic assessment.[165] DeTreville never taught again. He relocated to Houston, Texas, where he became the secretary of the Houston Cotton Exchange. He died there on June 30, 1910.

On May 3 a correspondent from Camden, South Carolina, wrote to *The Independent* that the resolution hinged on President Dunton requiring the students to "sign paper declaring themselves not in rebellion against the State Board of Trustees."

> Thus, you see, the students were forced to give up the position of manliness which they had maintained for nearly two months. After the students signed the paper referred to, Professor DeTreville sent in his resignation immediately . . . The students feel that they have been humiliated. But what could they do? Some few, I think, will not consent to graduate under the circumstances.[166]

What was William L. Bulkley's reaction? There is no documentation of his thoughts and actions. He would have known both Cardozo and Townsend well. Cardozo's father, Henry, was a lifelong friend of William's father. Townsend used Bulkley as a middle name for one of his sons, indicating a close or respectful relationship with the family. However, Bulkley did not resign with Townsend and Cardozo. In the surviving records he is silent on the matter, so we must take clues from two brief mentions of him in the newspapers. From the report that Bulkley tried "to pacify the students and have them go to work,"[167] he seems to have been working on Dunton's behalf. William I. Haven of the New England Conference, Methodist Episcopal Church, received a letter from Bulkley in which Bulkley "intimates that there may have been blame on both sides—that is to say, he does not in the least condone Professor DeTreville's action, but blames Professor Cardozo for his offensive speech in the faculty meeting."[168] Reading between the lines, his choices illuminate some of the values that remained hallmarks of his career. He was committed to integration and to Black and white people working together for their common good. He was often most interested in shorter-term outcomes—in this case, students staying in school and completing their degrees—rather than making points of principle. He was also committed through family history and long acquaintance to both Claflin University and to President Dunton. Nonetheless, Bulkley's behavior as reported in the white press does not seem to match the passionate rhetoric in his Emancipation Day speech three months earlier.

The State Board of Claflin College of Agriculture inflamed the situation by never condemning DeTreville's action, by stalling for weeks, and by focusing on "insubordination" of the students rather than on De Treville, the true culprit. The Claflin University Board, although in many ways powerless, met at its regular annual meeting on May 19 and passed ten resolutions, including the following:

> Whereas, the recent unfortunate conflict between two professors of the University, Profs. Wm. J. DeTreville and I. N. Cardozo has been the cause of great embarrassment and is to be greatly deplored; therefore, be it resolved: . . .

> While Prof. I. N. Cardozo may have been injudicious in speech, we unqualifiedly condemn the subsequent action of Prof. W. J. DeTreville, whom we had learned to esteem for his excellent intellectual qualities, for the personal injury he inflicted upon Prof. I. N. Cardozo.[169]

The board must have been extremely frustrated with their lack of control over DeTreville and perhaps their lack of control of Dunton and the Freedmen's Aid Society.

During these three months, the relationship between the state and the university was in danger of being severed. On March 8, J. C. Hartzell of the Freedmen's Aid Society wrote to A. G. Haygood that the current events "will probably force a careful discussion of the exact relations which exist between ourselves and the state, which will not be a bad thing."[170] Hartzell explained his reasoning further in his letter to a colleague in Greenwood, South Carolina, on March 28:

> It is of very great importance to our people in that state that the friendly relations between us and the state should continue. The work is so vast and we need such large help in every direction that we want to hold all friends as long as possible.[171]

Historian Gore explains the underlying feelings:

> It had probably not occurred to the many well-intentioned missionaries who came south to educate the freedmen that their charges would one day demand control of the institutions in which they were being taught. These churchmen could not have foreseen that their humanitarian efforts would finally be interpreted by some as benevolent despotism.[172]

Many things about this incident and how it was handled are appalling, not the least of which is that there was never any recorded consideration of filing assault charges against DeTreville. The Claflin University Board was in a difficult position—they could not fire or punish DeTreville because he worked for the State Board of the Claflin College of Agricultural Sciences. They surely would have liked to have been more outspoken in support of the students and the two professors who resigned. However, open conflict with the state board would undoubtedly have meant the severing of the Agricultural College from the University and the loss of state funding for the education program that was used to support students from both the university and the college. Members of the Claflin University Board may have considered such a move in 1890, but Dunton and Hartzell charted a different course.

President Dunton was in an even more difficult position. He was president of both the university and the college and committed to the survival of both. In a letter from Dunton to William B. Claflin, the university's private patron, Dunton wrote:

> If I should go against the State then I may lose the moral and financial support of the State. If I should go against the Claflin Board, I give an offense to the colored people that no argument could correct.[173]

Dunton's talent lay in his considerable force of personality and his commitment to Claflin University's survival and growth. The students seemed to like and respect him, returned to campus at his request, and eventually signed the pledges of "nonrebellion" at his behest. He was an excellent fundraiser, improved the curriculum and physical plant throughout his thirty-eight-year presidency, and was an excellent publicist. He did what he could to keep the institution alive and prospering, even when principle was compromised. In 1890 Dunton seemed to have gingerly handled the students, the Freedmen's Aid Society, and the state as well as both boards and come out with a positive outcome—he had to dismiss no students, got rid of DeTreville, and managed to keep Claflin's funding and reputation intact. However, Dunton may also have been responsible for prompting the resignations of Townsend and Cardozo. Townsend reported that Dunton blamed him and Cardozo for the students' refusal to report for class.[174] In 1995 Claflin University assessed Dunton's presidency thus:

> Dr. Dunton was sensitive to the political and economic climate of the times. He maintained the delicate balance of sensitivity to the outside world and ambition for his institution that allowed it to grow through funding and endorsements. . . . However, despite a discernible hostility in the social climate,

the number of graduates of Claflin's college and normal courses continued to increase. Many became teachers and ministers, greatly uplifting educational levels wherever they worked and resided.[175]

In 1896 Claflin University and Claflin College of Agriculture became two separate institutions. The College of Agriculture became the Colored Normal, Industrial, Agricultural, and Mechanical College, now known as South Carolina State University.

> Thus, we have the spectacle of southern whites, who wished to resegregate public education in South Carolina, joining with Blacks, who wished to ensure educational opportunity for their constituents, in an effort which would eventually destroy the marriage between Church and State at Claflin University.[176]

After his resignation Cardozo briefly joined the AME Church,[177] thus severing his connection with the Methodist Episcopal Church. He was elected to the faculty of the newly established college as professor of moral and mental science and pedagogy. He remained on the faculty until his death in April 1898 at the age of forty-two. The *News and Courier* wrote in Cardozo's obituary that he was "one of the most intelligent colored men in the State, and worked hard for his people."[178]

After his resignation Townsend served as a pastor in the South Carolina Conference of the Methodist Episcopal Church for the next forty years and retired from the ministry in 1931. In 1936 he was offered the honor of a gold-tipped cane as the oldest living alumnus of the University of South Carolina. When it was discovered by the university that it had offered the cane to an African American, the award was hastily withdrawn. He died in Sumter, South Carolina, in 1937 at the age of 83.[179]

The incident at Claflin, although local, attracted wide attention. The *Charleston News and Courier* provided major coverage of the event. It was of interest to both their white and African American readers. National newspapers picked up the story from the Charleston paper. The interest outside the South was primarily from publications affiliated with the Methodist Church, African American publications, and newspapers in Massachusetts, where the benefactor of Claflin was well known. With significant national negative publicity in newspapers from Boston to Texas, Dunton began damage control immediately after the settlement. On May 23 a full-page article in the *Charleston News and Courier* covered the commencement activities of the previous days. The resolutions of the Claflin University Board condemning DeTreville appeared at the end of the article, but otherwise the incident was not mentioned. In the fall he generated a spate of positive publicity. Among other reports, J. L. M. Curry, general agent for the Peabody Education Fund, called Claflin "the greatest institution in the South for the education of negroes,"[180] and the *Charleston News and Courier* published another full-page description of Claflin and its programs and achievements.[181]

Most of the events of spring 1890 at Claflin were reported in white newspapers with a predictable bias toward supporting DeTreville and justifying his behavior. The *Charleston News and Courier* reported on March 5, 1890, that Cardozo "got what he deserved." The *Watchman and Southron* printed an opinion that was probably widely held: "It is not to be expected that a fusion faculty composed of heterogeneous elements, naturally antagonistic, could get along peaceably. . . . We have always been opposed to the mixed faculty of Claflin and the present difficulties there are but the natural outgrowth of relations between members of the faculty that are necessarily strained." [182] DeTreville is often described as a "gentleman," whereas Cardozo is described as having a "reputation for being aggressive towards whites," [183] and both he and Townsend were described as "Republicans," which automatically carried a negative connotation to Southern white people. You can only imagine what would have happened and what would have been said if the situation were reversed and Cardozo had attacked DeTreville. Scattered among these majority opinions were reports from African American, religious, and liberal media.

> Any man who will pound a minister's head with a club because his [DeTreville's] low state of manhood rebels at the success the man of God is having in an institution of learning where both are members of the faculty, should be kicked and clubbed out of the country. There is no place in this country for such whelps as DeTreville.[184]

The *Southwestern Christian Advocate*, a Methodist publication edited by A. E. P. Albert, an African American, was slow to catch up with the story but then published a clear statement about the "murderous attack" that declared: "Our Church cannot continue him as a professor there without absolutely insulting every Negro in America."[185] Albert suggested Claflin would need to separate from the state school. On March 20, 1890, *The Independent* published a report titled "Why was he [DeTreville] not arrested?" The New England Conference of the Methodist Episcopal Church, home to Governor William Claflin, a major benefactor of Claflin University, passed a resolution on April 12, 1890, that read in part:

> While we have no excuse to offer for the offensive words of Prof Cardosa [*sic*] and regard them as a breach of courtesy for which their author should have made a frank apology, we have no words to express our chagrin that there should be found a professor in Claflin university who could see no way to resent an insult except by the cowardly use of the bludgeon. For this brutal outrage, Prof DeTreville should be promptly relieved of his professorship, or tried in court as a criminal. Nothing less than this will vindicate the honor of the university and of the state, and meet the demands of a Christian civilization.[186]

By the beginning of 1891 Episcopal Bishop P. F. Stevens, a white man in Charleston known for his work with African American congregations, had joined the faculty at Claflin University. He taught pure and applied mathematics. Henry Pearson, an African American Claflin graduate of 1888, was promoted from the industrial department to assistant professor of Greek and literature.[187] And Claflin moved on. In the end this incident faded from memory. Claflin University and Claflin College of Agriculture moved toward their inevitable separation, and Claflin University survived as an independent institution.

Within the space of six months William Lewis Bulkley's world brought into high relief the brutal repression of Black people in the South and the stark divisions of society that accepted, without punishment, the lynching of eight African Americans and the assault by a white professor of an African American one. He revealed his own attitudes and anguish through his Emancipation Day speech and his letter to *The Argus* about the lynching as well as his decision to remain at Claflin. He believed white and Black people should work together to achieve a world where racial caste was eliminated. He focused on the practical in his actions and the ideal in his speeches. He had an unwavering faith in education, religion, and hard work to solve racial problems. Through the lens of 1890 we can see in a microcosm the world of an African American in South Carolina and the "troublous times" of William L. Bulkley in particular.

Claflin University; Main Building, 2nd from left, and the steps where Cardozo was beaten with a cane

Proceedings of the Convention of Southern Governors, 1893

IV

LOYALTY TO THE SOUTHLAND, 1890–1899

Negroes who love their birthplace, love its balmy air, its sunny skies, its fertile fields, its luxuriant forests, the camaraderie of their kith and kin. To us there never cease to come times of yearning to revisit the old spots of our childhood and of our youth, to meet our brethren to hear their tale of woe, to weep with them over their distresses, to rejoice with them in their successes, to share with them the soul-refreshings that only a Negro revival can give.[188]

After the events of 1890, William L. Bulkley found his voice and went into action. It is as if he had repeated to himself, "Yes, I will."[189] He continued his education by earning an MA degree from Claflin in 1891.[190] He expanded his activities beyond teaching and university life. He sought to learn, serve, and teach. Bulkley spoke widely in South Carolina—at a Fourth of July picnic in Newberry, at Methodist Episcopal district conferences, at a Sunday school institute in Timmonsville, and at graduation at the Howard School in Columbia. One of the speeches that he gave was entitled "Despise Not the Day of Small Things."

> [Bulkley] showed that it is by accepting and mastering small things that the topmost round of the ladder of fame is reached. The subject was discussed from three points: First, No one should hesitate to seek greatness, resting with the belief that there is a lack of innate ability; second, Poverty should not be a barrier in the road to eminence; third, There is no room in the

world for a man who folds his arms and says, "I have nothing to do."[191]

His speeches elicited such compliments as, "His address was of a high order and appreciated by all" and "It was a masterly effort. Conservative, eloquent, humorous, pathetic."[192]

In an effort to spread skills and train others, Bulkley taught at a "colored teacher's institute," providing a professional development opportunity for about forty teachers.[193] Bulkley was not only interested in training others but also in bringing people together around common goals, foreshadowing later efforts. In 1898 Bulkley was part of the committee of representatives of the four Black colleges in South Carolina that called teachers to revive the Colored Teachers State Association, which had been inactive for many years. Its August meeting was attended by over 140 teachers. They recommended forming county and township associations to further the cause of education, extending the school term to at least six months, and increasing teacher salaries. Bulkley was appointed to serve on three committees: charter commission, bylaws, and publicity.[194]

Bulkley continued his interest in the Young Men's Christian Association (YMCA), first evidenced at Wesleyan in 1886 when he attended a YMCA Bible conference in Massachusetts. He was part of a conference of state and international YMCA representatives who discussed ways to increase the number of YMCA organizations in South Carolina that would be open to African Americans.[195] He also traveled in the South and to Mexico, lecturing and studying the "conditions of the people." "He is talking to the people on matters pertaining to their most vital interests."[196] In 1895 he attended the International Epworth Convention in Chattanooga, Tennessee. The Epworth League, founded in 1889, was a movement in the Methodist Episcopal Church for the spiritual education of young adults in the church. The meeting was a joint one of both branches of the Methodist Episcopal Church. The southern branch, which withdrew over the issue of slavery, was still a separate organization. At this meeting, "The treatment of colored delegates was far from Christian," noted Rev. E. B. Burroughs in the *Southwestern Christian Advocate*.[197] There were attempts to segregate seating in the hall and to marginalize the African American speakers. No record exists of Bulkley's thoughts or the role he played, but it surely was a disheartening experience.

In February 1896, at the South Carolina Conference of the Methodist Episcopal Church, Bulkley was elected as a lay delegate to the Methodist Episcopal General Conference in Cleveland, Ohio.[198] The order of business contained many mundane matters such as appointments and budgets but also faced issues about whether women delegates could be seated (they were) and whether to condemn a law recently enacted in Florida making it a "penal offense" to have an integrated school (they did).[199] Bulkley was appointed to two standing committees—Freedmen's Aid and Southern Education Society and the Committee on Missions.[200] His twin prescriptions for progress were religion and education. Religion was driving his teaching, speaking, and participation in groups that provided education or furthered his participation in the church. However, he did not neglect the educational side of his own life. He devoted three years of his time to his own education, two as a nonresident doctoral student at Syracuse University and one as a student at the best European universities.

Syracuse University, 1891–1893

In the fall of 1891 Bulkley matriculated at Syracuse University in New York as a PhD candidate in Latin language and literature. Syracuse was a Methodist school (like Claflin and Wesleyan) and had an active graduate program, primarily for nonresidents. The doctoral degree required a minimum of two years of study, an examination covering both years, and a thesis.[201] From the first year of its formal graduate program in 1873 through 1893, Syracuse awarded 127 doctorates, nine of which were in ancient languages.[202] Bulkley's PhD was only the fourth granted to an African

American in the United States and the first in classical languages. [viii] Bulkley's instructor Professor Frank Smalley had been at Syracuse University as a student and professor since 1871. His "teaching centered about the classics with special attention to Latin of which he became an ardent student, a skilled researcher, and the author of several books."[203]

Smalley reported that after "two years' hard study, [Bulkley] succeeded in passing the rigid exams."[204] Smalley described Bulkley's strengths: "He has the spirit of an investigator and an independent thinker, that refuses to take the conclusions of editors without careful examination of the reasons, for himself. He has done much work on the literature and toward the language, shows excellent ability in grasping the thought of an author, and has unusual facility in rendering into idiomatic English." [205] Bulkley described his own feelings about Latin in the *Claflin Catalogue*:

> At the *outset* our aim shall be not to crowd the pupils' minds with dry rules and tedious inflections, but to strengthen their knowledge of the English, while they are mastering the fundamental principles of the Latin. . . . The chief aim in studying this language is to vivify the studies supposed by the untutored horde to be forever dead; to show wherein they (Latin and Greek) form the beautiful in our own tongue; to cultivate a taste for literature of a high order; and to develop proper and effective expression of thought.[206]

[viii] Preceding PhDs were awarded to Edward A. Bouchet, Yale, 1876, in physics, John W. E. Bowen, Boston University, 1887, in theology, and A. O. Coffin, Illinois Wesleyan University, 1889, in biology.

Study Abroad, 1893–1894

Shortly after the Claflin University commencement exercises on May 24, 1893, Bulkley, his wife, and their infant daughter, Maude, left Charleston by steamer to travel to New York and then by train to Syracuse. He had a palpable sense of relief sailing away from Charleston on the *Iroquois*.

> I could not refrain from heaving a sigh of relief that for a few months at least I should not be sickened by the disgusting head[line]: "Lynched for the usual crime!" . . . Save for the loved ones, save for the great work of christian [*sic*] education, save for the vast opportunities of doing good among so large a population, I [would turn] my back upon the land that gave me birth. . . . I hate this spirit that will not recognize a man because forsooth! his Creator saw fit to make him Black. I hate with all the intensity of my nature that spirit which crushes every aspiration of a man; that forces the soul that could love and suffer for his native land to hate the spot that gave him birth[.] Alas! . . . nothing can here bring a man the just recognition of a man; nothing! Character, wealth, intelligence, all seem to fail in gaining the rights that any freeman has reason to claim.[207]

At Syracuse he took the examinations required for his PhD, but he did not stay for commencement. It was only the first leg of a trip that was to take him to Europe for sightseeing and post-doctoral study. On June 10, 1893, the little family sailed from New York harbor on the *Maasdam*. They arrived in Rotterdam more than a week later, where they boarded a steamer, which took them up the Rhine, passing through Cologne and Mainz to Mannheim. In Mannheim they boarded a train to Strasbourg, then part of the German Empire. Here Bulkley matriculated in the University of Strasbourg for the academic year to study Latin. He was expected to speak not only Latin but also Greek and German. The work was "the comparing of [manuscripts], the correcting of texts, discussing the origin and development of strange words and phrases, archaisms; in fact, everything that pertains to a through, ground-work understanding of the language."[208] At the end of his two terms he went to Paris for the summer to study Latin at the University of France at the Sorbonne. Just as he'd had to learn German to take advantage of his studies at Strasbourg, he had to learn to speak and understand French to get the most out of his studies in Paris.

Bulkley wrote letters describing his trip to the editor of the *Southwestern Christian Advocate*, a Methodist Episcopal Church publication aimed at its church members in the South, primarily African Americans. The letters were published in seventeen articles under the headline "Our Foreign Letter." These are the most personal of Bulkley's writings that survive and thus give an insight into his personality and his thoughts as a young man. He was interested in mechanics and science. He noted with precision the exact descriptions of a ship (2,577 tons burden, fifty-eight staterooms, triple expansion engines) and of fortifications (fifty feet wide at the base, twenty-five feet high and twenty feet broad at top). He was observant about the people around him, writing about the clothing the country people wore and the crops they were growing. He wrote about the farms, which were not plantations but "patches" like a block quilt or strips of carpet. He noted a woman pulling a cart harnessed next to a dog. This prompted the observation that European women's rights were not "such 'high diddle diddle,' election-time, will-o'-the-wisp twaddle"[209] as those espoused by feminists in the United States. He was also fascinated by novel and "quirky" things and spent as many paragraphs writing about salt extraction in Syracuse and barbering in Heidelberg as he did on more serious topics.

Bulkley visited Cologne Cathedral, Heidelberg University, and sites in Worms associated with Martin Luther. His deep grounding in his Protestant faith is evident. Standing on the hill above Heidelberg Castle, he looked over the town, the rivers, and the Alps.

> When I climb the Alps, when I cross the ocean, when I see
> God's finger-prints everywhere, I feel that the strongest, the
> most eloquent language possible to human tongue must fail to

give expressions to my emotions. I simply cannot. The words of men's lips are not made to express divine thoughts![210]

He revealed the anti-Catholic sentiments of his time, wishing the Cologne Dom could resound with less "Ave Maria" and more "Joy to the World!" Throughout, Bulkley brought to bear his deep knowledge of Greek and Roman history, the Bible, and literature and art.

Race was never far from his mind. Throughout his travels in Europe, he found no other Black people until he got to Paris. There were many people of color in Paris, but they were from places like Central and South America, Haiti, and Africa, not from the United States. This pained him greatly. Ironically, in May 1894, when Bulkley arrived in Paris, W. E. B. Du Bois was in Paris, viewing statues at the Louvre and seeing Sarah Bernhardt.[211] There is no indication their paths crossed, and Bulkley does not mention meeting anyone from America while he was there.

> In none of [these countries] can I find the prejudice one must meet under the stars and stripes. In the country where Protestant Christianity has its largest following; in the country where the English language, the boasted language of progress, is spoken; in the country where the constitution offers the right to enjoy life, liberty and the pursuit of happiness, there we see the most virulent type of Negro phobia.

> The more I travel, the more I'm getting convinced that the peculiar prejudicial environments we suffer make us fall behind our brethren of other lands. But if the Bible be true; if Christianity be not a farce; if Jehovah be not a myth, prejudice and its concomitant evils must pass away. It is an anarchy; it is a hydra-headed monster; it is a burning disgrace to the fair name of the most progressive land of the world; it is a child of the devil. We must work, we must wait. We must trust the Hand unseen.[212]

Bulkley ended his series with "Oh, that we had the opportunity to climb in America! On every side a barrier! God speed the right!"[213] His impassioned indictments of racism and turning to God for the solution reveal a deep source of energy for making change and a reliance on the triumph of the right. In the end the latter is a hope, not a guarantee.

Claflin University, 1894–1899

Bulkley returned to Claflin in September 1894 and started a night school that used the facilities of Claflin University, volunteer teachers, and a minimum charge (one penny per night) to cover heat, lighting, and janitor work. Thirty-two men from the laboring classes, aged sixteen to fifty, enrolled in the classes to learn "the three Rs." But that was not the only purpose of the course. Bulkley wrote that

> the object in starting this class was not only to help the two or three scores who may become members, but also, and chiefly, to set an example to the hundreds of [college] students who come to this school every year from every corner of this State and from adjoining States. They can, they ought, they will do a like work where they go. The lesson is one of helpfulness. It is easy; it is practical; it is Christian.[214]

This is a forerunner of the work he would do in New York City. It is interesting to imagine this initiative incubating in Bulkley's mind while he was studying advanced languages in Europe. It also demonstrates one of the principles Bulkley followed in his other work: train the teacher to multiply the impact.

1896 was a critical year for Claflin and Bulkley. Claflin College of Agriculture separated from Claflin University.[215] The US Supreme Court handed down a decision in *Plessy v. Ferguson* that affirmed the constitutionality of racial segregation.[216] Bulkley, while continuing to teach, was promoted to vice president of Claflin under the presidency of L. M. Dunton, his former teacher in Greenville, becoming Claflin University's first Black administrator.[217]

The Thirteenth, Fourteenth, and Fifteenth Amendments to the US Constitution abolished slavery, provided equal protection of the law, and ensured the right to vote. However, states continued to pass laws abridging these rights for African Americans. Litigation over these laws reached the Supreme Court in 1873. The court's decisions weakened the protection of these amendments. In 1896 the Supreme Court upheld a Louisiana law passed in 1890 requiring separate railroad cars for African American and white riders. Segregation in transportation had been a topic of editorial, legislative, and court action throughout the nineteenth century.[218] The decision in the case of *Plessy v. Ferguson* affirmed the doctrine that segregation by race was legal as long as equal accommodations were made. The ruling did not get widespread attention at the time, but it legitimized segregation and Jim Crow, setting the stage for the nadir of civil rights in the United States. The day after the ruling, a brief article appeared in *The State*, published in Columbia, which Bulkley certainly read. He may have realized the implications of this decision and begun his deliberations about leaving the South and establishing a new life in the North.[219] In 1897, emboldened by the *Plessy v. Ferguson* decision, South Carolina considered its own segregated cars bill. Bulkley wrote to the newspaper:

> Every vestige of authority has been taken from our hands. The ballot, the jury box, nearly every municipal and every State position is lost to us. Is that not enough? Is it necessary to deprive us of the comfort of a public conveyance and subject our wives and daughters to the indignities practiced on a "Jim Crow" car? Is it chivalrous to knock a man who is down?
>
> I have traveled in every State that has such a car. I know what indecencies are practiced there. I know to what dangers a helpless woman is exposed. I have always returned to South Carolina with the satisfaction that in my native State there was still that spirit of justice sufficiently alive to heed the appeal of even the humblest citizen.[220]

In 1898, when the Jim Crow car bill was introduced for the seventh time, it passed the South Carolina legislature. Six Claflin University teachers, including Bulkley, lobbied against the passage of that bill.[221]

The 1896 split between Claflin University and Claflin College of Agriculture cost the university $17,000 as well as land, buildings, equipment, and students. The university's very existence was threatened. Dunton managed the transition with fiscal belt-tightening and the help of the Freedmen's Aid Society. Bulkley wrote that Dunton's success was attributable to "his coolness, energy, perseverance, and constant work."[222]

One of Bulkley's new roles as vice president was traveling "in the interests of the University" to raise money in the North.[223] In 1871 the Fisk University Jubilee Singers had pioneered using the touring music ensemble to raise money. Entertainment was a good way to attract an audience. Bulkley often traveled with the Claflin's Plantation Melody Quintet[224] to lecture and raise funds. In the summers of 1897, 1898, and 1899, he toured Massachusetts, New York City, Brooklyn, and Long Island. During these trips Bulkley had sufficient opportunity to meet other people and see what life was like in the North.

By 1899 William was thirty-eight years old; had a wife and four daughters, aged two through eight; had been a teacher and professor for at least fourteen years; and had been the vice president of Claflin for three years. He had a bachelor's degree from Claflin (1882), two years of academic work at Wesleyan University (1884–1886), an MA from Claflin (1891), a PhD from Syracuse University (1893), and post-doctoral education at Strasbourg University and the University of France (1893–1894). He had lectured throughout South Carolina, traveled in the United States and abroad, and endured years of Jim Crow rule and violence. He was a leading African American voice, considered among the national leaders of the time. The *Independent* included Bulkley as one of those on a par with Booker T. Washington. "We do not give [Washington] any unique honor above what we give to Professor Crogman, Professor Dubois [*sic*], Professor Wright or Professor Bulkley." [225] William H. Crogman was professor of Greek at Clark University, W. E. B. Du Bois was professor of history and economics at Atlanta University, and Richard R. Wright[226] was a Republican politician and president of Georgia State Industrial College for Colored Youth.

Bulkley was also giving thought to his own future. He loved the South, but as repression, violence, and lynching escalated, it was harder and harder for him to stay. What came next for this talented, educated, dedicated, thoughtful man? Where were his children to be educated? Would they grow up in a segregated South? It was a long time before he was ready to say, "Enough," and leave the South, Claflin, and the church to move to the North.

Hall of Languages, Syracuse University, Syracuse N. Y.

Hall of Languages, Syracuse University   Collection of the author

William L. Bulkley   *Success*, 1899

Delftsche Poort

Rotterdam, The Netherlands   Collection of the author

Heidelberg, seen from the Hirschgasse, Baden, Germany   Library of Congress

Strasbourg University   Collection of the author

Sorbonne, University of France   *La France illustrée*, 1881

V

GIVING HIS MOST CAREFUL
ATTENTION, 1899–1923

It is to these children in New York that we are giving our most
careful, sympathetic, hopeful attention. [227]

In 1898, on one of his fundraising trips in the North, Bulkley took the examination for department head in the New York City school system.[228] He received a certificate and was ready to begin a new phase in his life. He arrived in New York City in November, 1899, to take a job as an elementary school teacher. It was the start of a twenty-three-year career in the New York City school system. He met racism with every step but eventually became the city's first African American principal of a school with white students and white teachers.

New York City School Desegregation

Bulkley was not the first, nor the last, to make progress toward integrating the staff and administration of New York City's schools. A long and deliberate process of legislative, judicial, and local actions affected African American students, teachers, and principals. Schools for African Americans had existed since the eighteenth century, run by organizations such as the English Society for the Propagation of the Gospel in Foreign Parts and New York Manumission Society. By the 1850s five schools for African Americans were run by yet another group, the Public School Society. In

1853 these private schools were merged into the New York City public school system. However, allocation of public resources to the schools was inadequate, far below that spent on white schools. African American churches attempted to compensate by adding Sunday schools where students could receive both religious and literacy instruction.[229]

In 1857 abolitionist Charles B. Ray and pharmacist and activist Philip A. White, both African Americans and representatives of the New York Society for the Promotion of Education among Colored Children, wrote a detailed examination of the "colored schools" for the state commissioners, who were examining the common schools of New York City. After a presentation of facts on population, attendance, expenditures, and taxes, they concluded that

> there is no sound reason why colored children shall be excluded from any of the common schools supported by taxes levied alike on whites and black . . . But if . . . common schools are not thus common to all, then we earnestly pray you to recommend to the Legislature such action as shall cause the Board of Education of this city to erect at least two well-appointed modern grammar schools for colored children.[230]

In response only modest actions were taken to improve the school buildings, and the schools remained segregated. In his 1859 annual report, the superintendent of New York City schools stated the public schools were open to both Black and white children. This had little practical impact, and the "colored schools" remained in the New York City system.[231] In 1864 the Common School Act authorized "separate but equal" schools.

In 1873 New York State passed a general civil rights law that provided that no person be excluded by race or color from accommodations and facilities, including public schools. The law was drafted by William H. Johnson, an African American who had been fighting for racial equality since before the Civil War.[232]

Months later the state Supreme Court ruled that the 1873 Civil Rights Act did not supersede the earlier act permitting segregated schools. Thus, the school system's segregated schools were still legal. Despite the fact that New York City schools were now technically open to all students, three "colored schools" remained. In 1884 the state legislature passed a law making the "colored schools" of New York City into ward schools, putting them on an equal footing with the other public schools. The schools were now open to all students without regard to race or color under state and local law. [233] As pupils chose to attend the formerly forbidden schools, enrollment at the segregated schools declined, and they were slated to be closed. If the "colored schools" were closed, the Black teachers would lose their jobs. Although student bodies were beginning to integrate, the faculty remained segregated, and Black teachers would not be hired in the integrated schools.

The teachers lobbied to maintain the "colored schools." Two of the schools, PS 80 and PS 81, remained open, and though they were ward schools, the students were almost entirely African American. Charles L. Reason and Sarah J. S. Garnet, principals of these schools, thus became the first principals of integrated schools in New York City, but few white students chose to enroll. In an attempt to attract pupils, the schools were promoted in the community, and car-fare was offered for pupils who would commute. In 1893 Reason died, PS 81 was closed, and Garnet was transferred to PS 80, bringing a number of teachers with her. [234] Thus, PS 80, where Bulkley was to become principal in 1901, was the legacy "colored school" in New York City and retained a virtually all-Black student body and many African American teachers.[235] In 1900 Roosevelt signed another bill into law making any public school in New York State open to all children regardless of race. The city schools already had that legal requirement, but the "colored school" remained—a result of custom and of residential segregation.

Since the 1873 New York State civil rights law, no new African American teachers had been hired, as they would have had to be assigned to schools with white children. In 1888 Susan Frazier placed fourth on the teacher examination but was passed over many times for appointment to a school. In 1895 she and T. McCants Stewart, a Black lawyer and civil rights leader, filed a writ of mandamus in the New York State Supreme Court, asking the court to compel the Board of Education to appoint her. The court denied her request on procedural grounds. [236] However, several months later, whether due to nationwide publicity or to political intervention, she was appointed to an integrated school.

Changes in the New York City school system that would affect Bulkley's career were also taking place. In 1896 the city's school system was centralized, a victory for the reformers who envisioned a professional elite running the schools and removing local control and the consequent patronage. With the consolidation of the boroughs in 1898, the reach of centralization extended to Brooklyn, Queens, and Staten Island as well. The details of the changes in Brooklyn were negotiated in the state legislature, and Brooklyn schools retained some aspects of local control, such as the local school committee. [237] Nevertheless, centralization initiated "a remarkable burst of energy and innovation, unparalleled before or since in the New York schools."[238] Reforms included appointment by examination, standardized curricula, and establishment of evening, trade, and industrial schools.

William H. Maxwell was the superintendent of schools for the newly consolidated system. He was a forward-looking, progressive educator from Ireland with teaching and administrative experience as well as experience as a reporter and editor. Maxwell enthusiastically implemented the provision for examinations, even though there was opposition among teachers as the rankings were to be used not only for initial teaching positions but also for promotions. Previously jobs were often granted through the local patronage system. In fact, when Maxwell immigrated to New York City in

1872, he had been unable to secure a position for himself because he did not have the necessary political connections. Maxwell supported the examination system with unqualified praise as "the sentinel at the city gate to keep unworthy persons out of the teaching ranks, and to obtain for the schools of the city the best qualified men and women in America."[239]

The city's schools faced enormous challenges. There were not enough seats in the schools for every child; thousands were turned away each day. Students of many ages came to school without being able to read. Children dropped out in large numbers to work to support their families or because they were discouraged with school. Finally, the school system had the enormous responsibility of acculturating the newcomers, especially foreign-born but also new arrivals from the South.

PS 114, Canarsie, Brooklyn

On November 13, 1899, William L. Bulkley, PhD, stepped before a classroom of eighth-grade boys to begin his new appointment as a teacher at PS 114 in the Canarsie neighborhood of Brooklyn. Canarsie was still a village with dirt streets. It was home to families that had lived there for generations as well as to newly arrived German immigrants. As in the rest of the city, the rapidly growing school-age population was outstripping school capacity. Teachers were desperately needed. In 1900 Brooklyn's population was 1,166,582, of whom 30 percent were foreign born and only 1.5 percent Black. Eleven percent of the foreign-born population was not literate in any language, and 9 percent of African Americans were illiterate. Eighteen hundred children under the age of sixteen were not able to attend school because they were employed in manufacturing, earning enough to be critical to their families' economic status.

In 1898, during one of his fundraising trips for Claflin, Bulkley had taken the new examination instituted by Superintendent Maxwell. He passed and received a certificate for a vice principal or department head position. He hoped to get an appointment as instructor of Latin at Eastern District High School, which was to be opened in February 1900.[240] The examination alone may not have been sufficient to get Bulkley a job quickly. However, the vestiges of the old patronage system in Brooklyn did the rest. A representative of the African American community had been on the Brooklyn school board since 1882. Samuel R. Scottron (ca. 1843–1911), an engineer, inventor, and activist, held that position in 1899. He was the kind of self-made man whom Bulkley admired. He was a barber and grocer; he invented and manufactured a barber's mirror. He then began manufacturing adjustable window cornices, curtain rods, and porcelain onyx. He was educated in Brooklyn schools and at Cooper Union.

Scottron was a member of the Board of Education's Local Committee for PS 114. Thus, he was in a position to help once Bulkley was on the eligible list of teachers.[241] Local committees were made up of three members of the forty-five-member school board and had the power to make recommendations to the teachers' committee for appointment of teachers in their schools. This vestige of the old patronage system was soon to disappear, but it gave Bulkley the leg up he needed to get an appointment in the schools.

Bulkley received his appointment, pending final board approval. On November 6, Bulkley observed eighth-grade classes at Brooklyn's Training School for Teachers.[242] One week later he stood before his own class of eighth-grade boys at PS 114. It was not long before the "color question" was raised.[243] Although the parents of the pupils raised no objection, the teachers demanded that the board deny him a permanent appointment because he was not white. The teachers declared they would resign if Bulkley's appointment was made permanent. They did not want to work with an African American, nor did they want an African American teaching their white pupils. The principal of the school, Mrs. Mary J. McHench, was satisfied with Bulkley's work and requested that the board approve him. However, it was the local committee that needed to recommend the permanent appointment to the teaching committee of the board. Committee member Edward M. Bassett withdrew his support for a permanent appointment, saying "he had thought it was a class of colored children he was to teach, and not white children."[244] The exam Bulkley had passed was for head of department. Another man made the specious argument that there would be no problem if his appointment had been made at the appropriate level, that of department head instead of classroom teacher. Borough Superintendent of Schools John Jasper responded to the controversy:

> Mr. Bulkley was here this morning, and said the whole matter was talk, and there was nothing to it. He remarked that he was doing good work as a teacher, and intended to present himself before Superintendent Maxwell at the next principals' examination. If he gets on that list we are bound to appoint him. It is about four years since colored teachers began to teach white children in Manhattan. The colored teachers stand on exactly the same footing as the white teachers. Everything depends on themselves.[245]

The question was not a legal issue as there was no legal segregation of pupils or teachers in the schools. There were already about twenty Black teachers in the schools of Greater New York.[246] However, when the school board met on January 2, 1900, Bulkley's name had been crossed off the list that the teachers' committee had submitted to the board for approval. The matter was urgent; Bulkley's appointment was set to expire on January 31.[247]

On March 1, Bulkley was surprised to discover that there was no paycheck for him. When he inquired at the Board of Education, he found his name had been dropped from the payroll.[248] Bulkley went to Scottron:

> They have dropped me . . . My name was not on the payroll which came out to the school on Thursday, and when I went down to the board rooms to get an explanation I was told that the teachers committee at its last meeting had seen fit not to appoint me. I tried to see Mr. Bendernagle [the chair of the

committee] at his home, but he would not even allow me in his house.[249]

Scottron was prepared to ask for an investigation.[250] Under that threat and having no way to legally stonewall the appointment, the teachers' committee finally approved Bulkley's permanent appointment in New York City schools on March 6. With his permanent position in New York secured at last, Bulkley submitted his resignation to Claflin University, which was accepted by the board on March 27, thus ending his over twenty-year association with the university.[251] Bulkley cannot have helped but wonder if he was leaving the Jim Crow South for the Jim Crow North. He had left home, his family, his people, and his college and now was immediately the center of controversy. Perhaps this did not surprise him, but nonetheless it was a rough way to start his northern educational career and one that prefigured the years ahead as he pushed against the color line.[252]

Further demonstrating the similarities of the North and South, in August 1900 there was a riot in the Tenderloin District in Manhattan, just across the river from Brooklyn. The Tenderloin was the area of Manhattan where most African Americans lived. It extended from approximately 23rd to 60th Street and Fifth to Eight Avenue. The area not only was crowded with housing but also bars, theaters, brothels, and dance halls. A young Black man killed a plainclothes policeman who was harassing his wife. Racial tensions exploded.

> The entire neighborhood went wild with rage. . . . Up and down the streets, through hotels and saloons, in cellars and streetcars, Negroes were attacked and beaten. White street gangs mobbed the electric cars on Eighth Avenue . . . pulled Negroes off at random and beat them.[253]

The police not only did nothing to stop the violence but also some were participants in the mayhem. Many serious injuries occurred, and in the ensuing days of unrest two people died. The violence looked different in

New York than in South Carolina, but it was nonetheless violence and was still motivated by race.

PS 80, Manhattan

Six months after the riot, on March 6, 1901, Bulkley was appointed principal of PS 80 at 265 W. 41st Street in Manhattan in the heart of the Tenderloin District.[254] This occasioned the notice of the media nationwide. PS 80 had been "Colored School No. 3," and by virtue of custom, location, and recruitment of pupils the school continued to be mostly African American. Sarah S. T. Garnet retired from PS 80 in 1900, leaving the principal's position vacant.[255] John Jasper, Manhattan superintendent of schools, turned to those on the eligible list of principals to fill the position. No one wanted to be principal in a former "colored school," which had always had a Black principal. Bulkley had taken the principal's examination and was near the bottom of the list (which was arranged by date of passing the test). More than thirty people on the list refused the appointment and waived their right to the job before Bulkley could be appointed.[256] Bulkley at age forty was optimistic, hardworking, and professionally prepared to take on the challenges of this poor district. He began to transform the school. He established a kindergarten to care for the children of working parents. He involved the parents in the school, essentially turning the school into a social center, meeting many needs of the very poor African American newcomers from the South.

Bulkley increased the usefulness of the school to both families and students. To involve the parents, the teachers visited homes and spoke in the community. The school had five evening meetings for parents in each term. The themes were home, school, industry, and education, with a social night added. Each two-hour event had a short literary or musical program and then a discussion of the subject of the evening with displays of children's work on industrial and educational nights. On social nights parents furnished the cake, and teachers brought the ice cream.[257] Miss Julia Richman, speaking about opportunities for social work in public schools at a meeting of the Association of Neighborhood Workers, described Bulkley's school in these words:

> That school in New York which perhaps more than any other does the best work for social service among its pupils is the school on Forty-first street. The principal of this school is Afro-American and so are many of his teachers. Ninety-eight percent of the pupils are Afro-Americans. It is here that we see the effort being made to make the school a social centre for the parent and the child, to stand for that neighborhood idea that this association emphasizes. And the effort has met with success.[258]

However, Bulkley saw that no matter what he provided within the walls of his school, the children faced a bleak economic future.

> With the white child in America, everything industrial, civil, political, and social is possible. What of the black? . . . They evidence the same interest, the same faithfulness, the same receptivity noticeable in other race varieties up to a certain age. Once arrived at that place where they begin to learn, to ponder over, to understand, that on every hand avenues of employment are shut tight, discouragement begins, further study ceases, books become distasteful, and they leave school to work at any menial employment that offers itself. A promising boy of fourteen said to me last winter, "Why should I finish my course? What can a colored boy find to do?" He dropped out and is now an errand boy.[259]

> The saddest thing that faces me in my work is the small opportunity for a colored boy or girl to find proper employment. A boy comes to my office and asks for his working papers [his ultimate goal to be head bell-boy.] . . . He must face the bald fact that he must enter business as a boy and wind up as a boy.[260]

Bulkley was concerned that even the students who stayed in school were not doing as well as their suburban counterparts. He administered a test at a suburban school and at PS 80; the results were decidedly in favor of the suburban school. He considered and dismissed a number of factors: the course of study, the board of education, the teachers, the pupils. He blamed the distracting, noisy environment of the city, the social environment on the street, and confined quarters at home. Overage students—ones who had arrived in the city with very little education and needing to start in the lower grades—were also a factor in urban schools. "We shall wrestle with our problem as best we may, and leave the rest to God."[261] His next task in making education more accessible and more relevant was to start an evening school for adults.

"The Industrial Condition of the Negro in New York City"

On April 7, 1906 William L. Bulkley rose before the American Academy of Political and Social Science to speak on "The Industrial Condition of the Negro in New York City."[262] In his usual logical fashion, he posed and answered questions to illuminate his topic.

"Is the Afro-American possessed of the necessary qualifications to hold his own in the strenuous industrial and economic conflicts of a city like New York?"[263] African Americans performed virtually all the skilled and unskilled labor in the South for two centuries, but when they came North most unions banned them altogether and others put obstacles in their way. In 1900 only 6 percent of working Black people in New York State were engaged in manufacturing and mechanical pursuits. The rest held menial jobs. "What kinds of employment are open to him?"[264] There were few opportunities for manual training, and Black people did not have access to on-the-job training if no one would hire them. Because of lack of access to jobs, education also suffered. He once again told the story of one of his promising students dropping out of school.

> A bright boy came to me one day for his working papers. I was sorry to see him want to leave school, but he had no father, and

his poor mother had the hardest sort of job to earn enough over the wash-tub to pay the rent for their two rooms and to buy their meager food and clothing. The boy earned what little he could by odd jobs in the afternoon, Saturday and holidays. Still, I felt that if I could get him to stay till he could finish he might chance to find something better; but that would mean at least three years more of school. In reply to my urgent request that he try to battle through, with sad face he said: "I am old enough now to help mother; she needs me. And again, there is nothing better for a colored boy to do if he finishes the course." The reply pierced my heart like a white-hot bolt. I shall remember that scene till my dying day. All the monster evils of prejudice passed before me in procession like the hideous creatures of an Inferno, and I thought of the millions of hopes that have been blighted, the myriads of human possibilities that have been crushed, the intellects that have been stunted, the moral lives that have been gnarled and twisted, all because the iron heel of this base, hell-born caste is upon the neck of every boy, of every girl who chanced to be born black.[265]

Bulkley asked, "Is there reason to . . . hope?" He offered reasons to hope: children of all races in New York State were educated together; there were many "stalwart friends of humanity" in the professions, business, and trades; immigrants were not raised in the caste system and had not learned to the core to hate; and socialism promised equal opportunity to all men. "Lastly, the determination of the people to rise is itself the highest and best encouragement."[266]

In closing, let me appeal for the establishment of trade schools in the cities of the North to do work similar to that done in our industrial schools in the South. And, then, let this be held out before every boy and girl of all the races as one of the fundamentals of our constitution—*the right to work;*

opportunity to work; encouragement to work in any sphere in which one may be useful.[267]

Evening Schools

Evening and industrial schools had been a part of New York education since 1825, when they were established by the Public School Society. In the 1840s the Board of Education took over responsibility for these schools, which were viewed as a means of acculturating the ever-increasing immigrant population of the city. By 1898 there were sixty-one evening elementary schools. These schools served primarily to offer education to children as young as age twelve who had left school to work in factories, shops, and offices.[268] The classes were in literacy for both native and foreign-born residents and in manual training. Attending evening school was voluntary. Thus, working (often a ten- or twelve-hour day) and attending evening classes required an enormous commitment. At Superintendent Maxwell's suggestion, five evening trade schools, particularly for adults, were opened in 1904–1905.[269] Bulkley saw the need for an evening trade school for adults that would specifically welcome African Americans, prepare them for work in the trades, and teach them to read. He felt evening classes could develop character, encourage men and women in learning a trade, and bring the attention of the community "to the better side of the Negro question."[270] Skill in a trade was normally developed through the apprentice system, but white people and foreigners "guard jealously the approaches to the trades."[271] African Americans needed a trade school.

In fall 1905 Bulkley opened an evening elementary school at PS 80 for students over age sixteen, expecting about two hundred people to register. It was a part of the free public education offered by the New York Board of Education. Students were encouraged to attend through public meetings in churches and articles in the newspaper. They were assured the school was for them. An announcement in the *New York Age* stated, "There is no color line here, just as there is no color line in the school system of New York. Here you have an equal chance with the other fellow, a chance to learn a trade, to get hold on useful knowledge."[272]

Fifteen hundred students, almost 90 percent of whom were Black, registered for evening school in the eighteen-room building. This was seven times the number of students Bulkley had expected. The classes met for two hours, four evenings a week, and students not only learned English and "English to foreigners" but also stenography, mechanical drawing, bookkeeping, dressmaking, millinery, cooking, woodworking, and embroidery. In October the school opened with thirteen teachers. By December nineteen teachers were on the payroll.[273] Mothers came with young children. Students sat on top of the child-size desks. Classes crowded into the assembly hall. Some students spent three hours on the train to get to and from the school. Some students came to learn to read. Carpenters needed to learn to read to follow blueprints and written contracts. Bellhops and scrubwomen came to advance their skills to get a better job. Domestic servants needed to learn to do "flat house cooking" (as opposed to Southern cooking). Maintenance men needed to learn to run steam boilers so they could progress to janitor's jobs.[274] Students at evening schools were also there for self-improvement, not employment. They learned to read, cook, and improve their needlework skills for the home. A crowning event of that first year was a centerpiece of Irish linen and Cluny lace made by the evening school embroidery class. It was presented as a wedding gift to Miss Alice Roosevelt.[275] She was the daughter of President Theodore Roosevelt, who was viewed as a champion of Black people. "The enthusiasm in the work, the faithfulness in attendance, the excellence of results so pleased the Board of Education that they are planning to enlarge the plant next year."[276]

The Clansman, a racist play by Thomas F. Dixon, opened on January 8, 1906, at the Liberty Theater on 42nd Street, which backed up to PS 80 on 41st street. The play was based on a novel by Dixon glorifying white supremacy and the Ku Klux Klan. Bulkley's evening school had been open for three months, had 1,100 African American men and women registered, and had 700 in attendance on the evening Bulkley sat in his office thirty feet from the theater and wrote these words in a letter to the editor of the *New York Times*:

> The curtain is possibly being raised at this moment in an effort to portray the negro race in the worst possible colors; within this building hundreds of the maligned race are at the same moment quietly but earnestly working at their books or in the trades. So far as I can note, not one of them cares a straw what slanders any marplot may heap upon them; happy, hopeful, busy, each and all.
>
> What a refutation to all pessimism would it be if the audience in the theatre would take a recess for a few moments and go through our classrooms! Suppose they could see these men and women, up to 67 years of age, present in full force this stormy night, hungry for knowledge determined to learn some trade that will make them worth more to the community—what an object lesson it would be! Not a room in the building is vacant. Even seats for baby pupils and kindergarten tables are occupied. Neither cold nor heat; snow nor moonshine, with all their attendant drawbacks or attractions, can keep these pupils away.
>
> In the theatre the audience is looking at the past; these people are looking into the future. To the one crowd despair; to the other hope.
>
> What may be the thoughts of the people who are witnessing the play I do not know, but of this much I am sure—there are not 700 happier people in any building in New York than those who are busy here to-night.[277]

The following year, in the fall of 1906, the evening school moved to larger quarters at PS 67, on 120 W. 46th Street, where it remained.[278] Bulkley was its principal for the next eighteen years. In 1907 the elementary evening school at PS 67 enrolled two thousand students. In 1913 he wrote that the things that would help the most to improve the evening school were better teachers, sufficient appropriation of money, and a longer term (length of terms for evening schools had been shortened to save money). In addition, Bulkley felt the evening *elementary* school should take its place with the other trade schools like Stuyvesant Evening Trade School, which was classed as a high school.[279] He was always fighting against the neglect and unequal treatment of a school that welcomed African Americans. Although evening schools were not new, having the school in the heart of the African American community, offering classes to adults, teaching useful trades, and having a talented and dedicated principal set it apart. The evening school attracted many visitors and much media attention. Bulkley's commitment is revealed in a 1918 letter to W. E. B. Du Bois. He declined a dinner invitation because "duty calls elsewhere."

> During thirteen years I have not been absent from my evening school except on one night when a fever forbade my going out into the snow. On this occasion quinine, castor oil and a few other delicacies were served out to me. If this dinner were given on an evening when my school did not demand my attention, I assure you it would give both my wife and me unfeigned pleasure to be present.[280]

Bulkley's success with the evening school prompted Samuel Scottron to establish a similar school in an African American neighborhood in Brooklyn. The *New York Age* reported in May 1908 that the two public industrial schools (PS 67 and the Brooklyn school) had educated 2,195 in the trades and 884 in common school subjects. Although the students at Bulkley's evening school in the early years were primarily African American, reflecting both the neighborhood and Bulkley's recruiting efforts in African American churches and newspapers, the student body was diverse. In 1907, certificates were awarded to 323 pupils from twenty countries.[281] PS 67 evening school offered skills, self-confidence, and hope to thousands of students during the eighteen years Bulkley was principal.

Evening School Students

An April 1909 program for PS 67's closing exercises recorded the names of the students.[282] They were born in North Carolina, Virginia, and Ireland, as well as in New York. They lived from 40th Street to 134th Street. Some, like Mrs. Matilda A. Vann and Frances E. Hebbons, were improving their professional skills. Vann was a dressmaker and taking embroidery classes. Hebbons had a millinery shop and was taking millinery classes.[283] Others took classes that never led to careers. James H. Norwood took architectural classes but worked as a salesman and shipping clerk.[284]

Lee A. Pollard used a course at PS 67's evening school to improve his situation. He had come to New York City from Virginia in 1899 at the age of eighteen. He advertised in the classifieds for a position of office boy or store work.[285] He was not content to stay in that kind of work. He took night classes at the YMCA and an electrical course at Bulkley's evening school. To move forward he had to go into business for himself, and he identified a niche in the automobile industry. With a partner, he opened Auto Transportation Company, then moved on to private work operating automobiles for the president of Columbus Shade Cloth Company. In 1909 he organized Cosmopolitan Automobile Company to train African American men to operate gasoline engines. These skills were important for chauffeurs in the age of the automobile, who not only had to drive a car but also to maintain it (much as a coachman was responsible for the horse that pulled the coach).[286] An ad for Cosmopolitan Automobile Company ran for several years in *Crisis*, the magazine of the NAACP, soliciting students who could learn "Shop and Road Work." The tuition was twenty-five dollars for a six-week course.[287] This also met a need, since the popular course at the YMCA would no longer admit Black people.[288] In 1913 Pollard and Benjamin E. Thomas were "considered two of the leading practical automobile colored men of New York City."[289]

Louise Fleming, born into slavery about 1840 in Florida, came to New York in 1872 as a single woman who had to support herself. In 1909 she heard about the evening school and entered to learn to read and write. The second year she learned arithmetic and progressed at least to the fourth year. In 1910 she lived in a tenement on West 40th Street (between 8th and 9th Avenues) in Manhattan and worked in the cigar business, probably from her home, and had two lodgers.[290] She was described as "bright, energetic, possesses an active mind, and vows she will stay in school until she graduates."[291]

Several of Bulkley's students wrote letters to him about their experiences at the evening school, which are in the papers of George Haynes at Fisk University.[292] They were probably used during the writing of Haynes' book *The Negro at Work in New York City*. Marguerite Randall wrote in 1908 that she was learning millinery and that her first hat was worth fifteen dollars. She became a milliner.[293] Martin V. Washington wrote that after being a pupil at PS 67's evening school, he had taken the civil service exam for a clerk in the US post office. In 1908 he was appointed clerk in the post office and retained that job for at least the next forty-three years.[294]

In 1909 Samuel Harris, perhaps fifty years old,[295] explained his situation in a letter after his first season in class 1B (spelling and punctuation as written):

> I believe that you would like me to state my reasons why I am attending evening school at this late date of my age as I am sorry to say it is owing to the sad lost of both mother and farther in my early days which lef me to under go the hard ships of life with no one to look up to for schooling and haveing to confess my own neglect in my early days I could not see or feel the need of it as I do today—and one great reason I am attending evening school now is because I realize this is a great opportunity opened up to me as I have in late years become associated with educated and business men along business lines I at times feel sadly in need of education.[296]

Walter H. Johnson, English class IIB, wrote of his experience and hopes for the future after a short time in the school:

> My advancement has exceeded my expectations, so that I am more ambitious than ever to become a graduate of this school. I have not as yet had an opportunity to put my learning to practice, as my position is one which does not call for much learning, so I am trying to prepare myself for something better in the future.[297]

Although Bulkley's work in education did not earn him much attention after the initial years, it is clear he provided a place where people could change their lives and develop hope in a very dark time. He was a model of energy, efficiency, passion, and respect for students of all ages and backgrounds. He provided them his most careful, sympathetic, and hopeful attention.

PS 80, Manhattan

New York City,
Municipal Archives

PS 125, Manhattan

New York City,
Municipal Archives

PS 67, Manhattan   New York City, Municipal Archives

Cooking Class, PS 67 Evening School   New York City, Municipal Archives

Steamfitting and Boilermaking Class, PS 67 Evening School
New York City, Municipal Archives

Tailoring Class, PS 67 Evening School   New York City, Municipal Archives

VI

NOT ALMS, BUT
OPPORTUNITY, 1901–1909

*We do not ask for charity; all we ask is opportunity. We do not beg
for alms; we beg only for a chance.*[298]

Bulkley was one in a long line of teachers in the New York City schools
who were involved in civil rights activism. New York State's Black
teachers in the nineteenth century were writers and editors for abolitionist
and Black protest publications. They campaigned for suffrage and other
civil rights legislation. They helped organize state and national conventions
as part of the National Negro Convention movement, lectured against
racial discrimination, aided fugitive slaves, published protest letters, and
protested specific and general acts of discrimination on account of race or
sex.[299] They were not just pioneering educators but also pioneering
advocates for civil rights. Bulkley joined this long line of activist educators
by joining and founding organizations, some of which are still active in
American civil rights today.

It is impossible to discuss civil rights and Black uplift in the early
twentieth century without discussing Booker T. Washington and W. E. B.
Du Bois. As rights for African Americans were disappearing, segregation
was solidifying, and violence was rampant, leaders had to figure out how to
be effective agents of change. Two different approaches developed. Booker

T. Washington was the voice of the conservative approach. He was the founder of Tuskegee Institute in Alabama and its president from 1881 to 1915. In 1895 he was invited to give a speech at the Cotton States and International Exposition in Atlanta, Georgia. [300] He offered the white audience a compromise: we won't ask for full social and legal rights (yet) if you allow us the opportunity to get on our feet economically, to grow into our role as new citizens. He advised every Black man to "Cast down your bucket where you are!" and assured the audience that "In all things that are purely social, we can be as separate as the fingers, yet one as the hand in all things essential to mutual progress." [301] His speech was initially hailed by most, including Du Bois, as a guidepost to the future. The approach that he proposed came to be described as "accommodationist."

W. E. B. Du Bois developed the more activist approach. In 1903 he included a chapter in his book *The Souls of Black Folk,* "Of Mr. Booker T. Washington and Others," in which he lambasted the accommodationist philosophy:

> Mr. Washington distinctly asks that Black people give up, at
> least for the present, three things, —
>> First, political power,
>> Second, insistence on civil rights,
>> Third, higher education of Negro youth, —
> and concentrate all their energies on industrial education, the
> accumulation of wealth, and the conciliation of the South.[302]

Washington had enormous power, due in part to the forcefulness of his personality and his relationships with wealthy white philanthropists who supported Tuskegee Institute and others of his projects. Du Bois was powerful as an intellectual and moral leader. He earned a PhD in history from Harvard University in 1895 and researched and taught at Atlanta University from 1897 to 1910. In 1910 he became editor of the NAACP's *Crisis* magazine. Du Bois demanded enfranchisement, civil rights, and access to higher education for all. Washington put the civil rights agenda aside, although secretly supported civil rights initiatives. Du Bois was viewed by some as arrogant. Du Bois had great skill as a researcher and a writer. Washington had great power and influence he could wield with favors, or money, or in the press. Both men knew how to get things done, but every movement and every leader from 1900 to 1915 needed to consider the implications of these two philosophies. This is a greatly simplified description of two complex men, their philosophies and strategies, and their followers' shifting alliances and multiple goals. For more information, begin with the biographies of both men[303] and their own writings.

Bulkley's appointment in 1901 as the principal at PS 80 started the most productive period of his career. His education, his mission, opportunity, and his growing leadership abilities came together in a decade of incredible productivity, not only as an educator but also as a leader in the exciting civil rights movements then underway. Parris and Brooks, in their book on the history of the National Urban League, assert that "Dr. Bulkley was in the forefront of race uplift in the first decade of the twentieth century. His wide vision of the needs of Blacks in the city, caused him to initiate and lead in reform and social service efforts."[304]

In 1902 Bulkley established the Carlton Avenue YMCA branch for African Americans in Brooklyn. In 1903 he was part of a group called together by the president of the Long Island Rail Road, William H. Baldwin Jr., to plan steps to improve the life of Black people in New York City. In 1905 he was a charter member and treasurer of the New York Association for the Protection of Colored Women (NYAPCW). In 1906 Bulkley established the Committee for Improving the Industrial Condition of the Negro in New York (CIICNNY). In 1909 he signed the call for the National Negro Conference, which became the NAACP in 1910. He was on the executive committee of the NAACP. In 1911 he was a founding member of National League on Urban Conditions Among Negroes (NLUCAN), which was later renamed the National Urban League (NUL). This was a heady time.

Carlton YMCA, Brooklyn

After his appointment at PS 80 in 1901, Bulkley set about transforming the school. In 1902 he took up another cause. In many urban areas, the YMCA was an important organization for meeting the needs of young men. The Brooklyn YMCA at that time was actively expanding its outreach by establishing branches for soldiers and railroad and trolley workers. They were agreeable to establishing one for Black men as well.

The idea for the branch extended back into the nineteenth century. Rev. Alexander J. Henry, who had been called as pastor of the Nazarene Congregational Church in Brooklyn in 1888, made investigations into the condition of the people in order to grow his church. He realized that a branch of the YMCA would be of great benefit to young Black men. He was never able to get his plan off the ground. In June 1901 he called a conference with several influential men, and they determined to establish the YMCA for African Americans and enrolled 250 men.[305] With this success in hand, they petitioned the Brooklyn YMCA for a branch. The men started meeting under Bulkley's direction. Shortly thereafter, the YMCA received a donation of $7,500 from George Foster Peabody for establishing a "colored men's branch," which was used to purchase a four-story building at 405 Carlton Avenue in Brooklyn. The Branch Y was organized on May 15, 1902, with William L. Bulkley as its chairman.[306] The secretary of the branch was Charles H. Bullock, one of the first African American professionals in the YMCA.[307] The building contained, among other amenities, parlors, a library, and a game room. The program featured educational and Bible classes; religious, literary and musical meetings; an employment bureau; a baseball club; and more. In the first year the Carlton Branch YMCA had 195 members, placed forty-four men in jobs, had eight students in educational classes and ninety-one in religious classes, and had a library of 175 volumes.[308] In the second year Bulkley reported 14,694 visits to the building.[309] In both years he was able to report a year-end positive balance in the treasury. A writer in 1904 described the Carlton Branch

YMCA: "All indications point to a great work for the uplifting of our people in body, mind and soul."[310]

Due to the "pressure of other duties," Bulkley resigned as chairman of the Carlton Avenue Branch in January of 1905, at the same time C. H. Bullock left for a new post in Louisville, Kentucky.[311] However, he remained active in public programs during 1905 and occasionally for many years after, including assisting with a fundraising campaign in 1915 for a new building.[312]

New York City Negro Conference, 1903

In 1903 William H. Baldwin Jr., president of the Long Island Rail Road and a close associate of Booker T. Washington, called a "private conference regarding the condition of the Colored people in New York City" at Mt. Olivet Baptist Church in Manhattan.[313] Twelve men, including Bulkley, attended the meeting, which was groundbreaking in its interracial makeup. Seven Black men and five white men sat down together to listen to one another. Bulkley reported on the necessity of publicizing education opportunities and urged the use of established vocational schools rather than the creation of separate schools for African Americans. Du Bois recommended that 30,000 homes should be surveyed to gather data so actions could be based on facts, similar to the survey he had made in Philadelphia in 1899.[314] Felix Adler, the leader of the Ethical Culture Society, also suggested an investigation "in order that it would be plainer what help could best be given." Du Bois proposed a social (not educational or religious) settlement house run by African Americans to help Black people from the South adjust to life in the city. Others identified the need to improve housing, as Black people were paying more than white residents for housing that was inferior.[315] There was at least one more meeting,[316] but as Baldwin's health declined, he was no longer able to take a leadership role, and no organized action resulted. Nevertheless, the vision laid out at this meeting was the one Bulkley embraced by establishing his school as a social center and by establishing the evening school at PS 80. Baldwin may have been trying to channel energies into reforms in the mode of Booker T. Washington, but he set loose a movement that would challenge them.

African American Suffrage

In 1903 African Americans were also focused on suffrage. Virginia had approved a new constitution limiting the right to vote by requiring three years of paid-up poll taxes and an understanding of the Constitution (which was used to keep Black people from voting), and exempting Union and Confederate veterans and their sons from meeting any requirements to vote.[317] On February 19, 1903, Black people in New York City held a public meeting to protest disfranchisement of the Black man in the South and to raise money to challenge the new Virginia constitution. In addition they adopted a resolution to support President Roosevelt's policy to appoint Black people to federal jobs in the South. Out of this diverse group of issues the attendees appointed a committee to be known as the New York Conference Committee on Negro Suffrage. The fifteen included African American members Bulkley, Rev. W. H. Brooks of St. Mark's Methodist Episcopal Church, Bishop Alexander Walters, of the AME Zion Church, Samuel R. Scottron, and Charles W. Anderson, a Black politician and public official. Bulkley probably already knew them and would work with in the future them.[318] Apparently no significant action came from this committee. A National Negro Suffrage convention was held in Louisville, Kentucky, that summer, but only thirty-eight people attended.[319]

Charity Organization Society

In 1904 Bulkley was named to the new Negro Sub-Committee of the Committee on the Prevention of Tuberculosis of the Charity Organization Society. They gathered information about tuberculosis and its treatment in Black neighborhoods and set up special clinics. Mary White Ovington, a white social worker newly interested in work among Black people, was also on the committee.[320] She and Bulkley worked together on many committees in the years to come. This committee conducted investigations, adapted current institutions to meet new needs, and sponsored public meetings. These were all important features of Bulkley's work.

New York Association for the Protection of Colored Women

In 1904 Frances Kellor, a lawyer and sociologist, published an exposé entitled *Out of Work* that detailed employment agencies' exploitation of foreign and Black women.[321] For women in the South, the system began with the vision of good wages, good work, and good times in New York or Philadelphia. As an inducement, "runners" provided a contract and the fare for the ship north. The young women arriving in the North were met by "employment agencies" that housed the women in crowded conditions, impounded their luggage, and steered the young women to prostitution rather than placing them in legitimate jobs. Kellor wrote: "When a girl without control over her person and baggage, $20 in debt, and a total stranger in the city, is sent to a disorderly place, upon threats or promises, can she be said to be anything but a slave?"[322] She knew there were well-organized efforts to protect immigrant Jewish women and felt young Black women arriving in the cities from the South were in desperate need of similar services. Victoria Earle Matthews's White Rose Mission had been doing some of this work since 1895, but Kellor envisioned a more comprehensive system of services and legal actions.

In the spring of 1905, she started the NYAPCW and mobilized her contacts and considerable energies. The association's efforts were divided into travelers' aid, lodging houses, education, employment agencies, finances, and membership. In many cases there were already institutions, such as the White Rose Mission, in place to house, train, or employ the women. The NYAPCW looked at the entire system, filled the gaps, and directed the women to safe places.

By June 1905 Kellor reported that the commissioner of licenses in New York City had closed five employment agencies that were sending women to houses of prostitution or to places where no jobs were available. More agencies were under review.[323] By July the league was distributing leaflets in the South advising girls to have a definite place to go before coming to New York. They placed agents at the docks to direct those who did come to organizations such as the Young Women's Christian Association (YWCA) that had housing and occupational training.[324] By October the NYAPCW and the YWCA of Brooklyn opened a domestic training department to prepare young women for work. Kellor also solicited funds through ads in the newspaper: "We Need Your Help: $2,000 Will Start a Good Work for Which There Has Long Been Urgent Need."[325] This was a committee that was getting things done. Bulkley was treasurer of the NYAPCW and is counted as one of the founders. Others on the executive committee included Fred R. Moore, editor of the *Colored American Magazine*; Dr. E. P. Roberts, physician in Harlem; Frances A. Kellor; Mary White Ovington; Dr. Verina Morton-Jones, physician and suffragist; and lawyer Wilford H. Smith.[326] The association held public programs to educate people about the situation facing young women arriving from the South and the services available for them. The first public meeting was held on December 24, 1905, at Mt. Olivet Baptist Church, with more meetings planned.[327] In 1906 the associations in Philadelphia and New York united to become the National League for the Protection of Colored Women (NLPCW). Kellor was secretary of both the New York association and the national league.[328]

In the NYAPCW and the NLPCW, Bulkley learned firsthand the important principles for the successful implementation of a program of action. It not only required energetic and visionary leadership but also it emphasized coordination of already existing services, work for structural change in agencies and unions, holding public meetings, and having both Black and white people with common goals taking action to implement their vision.

In the six or seven years Bulkley had been in New York, he had made a name for himself. He was well connected and known for his thoughtfulness, willingness to take action, and speaking abilities. The *New York Age* described him as

> a useful citizen of the sort we need all over the great
> metropolitan district. He has character, brains, public spirit

and nervous energy in large measure. . . . [W]hile making an honorable reputation for himself in the public school system, [he] has taken a leading part in work for the betterment of the condition of the people which has drawn heavily upon his time, the good results of which are beginning to be seen and appreciated by the public.[329]

Afro-American Council

One of the organizations with which Bulkley was briefly affiliated was the Afro-American Council. In 1898 Bishop Alexander Walters and T. Thomas Fortune, editor of *New York Age*, founded the National Afro-American Council to fight against lynching and racial violence, disfranchisement of Southern Black voters, and Jim Crow laws, especially the segregation of transportation. They filed court cases and worked to influence legislation. It was the first national civil rights organization to address social and political issues.[330] Bulkley was on the Committee of One Hundred that planned the council's conference held in New York in 1906. He gave a speech of welcome on behalf of educators and gave an address, "The Attitude of Northern Opinion," which was "one of the gems of the convention and won vigorous applause."[331] Booker T. Washington gave an address at the close of the session, rousing the crowd with his oratory:

> Let us not become unduly alarmed or depressed when seasons of disturbance and riot overtake us. In the future, as in the past, we are going to have long periods of contentment and happiness and those will be followed by waves of trouble and disappointment, be we must pursue the even tenor of our way with a stern and unconquerable determination never to fail.
>
> Has anything occurred in recent years that will begin to compare with the horrors of the middle passage, the trials of reconstruction, the season when Ku Klux Klans in a large measure, seemed to rule the destiny of our race?[332]

The resolutions of the council condemned the race riot in Atlanta that had occurred the previous month. They urged "upon the colored people a manly, sensible, and unceasing insistence upon every right guaranteed by the Federal Constitution."[333] They called for testing the degrading Jim Crow car laws in the Supreme Court. They called for national aid to education. "We feel that we are entitled to the encouragement of all patriotic Americans in our endeavor to uphold the fundamental law of the land."[334]

Despite the success of the New York meeting, the National Afro-American Council collapsed within a year due to internal friction, lack of funding, and lack of a public voice. Bulkley's energies were channeled into the Niagara Movement and then into the CIICNNY.

The Niagara Movement

The Niagara Movement was initiated by W. E. B. Du Bois in 1905 as a way to form an activist committee that would stand for civil rights, putting racial issues on the Progressive Era table. They were forging a Black voice and identity but were integrationist in practical matters. The Niagara Movement used words to change the uplift agenda and win hearts and minds.[335] In 1907 Bulkley publicly affiliated himself with the movement. In August of that year, he attended the annual meeting in Boston, where he was confirmed as chair of the education committee.[336] He joined this movement in its waning days. By 1910 many Niagara Movement members had turned their attention to the new NAACP.[337] Although Parris and Brooks list Bulkley as a founding member of the Niagara Movement, I don't find any concrete indication of that. He was not at the first meeting held in Niagara Falls in July 1905 nor at the second meeting in 1906 at Harper's Ferry. He may have been a behind-the-scenes participant as an associate of Du Bois.

Committee for Improving the Industrial Condition of the Negro in New York

Bulkley had addressed educational and training needs at PS 80 and in the evening school, but he wanted to expand his influence. Three years after the

Baldwin conference, he founded the CICCNNY,[ix] along the lines outlined by those in attendance at Baldwin's 1903 meeting. "[T]he development of the committee is in a sense the fulfillment of a plan long cherished by the late William H. Baldwin."[338]

Bulkley invited a group of people to meet at PS 80 on April 20, 1906. He and Mary White Ovington read "interesting papers," no doubt outlining the problems of economics, education, and labor and what could be done about them. The group "resolved themselves into a permanent organization to consider the political, economic and social condition of the Afro-American." William Schieffelin, a white businessman and philanthropist, and Charles W. Anderson, close associate of Booker T. Washington, were tasked with nominating officers and defining the scope of the body.[339]

Schieffelin called the first official meeting of the committee for May 11, 1906. [340] Forty white and twenty African American people met at Schieffelin's East 66th Street French Renaissance mansion "in the cause of industrial opportunity for the New York Afro-American." The committee's scope was to be the "economic phase" of the "problem of the New York Afro-American,"[341] with a consideration of a larger organization with a broader scope at a later time. Schieffelin was elected president and Bulkley, secretary. They formed as an affiliate with the New York Armstrong Association, which provided instant structure, contacts, and

[ix]The committee's name had several minor variations. This is taken from the cover page of a pamphlet published about 1906 and the earliest newspaper articles. Also known as the Committee for the Improvement of the Industrial Condition of the Negro in New York (*Brooklyn Eagle*, June 19, 1906); the Committee for Improving Industrial Condition of the Negro in New York [sic] (cover of pamphlet in the Stokes Papers published about 1906 by the committee); the Committee for the Improvement of the Industrial Condition of the Negro in New York (running head on 1906 pamphlet); the Committee for Improving the Industrial Condition of Negroes in New York (letterhead used 1906, 1907, 1909); the Committee for Improving the Industrial Condition of Negroes of New York (letterhead used in 1910).

access to funds. Armstrong Associations had the support of prominent politicians and philanthropists. They were fundraising arms for Hampton and Tuskegee Institutes and industrial training schools for Black people in the South. They had been considering expanding their mission to include needs in northern cities, so Bulkley's proposal was timely. The affiliation seems to have been rather loose, as the committee remained autonomous in its affairs.[342]

Just five days later, on May 16, Bulkley called a strategy meeting at PS 80 of the African American members of the new committee. They clearly wanted to maximize their influence on the new organization. He once again outlined the problems facing Black people in New York and laid out his vision for the committee by proposing that the new organization form eight committees:

1. Committee on publication to print items for the organization, "but particularly aiming to inform the public through the press" and "to secure the friendship of the press to our cause."

2. Committee on public meetings for Black people to "enlighten them as to their needs, their duties, their opportunities" and for white people to learn how they might help and know the capabilities and achievements of the Black man.

3. Committee on securing employment, with the objective of investigating the "colored craftsmen in our city" and the "attitude of employers and labor organizations." It was also to be "to a certain extent, an employment bureau."

4. Committee on the employment of women.

5. Legal committee to investigate "enactments which will be of interest to the colored craftsmen and shall further stand ready to protect him in his rights as a workman."

6. Finance committee to raise funds.

7. Committee on trade schools and social centers.

8. Committee on membership.[343]

When the CIICNNY next met, they laid out their purpose: to get the facts of industrial conditions affecting African Americans in the city and to take actions that would improve these conditions. "A square deal," the committee announced, "in the matter of getting a livelihood is held to be fundamental."[344] This was to be an action committee, not one about raising money to support other programs. Roscoe C. Simmons, nephew of Booker T. Washington and a reporter and orator, was selected to make a study to establish a foundation from which the CIICNNY could plan its work. The committees created to carry out the work were public meetings, publication, legal, craftsmen, tradesmen, social centers and trade schools, and neighborhood work. This is based on the structure outlined by Bulkley, but there were no committees on women, finance, or membership.[345] It is interesting that membership, the grassroots component that was later to be such an important aspect of the NAACP, was not included.

Ovington reported to Du Bois: "We put it first [as the] 'economic' question, but Mr. Seligman, the banker, for some reason changed it to industrial which we may have to stretch a little."[346] Bulkley, Ovington, and others saw industrial training as a component of a larger economic program for uplift and rights. Not all the committee members did. The groundbreaking nature of the CIICNNY was noted in the press. "So far as is known, the committee is unique as a compact working body in which representatives of progressive elements among both white and colored populations meet on an equal footing. The common ground lies in the two words 'economic opportunity.'"[347] In June 1906 the *Springfield Republican* summarized the purpose of the new committee:

> There has been little or no chance for negro youths to become skilled workers, and this committee for the betterment of the industrial condition of the negro in New York proposes to get at the facts, and so set forth the condition as it is, and then to enlist public opinion and the co-operation of the colored people themselves, in ways that will develop opportunities where they are now denied.[348]

White people held the positions of chairman (William Jay Schieffelin), vice chairman (Seth T. Stewart, superintendent of schools in Brooklyn) and assistant secretary (Mary White Ovington). Black people held positions of vice chairman (S. R. Scottron) and secretary (Bulkley). The subcommittees were headed by two African Americans and five white people. Although Black people were making progress in power-sharing, white people still held positions two to one. Parris and Brooks wrote that although the committee was firmly based on principles of industrial training and investigation, the interracial makeup of the group was groundbreaking because a group of knowledgeable Black leaders had proposed the structure of the committee.[349]

Bulkley unofficially opened the campaign on May 21 when he spoke to an overflowing crowd at educational night at Mt. Olivet Baptist Church. He urged those present to take advantage of the opportunities available and promoted the evening industrial classes that were to open at PS 67.[350] The CIICNNY Committee on Public Meetings began making plans for meetings in the fall. "Dr. Bulkley, the author of the movement, will speak at every meeting and outline the ideas which he has at heart." The CIICNNY "has the aim of breaking down color caste in the gainful occupations in New York."[351]

The first public meeting of the CIICNNY was held on the hot, sultry evening of September 20, 1906. [352] Eight hundred men and women gathered at Mt. Olivet Baptist Church to hear Booker T. Washington, a last-minute substitute for Charles W. Anderson, address the crowd. He encouraged industrial training at the expense of literary training (which, he said, makes one desire a better house but not the means to make the money to buy it). He chided Black people for wanting more and not being willing to work for it. "He made a speech along his usual lines in advocacy of hand training, but his casual criticism of the general policy of Afro-American newspapers attracted most attention. He deprecated their tendency toward yellow journalism in featuring news about oppressions and wrongs at the expense of news of a more encouraging complexion."[353] Mary Schenck Woolman, a professor at Teachers College and the founder of the Manhattan Trade School for Girls, gave a practical talk about trade school training for girls and the successes that good workers have in the workplace.

Bulkley also spoke. He explained the purpose of the committee:

> It is fundamental to the best development that every man should feel that he has an equal opportunity to compete with all other men in the struggle for existence. Close up any avenue for honest and remunerative employment, and you in just such a degree restrict one's usefulness as a citizen. Carry that restriction into nearly all the avenues of employment where intelligence and skill are required, and you stifle laudable aspirations, provoke discouragement and invite all the evils that an idle brain can conceive.

> The exact status of the Afro-American of this city we hope to know when our investigations are completed. Taking the last census [1900] however, for our present guide, we find that out of 57,000 Afro-Americans over ten years of age at work in this State, 49,000 were engaged in service more or less menial. We do not attack menial service as a thing bad of itself, for till the end of time there must be hewers of wood and drawers of water. What we do deplore is the too common practice of restrictions of the Black man to certain kinds of employment.

> That the door of hope and of opportunity should be closed against any man anywhere in this land is unfortunate. That there should be such restrictions in this great and glorious city of ours is to me a cause of deep regret. This magnificent haven of the oppressed of all lands! What a satisfaction it would be to know that the day was not far distant when the only test required of any man for any employment would be ability and character![354]

In *Charities and the Commons*, journal of the New York Charity Organization Society, Bulkley summed up the success of the meeting:

> There were stirring speeches from the platform and more than that, a live interest among the people who had gathered. They were not told the usual political claptrap that they are progressing as no race has progressed. They were told that from an economic standpoint they are dropping behind in the great cities and that only by working together and standing for high standards of workmanship, is there a chance—and a large chance—for better conditions of living.[355]

The second public meeting was at St. Mark's on October 25, 1906. Ovington, Scottron, and J. Douglas Wetmore, a civil rights lawyer from Florida, spoke. Mr. Wetmore touched on the discriminations practiced against African Americans in the South. Schieffelin, who presided, chided him for discussing "race 'hatred'" and said "Afro-Americans were disfranchised in order to purify politics in the South, as they were in the habit of selling their votes by wholesale."[356] Purifying the vote by denying it to "undesirables" was a common tenet of the Progressive Era agenda, one used with racist intent. Wetmore made an eloquent reply defending the race. It was plain the audience supported Wetmore, and the *Age* opined, with some understatement, "It is feared Schieffelin did not enhance the popularity of his committee by the positions he took."[357] Herein lies a disagreement at the core of the CIICNNY. Bulkley and others wanted to offer Black people hope and empowerment, to give them the dignity of aspiration, truth, and choice. They were putting the matter of denial of employment and underemployment on the agenda as a racial justice issue.[358] Schieffelin and others, besides revealing their own racism, were trying to keep the movement attractive to white donors and limit the aspirations and influence of Black leaders.

April 25, 1907, was the first annual meeting of the CIICNNY. For a fledgling organization, the previous year had seen major accomplishments. Public meetings had been held every month to direct people toward schools for learning skills and elementary studies. In June 1907 *Colored American Magazine* stated that:

> The feeling largely prevailing among the colored people, especially those from the South, that they are not welcome in these schools on account of indifference, or where the notion prevails that the time spent in acquiring the knowledge or skill in a trade will not later on be of service to them, is being largely overcome and dispelled by the work of the Committee on Public Meetings quietly, surely, effectively.[359]

Frances A. Kellor of the NLPCW appealed to the CIICNNY for help. A subcommittee of the CIICNNY was appointed to contact the steamship companies to end abuses.[360] Superintendent Seth T. Stewart's Committee on Social Centres and Trade Schools sponsored petitions requesting the formation of a Brooklyn evening trade school along the lines of Bulkley's school. Two thousand people signed. The Committee on Tradesmen met with Black ministers to plan meetings of storekeepers and tradesmen to discuss how to begin and run a business. Mary White Ovington and the Committee on Neighborhood Work brought together neighborhood workers of all kinds in all areas of the city. John W. T. Nichols, dry goods merchant, and the Committee on Employment placed dressmakers and seamstresses in jobs. To promote more employment, they were planning to test and then recommend qualified women to employers. Miss Helen A. Tucker, researcher and settlement worker, identified sixty-two craftsmen and called a meeting of Black carpenters. James L. Wallace, Central Federated Union and a member of the committee, advised against a segregated union. He said the United Brotherhood of Carpenters and Joiners was open to every man, including those of color. He himself was a Black union man, but others made few inroads into the unions.[361]

For the next three years the work of the CIICNNY continued. By 1909, in cooperation with the evening schools, they had trained over 1,000 Black people in a trade.[362] They faced discrimination head-on instead of ignoring it, not only by providing training in kinds of work usually reserved for white people but also in their insistence that "the denial of equal economic opportunity [is] a fatal blow to the morale of the race."[363] They formed a mechanics' association in January 1909, which had fifty-three African American members. The committee reached an agreement with the City and Suburban Homes Company, then building apartments in Harlem, to employ African American bricklayers and carpenters. The NLPCW task of meeting arriving steamships at the docks had been made part of the CIICNNY.[364] They had worked "very quietly but along very practical lines"[365] cooperating with other agencies, the city board of education, and private businesses to make significant progress.

In the first decade of the twentieth century, Bulkley was active in the New York City Negro Conference, the cause of Black suffrage, the Charity Organization Society, the NYAPCW, the Afro-American Council, and the Niagara Movement. He established the Carlton Branch of the YMCA and founded the CIICNNY. He was having an impact not only on his students but also on the larger issues related to industrial education and civil rights.

Meeting of the Niagara Movement, 1907, Boston

Bulkley: top row, 6th from left   W. E. B. Du Bois Papers

Amenia Conference, 1916

Bulkley: front row, 3rd from right, hat in hand   NAACP Records

VII

GRACE AND GUMPTION, 1909–1916

Be somebody . . . for without the ambition to become somebody,
backed by grace, gumption, greenback, grit and glue, all effort
sinks like he who makes it into nothingness.[366]

Bulkley's ambition, talent, grit, and gumption made him a successful educator, orator, and activist. In 1909 he was approaching fifty years old and had invested his whole life in his own education and in sharing it with others through schools and uplift organizations. It was to be a watershed year for him. He helped form the organization that was to become the NAACP and was moving forward with the CIICNNY and NLPCW to form the NLUCAN. He was also transferred to a school in lower Manhattan, where he broke new educational ground.

Schoolma'ams Rebel, PS 125

In 1909 Bulkley had been at PS 80 for eight years. The area around the school was changing rapidly; housing was being replaced by commercial development,[367] and displaced African Americans were moving north to Harlem. In 1901, when Bulkley was made principal, there were eighteen classrooms in the school and 327 students registered.[368] The number of students at first increased and then gradually decreased to below 300. Only ten classes were formed for the school year 1909–1910. Principals in schools with less than thirteen classes earned 30 percent less than those whose schools had thirteen or more.[369] Bulkley had a family with four children under the age of fourteen and could ill afford a decrease in salary.

The board of education transferred Bulkley to PS 125, located at 180 Wooster Street in Greenwich Village. It was on the edge of the wholesale dry goods district and near Minetta Lane, site of a historic Black community. However, less than fifty Black children attended the school, most of the rest being Italian or children of Italian immigrants.[370] That summer, before he left for a European vacation, Bulkley visited his new school, inspected the building, gave instructions to the janitor about improving sanitation, and then sailed to Europe for the summer.[371] His visit made headlines.

Schoolma'ams Rebel Against Negro Chief

> A bright, snappy acting person appeared at the school. He was almost as white as a native Yankee, but was unquestionably a negro. He said he was the new Principal of the school. The flutter into which those at the door were thrown went all over the school in a jiffy.[372]

The teachers called an "indignation meeting" to discuss their options, and more than half stated their intent to request transfers so they would not have to work under a Black principal. The *Hebrew Standard* took an editorial stand on the controversy that was reprinted in *New York Age* on July 22:

> The women teachers of Public School No. 125 who object to the recently appointed principal solely on the ground that he is a Negro have set a very bad example of race prejudice and should by no means be allowed to have their own way in this matter.
>
> In this city such discrimination against the Negro is absolutely a disregard of the eternal principles of right and justice and is to

be condemned as a wanton and malicious attempt to introduce the race question into our public schools.

The bigoted teachers referred to, should be brought to their senses. Public schools are the bulwark of our civilization and must be kept free, at all hazards, from the poison of race prejudice.[373]

Days later *New York Age* downplayed the event. Reporters checked the facts, and no one had yet applied for transfers.

There need be no alarm over the reported "rebellion." The merit of the new principal, the courage of the school authorities, the wisdom and culture of the rank and file of New York teachers will confine the trouble to the minds of the energetic newspaper men.[374]

Two weeks later *New York Age* was one of the few papers that reported the outcome of the tempest. Superintendent William H. Maxwell and the board of education refused to draw the "color line" and confirmed Bulkley would be the principal of PS 125 when it opened in the fall.[375] Three weeks after Bulkley's visit no transfers had been obtained.

Bulkley returned to New York on August 30 and began the school year at PS 125 with thirty-three teachers and 1,287 students. This was the first appointment in New York City of an African American principal to a school with predominantly white pupils and teachers. It would be twenty-six years before another such appointment was made, when Gertrude Elise Ayer was named principal of PS 24 in 1935.[376]

Bulkley's career in New York schools continued for another fifteen years without controversy. In March 1911 he became the boys' principal at PS 65, located at 48 Forsyth Street. This neighborhood on the Lower East Side of Manhattan was filled with new Jewish immigrants from Russia living in a neighborhood of tenements, synagogues, and factories.[377] The school had sixty-six teachers who served more than 2,400 students and included a kindergarten. Five years later he was appointed principal at PS 79 at 38 1st

Street near 2nd Avenue in the East Village, which was later known as the Joseph J. Little School. In 1916 the area housed eastern and southern European immigrants. The neighborhood included a large Roman Catholic church, a small synagogue, and a nondenominational church, Olivet Memorial Church.[378] Bulkley was now principal of a school of thirty-three teachers who served 1,221 pupils. He remained here for the rest of his career, retiring in September 1923 after almost twenty-four years of service.[379] He had taught African Americans who had lived in New York for generations, African Americans newly arrived from the South, and Italian, Russian, and eastern European immigrants who had come to the city of opportunity. Bulkley is best remembered for the very exciting and innovative years he was the principal at PS 80 and for his evening school, first located at PS 80 and then at PS 67, but his service in creating a learning environment for children of all ethnicities is a silent legacy to each of the pupils he taught. In 1908 his friend Dr. E. P. Roberts rightly introduced him as "the father of 2,000 children."[380]

National Negro Conference, 1909

In August 1908 a vicious riot raged for two days in Springfield, Illinois, Abraham Lincoln's hometown. White people attacked African Americans, and in the ensuing violence seven people died and forty homes and twenty-four businesses were destroyed. William English Walling, a wealthy white reformer, wrote a scathing indictment of the riots in *The Independent* that ended with a rallying cry:

> Either the spirit of the abolitionists, of Lincoln and of Lovejoy must be revived and we must come to treat the negro on a plane of absolute political and social equality, or Vardaman and Tilman will soon have transferred the race war to the North. . . . Yet who realizes the seriousness of the situation, and what large and powerful body of citizens is ready to come to their aid?[381]

Mary White Ovington took up the gauntlet thrown down by Walling. In January Walling, Ovington, and Dr. Henry Moskowitz, a social worker and activist, all white, met in Walling's apartment. They each had a broad knowledge of the problems faced by African Americans as well as the vision to know that no organization already in existence could address the fundamental issue of civil rights. The Niagara Movement had fizzled; the active groups in New York, such as the CIICNNY, were focused on social and economic issues. On Lincoln's birthday, 1909, the group issued a call for a national conference on the "Negro question." Oswald Garrison Villard, editor of the *New York Evening Post*, wrote the call and solicited sixty people to sign it.[382] He wrote:

> Discrimination once permitted cannot be bridled; recent
> history in the South shows that in forging chains for the
> Negroes the white voters are forging chains for themselves. "A
> house divided against itself cannot stand"; this government
> cannot exist half slave and half free any better to-day than it
> could in 1861. Hence we call upon all the believers in
> democracy to join in a national conference for the discussion
> of present evils, the voicing of protests, and the renewal of the
> struggle for civil and political liberty.[383]

Sixty people signed the Lincoln Day call. Seven of these, including Bulkley, were African Americans. The news of the call was released from New York, but it received scant attention there and scattered attention nationwide. Villard was discouraged by the lack of response from the newspapers and hesitated to take responsibility for planning a conference no one might attend. Nevertheless, Ovington and Moskowitz, now joined by twelve others, a mix of descendants of abolitionists and frontline reformers, continued to plan for the conference. Four people active in the CIICNNY were on the committee: Ovington, Bulkley, Waller, and Villard. The conference was scheduled for May 31 and June 1 at the Charity Organization Hall in New York City.

The first day of the conference confronted head-on the idea of "Negro inferiority." The presumption was a total rejection of racism. In the early 1900s, despite the pioneering work of anthropologists such as Franz Boas, there was widespread support among scientists and scholars for the idea that non-white races were inherently inferior. [384] At the conference 300 people listened to a wide range of authoritative speakers who soundly refuted those theories. The audience heard from professors of anthropology, neurology, political economy, philosophy, and history. There were also pastors, bishops, judges, an editor, and people from the front lines like Bulkley and Celia Parker Woolley of the Frederick Douglass Centre in Chicago. W. E. B. Du Bois, who was to play such an important role in the NAACP, spoke on "Politics and Industry." [385] Du Bois reported later that the 1909 Conference "left no doubt in the minds of the listeners that the whole argument by which colored people have been pronounced absolutely and inevitably inferior to whites is utterly without scientific basis." [386]

Bulkley presented an address, "Race Prejudice as Viewed from an Economic Standpoint." He pointed out the short-sightedness of

> driving out of the South a host of the best Negroes, best in culture of mind, best in sturdiness of character, best in skill of hand. . . . but when the Southern whites, by every conceivable means, humiliate, proscribe and hamper the best of us, there should be no surprise if we seek more congenial climes, where we can at least protect our wives and daughters from the contumely that the lowest white man can heap upon them with absolute impunity.

He summed up his points:

> We do not ask for charity; all we ask is opportunity. We do not beg for alms; we beg only for a chance. The right to work; opportunity to work; encouragement to work; reward for work; this is all we ask; less than this should not be given. [387]

The following day there was a mass meeting at Cooper Union in the afternoon. Ovington wrote later about the conference:

> These men and women, engaged in religious, social and educational work, for the first time met the Negro who demands, not a pittance, but his full rights in the commonwealth. They received a stimulating shock and one which they enjoyed. They did not want to leave the meeting. We conferred all the time, formally and informally, and the Association gained in those days many of the earnest and uncompromising men and women who have since worked unfalteringly in its cause.[388]

The evening session focused on creation of the new organization. Resolutions were passed establishing the goals of the new association, and the Committee of Forty on Permanent Organization was formed. There were arguments over the resolutions and the nominations for the committee, but in the end, they came to agreement on a plan that could be implemented. The Committee of Forty to plan for the future of the organization included Bulkley and at least a dozen colleagues Bulkley had worked with over the past decade. Many were involved in the CIICNNY. Charles W. Anderson reported to Booker T. Washington, "Du Bois, Waldron, Walters, Sinclair, Max Barber, Wibecan, Dr Mossell[,] Bulkley, Milholland[,] Ida Wells[x] and entire cosmopolitan dinner crowd in Secret conference to-day. Public meeting tonight have had newspapers cover it."[389] Washington had been invited, but both he and Villard knew this would not be a "Washington" organization, and he did not attend.[390]

---

[x] Revered J. Milton Waldron of Shiloh Baptist Church, Washington, DC, Bishop Alexander Walters, AME Zion Church, William A. Sinclair, physician, Max Barber, journalist, George E. Wibecan, postal clerk, Nathan F. Mossell, physician, John E. Milholland, businessman, and Ida Wells-Barnett, journalist. All were activists and became founders of the NAACP.

The committee planned a second conference for May 1910. At that time the group created the permanent organization to be known as "The National Association for the Advancement of Colored People (NAACP); its object to be equal rights and opportunities for all."[391] Despite minimal funding, by the end of 1910 the new organization had held four mass meetings, distributed thousands of pamphlets, and signed up hundreds of members. They planned a celebration of the hundredth anniversary of the birth of Charles Sumner, the abolitionist senator, and published the first issue of *Crisis*. With Du Bois as director of research and publicity and Frances Blascoer, a settlement house worker, as secretary, the organization had a solid start and was making news.[392]

Bulkley had an active role in those first two years. At a meeting of the Committee of Forty in November 1909, Bulkley was appointed (with Villard and Ovington) to a committee to select an executive secretary for the Committee of Forty.[393] Bulkley was also named to the general committee and a member of the executive committee.[394] He remained on the executive committee through 1911 and was a member of the advisory committee from 1912 through 1916.[395]

National League on Urban Conditions Among Negroes

In January 1910, Ruth Baldwin, widow of William H. Baldwin, called a meeting of thirty-eight people. It included leaders from the major groups working with African Americans in New York: the CIICNNY, the NLPCW, the White Rose Mission, the Negro Fresh Air Committee, and the YMCA. Journalist Ray Stannard Baker was the featured speaker. The ideologies of those present included adherents of both Washington's and Du Bois's theories of advancement. The wide-ranging discussions included topics from migration from the South and Jim Crow to the dangers of cocaine and dancing. [396] It was apparent that coordinating these organizations was going to be necessary to maintain effectiveness of the various missions. Over the next few months Baldwin and Frances Kellor met with George Haynes, a young African American man who had come to New York to study for his doctorate at Columbia. He had been employed by the CIICNNY to interview students at Bulkley's evening school and assist in placing them in work through employment agencies. The information about the city he was gathering was being used by the CIICNNY and formed the basis of his doctoral dissertation.[397] Haynes and Baldwin were convinced the field of social work was critical to the work going forward in the city and that trained Black social workers were needed. A subcommittee of the CIICNNY was considering enlarging the program of the CIICNNY. Haynes and Baldwin saw an opportunity and proposed adding social work training as a component of the organization.[398] The CIICNNY subcommittee approved the idea, but the board turned down the proposal. Haynes later wrote, "Miss Kellor, Mrs. Baldwin and I were stunned. <u>The original idea had collapsed</u>."[399]

Bulkley, despite being the founder of the CIICNNY, did not have the power to make his vision of a more comprehensive organization come true. Many associates of Booker T. Washington were on the CIICNNY, and it is possible Washington did not want to see the organization gain more power and influence. In 1906 Washington had been concerned that "Bulkley and his crowd"[400] would dominate the CIICNNY, but Charles W. Anderson, a close Washington lieutenant, assured him at the time that Washington's allies were in control of the organization.[401] The new organization contained many of his allies, and there was little danger of the militants taking over the committee.[402] In 1910 Washington was concerned about the erosion of his influence with the rise of the NAACP.

In response to the refusal of the CIICNNY to broaden its mission, Baldwin and Haynes established a new organization, the Committee on Urban Conditions Among Negroes (CUCAN), on May 19, 1910. Members of the spurned subcommittee of the CIICNNY, including Bulkley, joined them.[403] Frances Kellor of the NLPCW also joined the new organization. Edwin R. A. Seligman, Haynes's professor at Columbia, was chair. Their first formal meeting was on September 29, 1910. Haynes was named director of the CUCAN and a nominating committee of three, including Baldwin and Bulkley, was appointed to name officers and an executive board. E. E. Pratt, an economist and educator, was named secretary.

The CUCAN's agenda was outlined in the minutes of the first meeting, held on September 29, 1910. The first objective was the careful study of the conditions that result from the growing concentration of African Americans in cities with a view to encouraging helpful cooperation between betterment agencies already in existence and the establishment of such agencies where necessary. They noted that the employment problem, heretofore addressed by the CIICNNY, needed attention. The second objective was the training of young Black men and women for social work among their own people. [404] Haynes had been offered a job at Fisk University and made that the headquarters of the training.[405]

The CUCAN moved its agenda forward rapidly and in its first year took over fresh air and summer recreation work, began its survey of social service agencies in Black communities, and established two graduate fellowships for Black social workers.[406] In February 1911 leaders of the CUCAN and NAACP agreed to cooperate without duplicating each other's efforts. The NAACP would "occupy itself principally with the political, civil and social rights of the colored people,' while the Committee on Urban Conditions would deal 'primarily with questions of philanthropy and social economy."[407]

This laid out the course of work for each organization for decades to come and allowed two different models of fundraising—from wealthy white donors for the CUCAN (and eventually the NUL) and from grass roots donors for the NAACP, the activist group.

In April 1911 members of the CUCAN, CIICNNY, and NLPCW met and recommended consolidation. The original plan was the CUCAN would cease to exist and the other two committees would become subcommittees of the new organization. The new agency was to have "power of supervision and recommendations as to the general plans, policies, budgets and financial appeals" of the committees. [408] The CIICNNY objected to the call for supervision by the new agency. Samuel H. Bishop, of the Brooklyn Bureau of Charities, suggested "examination" instead of supervision. The CIICNNY also wanted to make sure the CUCAN continued its local work and not become a powerful administrative arm without specific duties. They envisioned that the new organization would be a confederation of the three organizations, not a union, and that it would be a one-year trial, and under these assumptions gave their approval at the meeting on September 26, 1911, just one year after the formation of the CUCAN. Thus, the NLUCAN came into being. In 1920 the NLUCAN became known as the National Urban League. [409]

On October 16, 1911, the new group was officially organized. Professor Edwin R. A. Seligman, economist from Columbia University, was chair, and Ruth Baldwin and Bulkley were vice chairmen. In December 1911, the first public meeting of the NLUCAN was a conference of social workers among African Americans. Du Bois and Bulkley both spoke. Bulkley's opening address was titled "School Facilities."[410] In 1912 George Haynes proposed to Secretary E. E. Pratt: "The motto 'not alms but opportunity' is one I suggest for a slogan in all our literature." Pratt's margin note reads: "Let's do it."[411] The slogan was first used in 1913. It is believed to be paraphrased from the last paragraph of Bulkley's 1909 speech at National Negro Conference: "We do not ask for charity; all we ask is opportunity."[412]

The next challenge was the official incorporation of the NLUCAN. In December 1912 Secretary E. E. Pratt sent a message to the members of the NLUCAN announcing a meeting for December 4, 1912, to act on "a proposition of incorporating this association."[413] The CIICNNY, still a separate committee, was again reluctant to take this next step in the consolidation. Although the details are not clear, apparently Bulkley was the major stumbling block. Eugene Kinckle Jones, assistant director of the League, was distressed Bulkley was being criticized, but L. Hollingsworth

Wood, Quaker attorney and on the executive board of the NLUCAN, felt that Bulkley was "getting an idea of the work which he never had before."[414] Bulkley had had frontline experience in "the work" for over a decade and clearly had a good idea of the work that needed to be done.

In May Haynes wrote to Ruth Baldwin to clarify points about the trouble with the CIICNNY. Their opposition grew out of "the old desire for independence and pride in their age and standing." He claimed they were not interested in focusing beyond New York. ("Their vision is considerably limited.") "They have signed for incorporation against which they held out for a long time. We will gradually bring them around in these two matters of standards for workers and the national scope of the work."[415] To Wood, Haynes mentioned a conference with Bulkley, Dr. E. P. Roberts, and Rev. W. H. Brooks—all original members of the CIICNNY and close associates. Haynes wrote, "Dr. Brooks . . . said that a little patience and tack [*sic*] will gradually bring them in the line if we keep their confidence. He emphasized the importance of keeping them assured that we mean to deal opening and fairly."[416]

There was an issue of the role African Americans would have in the NLUCAN and how much power the original committees would have. Issues of control extended to staffing as well. In March Pratt wrote to Haynes scolding him for not taking care of a personnel issue. "This matter of the Industrial Committee man is an absolute shame and I think that you are in large part responsible. You are the executive officer in charge of the staff and I do not understand why you are willing to submit to an incompetent subordinate."[417] One week later Pratt reported he had been told the new worker was doing very well; they had moved quickly to replace the "troublesome" worker.[418] Without knowing more, we can't know whether the worker was indeed incompetent or whether his behavior did not please his white supervisors. In another case, Grace Campbell was an African American NLUCAN probation officer who worked with women in the criminal justice system and was praised highly for her work. However, she was considered disruptive within the organization and "not able to fall into line." Despite community protest the executive board dismissed her in 1913.[419]

The CIICNNY agreed to approve the incorporation of the NLUCAN, but Bulkley was eased off the executive board. In October 1913 Wood wrote Haynes he would rather drop Bulkley than Fred R. Moore. By November Haynes was talking about Bulkley's replacement.[420] By the end of 1914 a major reorganization of the NLUCAN had occurred, changing its focus from Haynes's project to increase the number of trained Black social workers to a focus of providing organization and services in northern cities. The leader in this was L. Hollingsworth Wood, now secretary of the organization. Even though this was the area of Bulkley's interest and expertise, he was no longer considered relevant. It is not possible to tell how much was his choice and how much he was the victim of Wood's consolidation of power. In 1914 Kelly Miller, educator and author, was added to the board and assumed the role of vice chairman previously held by Bulkley.[421] When Bulkley's term expired in 1915, it was not renewed, thus ending his role in the NLUCAN.[422]

Bulkley's role in the CIICNNY needs further examination. How influential was he in the organization that he founded? The independence of the CIICNNY was clearly an issue during the negotiations over incorporation of the NLUCAN. How much independence did they have after the formation of the NLUCAN? Wood and others may have resented Bulkley's leadership role and competence. The leaders may have had differences of opinion about priorities. How much grassroots organization should there be? Who should control staffing, and how should they be evaluated? In any organization there are power struggles, but racism seems to have also played a role. It is clear that both Pratt and Wood, as secretaries of the NLUCAN, were frustrated with Black workers, including Haynes, at times. The NLPCW, CIICNNY, and NLUCAN had to work out how Black and white people were going to work together without the white people being in control all of the time. Bulkley played a part in defining these organizations and how they would work. But in the end, he was no longer able to work within them.

Amenia Conference

Booker T. Washington died November 14, 1915. Du Bois realized this was an opportunity to heal the rift in the two camps and to find common ground. Du Bois felt a meeting of the major people of all philosophies in the civil rights movement could give new direction and unity to the movement. Du Bois wrote after Washington's death,

> The wall between the Washington camp and those who had opposed his policies was still there; and it occurred to J. E. Spingarn and his friends that up in the peace and quiet of Amenia and around this beautiful lake, colored men and women of all shades of opinion might sit down and rest and talk and agree on many things if not on all. . . . We all believed in thrift, we all wanted the Negro to vote, we all wanted the laws enforced, we all wanted assertion of our essential manhood; but how to get these things,—there of course was infinite divergence of opinion.[423]

Fifty African American leaders of all philosophies met for three days in August 1916 at the country home of J. E. Spingarn in Amenia, New York. Spingarn was a scholar of independent means and a racial justice worker. The leaders camped out on Spingarn's estate and were fed in a large tent on the grounds. They had opportunities to talk to one another informally, address the group as a whole, and play together, including swimming, hiking, singing, and fellowship. In 1916 Bulkley, still a member of the NAACP's advisory board and recently finished with his position with the NLUCAN, was one of the people Du Bois invited to the Amenia Conference. In a photo taken in front of the dining tent, Bulkley is seated on the ground, hat in hand, surrounded by his peers.

The conference produced a unanimous set of resolutions that established a basis of agreement on the goals of the civil rights movement that strengthened the NAACP, still struggling for legitimacy. World War I, then raging in Europe, soon involved the United States and changed the nation's priorities, but not for African Americans. They went abroad to fight for freedom and came home to no more freedom than they had had before. James Weldon Johnson, later to be field secretary of the NAACP, wrote of the Amenia conference:

> The conference was held at a time when the fundamental rights of the Negro were in a state of flux. At no time since the days following the Civil War had the Negro been in a position where he stood to make greater gain or sustain greater loss in status. The great war in Europe, its recoil on America, the ferment in the United States, all conspired to break up the stereotyped conception of the Negro's place that had been increasing in fixity for forty years, and to allow of new formations. What new forms these conceptions would assume depended largely upon what attitude and action the Negro himself and the white people willing to stand with him would take. Those gathered at the conference determined to help shape them more in accordance with real democracy and the heart's desire of the Negro. The Amenia Conference came at an hour of exigency and opportunity, and took its place in the list of important events in the history of the Negro in the United States.[424]

VIII

HIS OWN EFFORTS

There is no such thing as progressing by nature. Like the tree, we have to grow from our own efforts.[425]

Retreat

After his final affiliations with the Urban League (in 1915) and the NAACP (in 1916), Bulkley ceased being actively involved in civil rights and uplift organizations. He continued to focus on his work as principal of his elementary schools and evening school. He occasionally gave speeches on African American topics. Where many of his colleagues remained active in civil rights and uplift organizations throughout their lives, Bulkley chose to retreat to private life. Without personal papers we cannot know his reasons. A contributing factor must have been that he was never able to assume the leadership role of which he was capable. He believed multiracial organizations could work with true equality. He eventually had to accept this was not true.

In a letter that Bulkley wrote to Du Bois, he raised the veil on his feelings and raised questions as well. In the summer of 1921 Bulkley was vacationing in Quebec, Canada, at the Chateau Frontenac, a sprawling, luxury hotel built in the style of a French château. Du Bois had written to Bulkley to request a photograph. Bulkley demurred, "I have no recent photo. Indeed, I doubt that I could find any kind of photo of myself. Publicity is a fate I have always dreaded. I want to die quietly; no flowers;

simplest burial service." He transitioned quickly to, "How are you, anyhow? I hope the strain of hard work will not shorten your useful life."[426]

"I want to die quietly." Those words can be read so many ways. It is obvious he was a modest man. Was he also disillusioned and depressed? Or was he merely content to have made his contributions and passed the torch to others? He still cared about the cause and was concerned his younger colleague's life's energy would be destroyed in ceaseless amounts of hard work. This was not a new theme for Bulkley. In 1906, when poet Paul Laurence Dunbar died at the age of thirty-three, Bulkley wrote no one was guaranteed "the desired three-score years and ten. Indeed, the hope of such a goal is increased or diminished according as one is, or is not, conservative of his strength. Burn up the oil, the light goes out."[427]

Bulkley's admiration for Du Bois and support of his work is evident in another letter from 1923 in which Bulkley expressed his regret Du Bois was unable to visit him in France. "How moves the world with you? I hope you feel that progress is being made in that herculean task in which you are engaged—I had almost said Sisyphean task. May you have many years of strength and vigor for the job before you!"[428] Bulkley's mention of Hercules and Sisyphus is revealing. Both Sisyphus and Hercules carried tremendous burdens, both in service and as punishment. These classical allusions to two mythological figures whose energy was spent in endless efforts were immediately understood by all those who were educated in the classics. Hercules succeeded after many trials and for his work gained a place on Mt. Olympus. Sisyphus, by contrast, suffered the eternal punishment of rolling a rock uphill only to have it fall back down again and again. It is interesting to note that the man in command of several modern and ancient languages used the colloquial in his correspondence. Bulkley opened his 1923 note to Du Bois: "So sorry you did not drop in and say 'howdy.'"[429] There is a folksy familiarity in that which reveals a man comfortable with himself and at ease in his language.

At the end of the 1922–1923 school year, Bulkley retired from his position with the New York City Board of Education. He had worked for the grammar schools from November 1899 to June 1923. He was a teacher for one year and a principal for twenty-two years, as well as principal of the evening elementary school for eighteen years. By the time the announcement of his retirement appeared in the *Amsterdam News* on August 29, he was already in France, "where he intends to make his future home."[430] He initially lived in the Riviera resort community of Juan les Pins. Later the family moved to Nice. It has been reported that Bulkley opened a school in France, but there is no evidence he had a school or worked as a teacher.[431] Bulkley returned to the United States only once. He arrived in New York on May 29, 1925, headed for Maude and John Dancy's in Detroit.[432] Bulkley's daughter Maude had suffered a stroke. Surely he also went to Jefferson City, Missouri, to see his mother, who was in the last weeks of her life. Madora E. Wilson Bulkley died July 2, 1925.

Five years later Bulkley was invited to return to New York as a guest of honor at the National Urban League's twentieth-anniversary dinner on May 3, 1930. He failed to get his passport renewed in time to make the trip.[433] On August 5, 1933, at age 72, Bulkley died at his home at 205 Promenade des Anglaise in Nice. There was little fanfare. He received a small notice on the front page of the *New York Age* and another in the *Sun*.[434] Ironically, in August 1933, representatives of the African American race were meeting in Amenia, New York, to once again discuss the state of civil rights and promote unity. One hopes the group took a few minutes to reflect on Bulkley's passing.[435]

Intellectual Life

In contrast to small-town Orangeburg, South Carolina, many Black people in New York City were interested in intellectual challenge, serious discussion, and learning. Bulkley's contacts with them were important throughout his first decade in New York.

Student's Club

The Students' Club in Brooklyn, a group of about a dozen Black men, met twice a month in members' homes. Each member was required to be an active participant "able and willing to contribute papers of approved ability and painstaking research" and to participate in lively discussions of the presentations. [436] They discussed "questions of timely interest, science, social and political economy, pedagogy, history and questions affecting the colored American."[437] Their study "develop[ed] careful, close, and accurate thinking, which is essential to the cause of right, justice and truth in the adjustment and solution of the grave questions and problems which confront the American people today." Topics were as diverse as the history of the incandescent lamp, the nature and authority of conscience, the Constitution, and the growth of trusts.

Bulkley first attended the Students' Club in 1901 at S. R. Scottron's house. Scottron read a paper, "Education, Its Relation to Our Future." He promoted entrepreneurship as an alternative to classical education or menial labor.[438] Bulkley joined his cousin, Rev. George Frazier Miller, rector of St. Augustine's Protestant Episcopal Church; lawyer D. Macon Webster; Jerome B. Peterson, managing editor of the *New York Age*; and others, among whom were inventors, physicians, pastors, educators, and businessmen. In April 1905 members of the Students' Club arrived at Scottron's home in evening dress. The speaker of the evening was one of their own club members, Lewis H. Latimer, a draftsman and inventor, whose paper "From Another Point of View" discussed the history of slavery and that there is "no real difference between the negro and other races." The guest of the evening was Oswald Garrison Villard, who said, "The colored man should have faith in his race; that no man can limit the human soul."[439] Bulkley must have thrived on the stimulation of learning, discussing, and debating with other thoughtful people of his race. Even more importantly, it put him in a position to meet not only the other members of the club but also guests such as Villard, who was to become important in the NAACP.

Bulkley worked at the CIICNNY or the NAACP with Scottron, Webster, and O. M. Waller.

Cosmopolitan Club

Another group was the Cosmopolitan Club, an informal interracial group called together by Mary White Ovington in 1906.[440] They met in homes of Brooklyn's elite—both white and Black—to discuss topics of the day, including race.[441] On April 27, 1908, Bulkley was present at the interracial dinner meeting of the Cosmopolitan Club held at Peck's Restaurant in Manhattan. The topic of the evening was "The Spirit of Caste in a Republic." Men and women of both races and with a wide range of opinion spoke to the issues. Among the many speakers, Hamilton Holt, editor of the *Independent*, said intermarriage among the races was one of the solutions to the "race problem." A reporter filed a report on the dinner with the United Press Association newswire, and newspapers across the country reported the event. The *Rockford (IL) Daily Republic* proclaimed, "Whites to Marry with Negroes" and reported:

> The spectacle of a young white woman seated between two negroes, and enthusiastic acclamations by the diners of the proposition of the intermarriage as a solution of the race problem, have proven too much. The prominent negro educators, the leaders with foresight sufficient to see the damage worked by last night's affair felt more injury had been worked to the race than by any event occurring [*sic*] in the north in recent years.[442]

In response, Mary White Ovington declared her "perfect willingness to meet negroes on [an] equal social plane. . . . New York is a cosmopolitan city, and I want to see it like London, Paris, and Berlin, where people of any race can meet without being [the] subject of criticism. That day is near at hand."[443] The *New York Age* ran the headline "Cosmopolitan Society Dinner: The Spirit of Caste Discussed Before a Unique Gathering" on April 30, 1908. The article details the variety of people who spoke and their topics, without reference to the furor it caused. Villard said, "Many of the newspaper accounts of the dinner are malicious and false. The subject of intermarriage was not discussed by any of the speakers save by one in passing, and he declared it to be impossible. The object of the meeting was merely for the purpose of exchanging ideas on how best to help forward the colored people."[444] It is now known that Booker T. Washington, feeling threatened by this interracial group, had secretly arranged for the press coverage.[445]

St. Mark's Lyceum

St. Mark's Lyceum was another venue for the thoughtful African American. St. Mark's Methodist Episcopal Church on West 53rd Street in Manhattan had a large African American congregation. The Rev. William H. Brooks was the pastor from 1897 to 1923 and became a close colleague of Bulkley. St. Mark's Lyceum, founded as St. Mark's Literary in 1882, met on Sunday afternoons and Thursday evenings. The lyceum was a nondenominational forum for current topics and music. It played a "commendable part in moulding the lives of many a young man and woman who have felt its healthful influence." [446] Topics included "Hymnology," "The Reduction of Southern Representation," "Life Through Christ," and "John Greenleaf Whittier: The Quaker Soldier," as well as current topics such as the Atlanta race riots in 1907. Bulkley first spoke at the lyceum in March 1905 on the neglect of educational opportunities. In spring 1907, he and Booker T. Washington shared the platform. Bulkley spoke there occasionally over the next decade.

Family

The previous chapters have reported little of Bulkley's personal and family life. Along with his career as an educator and his work in civil rights organizations, family is the third thread that creates the whole picture of the man during his New York years. When he took his first job teaching at Canarsie, he moved his family to a modest rental house at 269 Skillman Street in Brooklyn, near DeKalb and Bedford Avenues in the Bedford-Stuyvesant section, then a middle-class mixed-race neighborhood. In 1900 his household consisted of Mary and himself, their four daughters (ages ranging in age from two to nine), and his sister and mother.[447] In 1903 a son, William Jr., was born, and the family was complete with five children (two others died in infancy). At about that time he moved his family to a nearby brownstone at 826 Lafayette Avenue in another mixed-race neighborhood.[448]

Ridgefield Park

In 1905 Bulkley published "The School as a Social Center" and started the evening school at PS 80. He also made the big decision to purchase a home in the New Jersey suburb of Ridgefield Park. The space, quiet, good schools, and ease of commuting by railroad probably attracted the Bulkley family to this suburban community as it had many others. The eight-room Victorian house with gingerbread trim at 65 Bergen Street in Ridgefield Park was a short walk from the railroad station and the general store. It had "all modern improvements," including gas, electricity, steam heat, and was in the "best section of town."[449] The town boasted a new school.[450] The Bulkley children attended the local schools, played with the local children, and in June 1910 Maude, the eldest, graduated from Ridgefield Park High School.

The New Jersey suburbs of New York City were strictly segregated. Some deeds carried racial restrictions, excluding Black, Jewish, and Asian people. How Bulkley was able to purchase a home and live in a white community, while he was being featured as a Black educator and civil rights activist in New York, remains a mystery. His activities were widely reported in the New York papers. His affiliations and racial identity had to be known to his neighbors. In 1906 Roscoe Conkling Simmons, who was consulting with the CIICNNY, visited the Bulkleys in Ridgefield Park. The New York Age reported Bulkley and Simmons "made a round of the village and were cordially received by many of the residents, all of whom are very proud of their townsman, Dr. Buckley [sic]."[451] It is hard to tell if this was wishful thinking on the reporter's part or if indeed some in the village were fascinated by their unusual neighbor, a fair-skinned Black man living in one of the biggest houses in a virtually all-white town and active in the work of improving the lives of African Americans.

The Bergen County, New Jersey, suburbs welcomed Black people in service occupations and segregated their living areas. A 1908 article in the New *York Age*[452] about lots available in Englewood, near Ridgefield Park, lauds the benefits of country living with city comforts. Toward the end of the article, it is clear what kind of buyers they were looking for. It mentioned "three colored churches" and that laborers could earn two dollars and fifty cents per day and women could get work as hairdressers, seamstresses, and day workers. The focus was not on professional African Americans but on service workers and laborers.

It was also an era when attitudes were not far different from those in the South. In 1910, in nearby Hackensack, William Lightfoot, an African American, was accused of insulting Miss Minnie Metz, the white daughter of a local butcher, with a few "short and ugly" words. The newspaper article said, "The color line isn't quite as heavy in this city as it is in the Carolinas, where Bill hails from, or he might have had the extreme pleasure of climbing a tree with the help of a rope." Threatened with thirty days in jail or a five-dollar fine, Bill paid up and went on his way, but the message was clear to him and to all the readers of the newspaper.[453]

Europe

Bulkley was most comfortable in Europe. As early as 1893 he described the relief he felt going to Europe, where the color line was not drawn against him. Author and civil rights activist James Weldon Johnson described this eloquently:

> From the day I set foot in France, I became aware of the working of a miracle within me. I became aware of a quick readjustment to life and to environment. I recaptured for the first time since childhood the sense of being just a human being. I need not try to analyze this change for my colored readers; they will understand in a flash what took place. For my

white readers . . . I am afraid that any analysis will be inadequate, perhaps futile. . . . I was suddenly free; free from a sense of impending discomfort, insecurity, danger; free from the conflict within the Man-Negro dualism and the innumerable maneuvers in thought and behavior that it compels; free from the problem of the many obvious or subtle adjustments to a multitude of bans and taboos; free from special scorn, special tolerance, special condescension, special commiseration; free to be merely a man.[454]

France had been a refuge for Black people since the early nineteenth century. In the twentieth century, after World War I, the African American expatriate community grew rapidly. In 1909, the year Bulkley was appointed as principal to PS 125, he sailed for Europe in the summer. While in Europe he investigated educational opportunities for his children. Four years after his move to the suburbs, he was seeking alternatives for his family. The following summer, 1910, he escorted Maude, age nineteen, and Ethel, age sixteen, to Europe to enroll them in school, where he left them when he returned to New York in September.[455] The next summer, 1911, William sailed with the rest of the family to Europe. They joined Maude and Ethel and established a home in Lausanne, Switzerland, "for the purpose of their education."[456] Lillian was thirteen, Wilhelmina was fifteen, and William Jr. was eight. William returned to New York City and boarded at the home of his friend and fellow activist Dr. E. P. Roberts.[457]

The rest of the Bulkley family lived a comfortable life in the suburbs of Lausanne. The girls attended École Vinet, a rigorous, progressive school for girls ages eight to seventeen, founded in 1839 by Alexandre Vinet, a prominent Christian theologian. The school offered far more variety of classes than could be had in the United States: French, German, English, singing, drawing, botany, physiology, and bookkeeping, in addition to the usual grammar school subjects. Advanced topics included church history, ancient history, and cosmography.[458] In the Bulkley family photo album is a photograph of Hélène Monastier, a teacher at the school, who was a Christian socialist and a free thinker.[459]

Bulkley visited his family in Lausanne in the summers from 1912 through 1915. He returned to New York each year in time to start the next school year. He arrived in Switzerland in the summer of 1914, shortly before Archduke Franz Ferdinand of Austria was assassinated, the beginning of World War I. Bulkley felt marooned in the center of the war districts, but he was able to return to New York at the beginning of September.[460] The rest of the family remained in Switzerland. Living in a Europe at war was better than returning to the United States. He was able to visit in 1915 but not in 1916.

Mary and her children Wilhelmina, Lillian, and William Jr. remained in neutral Switzerland, but war raged all around them. As it became clear the United States would enter the war, they made plans to return to the United States. In early 1917 Ethel went to Switzerland to assist her mother in closing the house. On April 6, 1917, the United States declared war on Germany, and in June 14,000 US troops landed in France. Heretofore, the Bulkleys had been citizens of a neutral country living in neutral Switzerland, but now they were enemy aliens if they were to travel through German-held territory.

Early in the summer of 1917 they made their way from Lausanne across southern France to Bordeaux, where Mary, Ethel, Wilhelmina, Lillian, and William Jr. sailed for the United States on the *S.S. Chicago* on July 8 and arrived in New York harbor on July 19, leaving the war behind them. Although they initially went to Ridgefield Park, by the end of August they were established in their new home in Brooklyn, a three-story brownstone Bulkley had purchased at 118 MacDonough Street, now in the Stuyvesant Heights Historic District.[461]

The Bulkley women were active in war efforts, entertaining African American troops and raising money for Liberty Bonds.[462] Mary became involved with the Brooklyn Urban League and attended events such as a breakfast for Mrs. C. D. B. King, the wife of the president-elect of Liberia, joining "some of the most distinguished and progressive colored women in New York City and its environs."[463] Thus, the family picked up the threads of their lives. Maude and Ethel both married in 1917 and Lillian in 1920. Maude and Ethel stayed in the United States. In 1921 William Jr. started his career with a coffee company in Santos, Brazil. Wilhelmina returned to France about 1922 and never returned to the United States. In 1923 William and Mary moved to France. Lillian lived in the United States and in France. For more on the Bulkley family members, see Appendix 1.

Finances

One of the questions anyone looking at Bulkley's life might ask is how he could afford the lifestyle his family pursued. First, there is no evidence he accepted money from anyone and strong evidence in his speeches he would not have done so. What he spent he either earned or borrowed. Second, he was not extravagant. His housing for much of the time while his family was in Europe was a rented room. Bulkley had a solid middle-class income—his salary as a principal, his stipend from the evening school, and, when they were not living there, rental income from the Ridgefield Park house.

In 1904 Bulkley was on the board of directors of the Afro-American Investment and Building Company, which had been in business since 1892. It was a very small building and loan association, with members contributing one dollar monthly and in turn earning interest and eventually becoming eligible for a mortgage. In its first twelve years it issued nine mortgages.[464] His association with the Afro-American Investment and Building Company reveals an interest in investment and finance, and it is possible he invested money in the stock market. Mary inherited two properties in Columbia, South Carolina, when her mother died in 1910. The money from the sale of those properties may have made it possible for the family to afford school tuition and living expenses in Switzerland. From 1905 to 1921 Bulkley had four different mortgages on the property in New Jersey. In 1917 he purchased a town house property in Brooklyn with a mortgage. The family lived there until he sold it in 1920, after which they lived in Ridgefield Park for a year or two and then settled in a less expensive area of Brooklyn. In Switzerland Mary and the children lived in a nice house with servants and a governess. At least some of the children went to private school.

When Bulkley moved to France in 1923, he lived in the Riviera towns of Juan les Pins and Nice. By this time he was receiving a pension and no longer needed to support any of his children. Without more details, it seems fair to say Bulkley afforded the upper-middle-class lifestyle for his family by his earnings and possible investments, rental income from the Ridgefield Park house, and the possible advantage of the strong dollar/exchange rate in Europe.

Directors, Afro-American Investment Company
Bulkley: standing 3rd from left   *The Negro in Business,* 1907

826 Lafayette Avenue, Brooklyn
New York City, Municipal Archives

Childhood House

65 Bergen Avenue, Ridgefield Park, NJ   Private collection

Train Station, Ridgefield Park, NJ   Collection of author

Promenade des Anglais, Nice, France Collection of the author

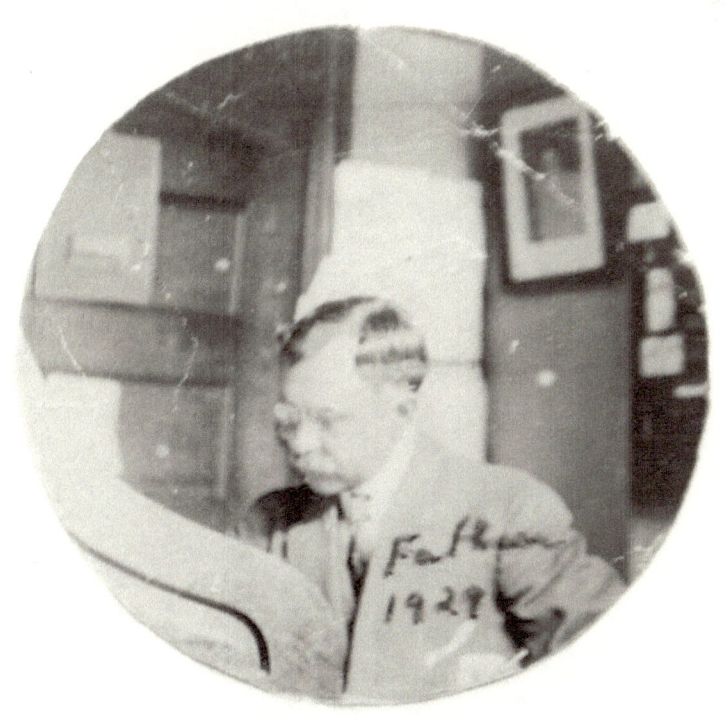

William L. Bulkley, 1929 Private collection

IX

THE QUIET LEGACY

Lives of great men all remind us
We can make our lives sublime,
And, departing, leave behind us
Footprints on the "adamantine hills of eternity."[465]

Over the years Bulkley provided various assessments of the ingredients of a successful life. He mentioned "grace and gumption" several times. Bulkley meant grace in its Christian sense: an unmerited blessing from God. Others might call it luck or karma. But in the Christian sense it is more of a gift. The ambition to become somebody is both chosen and a gift. Grace appeared in the form of Lewis Dunton, the missionary teacher in Greenville who ignited Bulkley's love of learning, in the opportunity to go to Wesleyan, in his first trip to Europe, and in Scottron's activism that got Bulkley the job in the Brooklyn school system. But of course these graces alone were far from sufficient. Bulkley was driven to be somebody. He had the gumption to stand for his beliefs, try new things, push himself forward in his education and career. He was motivated to rise out of poverty and did so through hard work and economy. Grit kept him moving forward in the face of adversity. Money not only provided the necessities for life but also social standing. Family, values, and his Christian faith were the glue that held it all together.

Bulkley's philosophical foundation was important to his achievements. At a lecture at St. Mark's Lyceum, he said, "Like a man lost in the Catacombs of Rome, we colored people have been [groping] to find the way out of our difficulties. This way out is a cord composed of several strands. The first is religion; the second a sound, strong body; the third a good education, and the fourth, altruism."[466]

The Foundations

Religion

The first foundation for Bulkley was always religion and his Christian faith. Bulkley was born into a home where prayer, devotions, and the Bible were part of its fabric and in a church that embraced freedom and the new world order after emancipation. From this faith grew his unwavering commitment to service for the advancement of his race and for the advancement of individuals.

The Methodist Episcopal Church put forth a model of freedom based on integration of the races.[467] It was very imperfect; white people held most of the leadership positions, but not all. The ideal was a church based on equal representation and equal opportunity. This view formed the bedrock of Bulkley's faith and, even more critically, the foundation of his philosophy of life. Religion and his commitment to integration influenced his decision to stay at Claflin University when Cardozo and Townsend resigned after the caning incident in 1890. It informed his commitment to institutions that were color-blind. He accepted the transition of his evening school, which had always been integrated, to a majority of white students. He accepted his appointment to a predominately white school in lower Manhattan. Children who needed his "most careful, hopeful, and sympathetic attention" were in desperate need of his attention whatever their race—the Russian and Italian immigrants as well as the African American migrants from the South. Early in his career Bulkley wrote, "My duty is only to work in my feeble way for the development of the mind, for

158

the inculcation of moral principles in the youth of to-day, the men of tomorrow. It must come or civilization is a failure, Christianity a farce, the Bible a lie."[468]

Education

Faith provided the hope for freedom and the future, but education provided Bulkley with the ladder out of poverty to a life unimaginable in the humble cabin in Greenville. Bulkley's youthful attitude was that hard work and education would overcome the barriers of racism. How understandable a belief it was and how naive. In *The Education of the Negro in the American Social Order*, Bond wrote:

> The passionate New England faith in the common school as the creator of all civic virtues transferred itself to the Southern scene with redoubled enthusiasm. "The brother in Black" needed, it was thought, but the touch of education to prepare him for his new duties. It was, perhaps, a naive faith, but simple only in the pathetic assumption by Negroes and whites that this transformation could be achieved in the course of a few years. It was certainly the flowering of the American ideal in a time when idealism was most needed, and the tragedy is more in the fact that the ideal was not maintained than in the enthusiasm with which it was initiated.[469]

This faith in education propelled him into the ranks of the very best educated men in America. It put him on an equal footing with anyone, whether they were willing to recognize that or not. His faith and education took him to Europe, where he found he could escape the caste system that infected every aspect of life in the United States, North and South. His faith in education informed his career, which was one of service to students of all races. Faith in education informed the choices he made for his children. He moved to Ridgefield Park for the schools available in the suburbs and sent his family to Europe, where the children could be educated in an environment free of racism and learn the multiple languages that enabled them to become world citizens.

Personal Responsibility

Along with religion and education, Bulkley's philosophy of life included a commitment to the individual's responsibility for developing his own wealth and physical fitness. This is perhaps also a reflection of that most American of ideals—the perfectibility of man, the boundless limits of self-improvement. The arc of Bulkley's life ends in retreat, but it started in the full optimism of Reconstruction, youth, and his faith in God. Bulkley created his life. He had the determination that allowed him to provide handsomely for his family and afford a lifestyle little imagined by his father and unimaginable to his grandfather.

Altruism

Bulkley's life was one of service to others. As a teacher he chose a service profession. Beyond his profession he used his talents and time to create organizations that supported people and advocated change. Without this commitment to altruism, he would not have created the school as a social center, spoken widely, founded organizations, or struggled to define them and make them work. Bulkley's personal foundations were religion, education, self-improvement, and service. They were not enough, as the young Bulkley hoped, to overcome the racism of larger society he worked in.

Race and Identity

Richard Greener said, "In this country it is well known to many that any one is white who dares to assert and maintain his assertion." [470] He experienced this firsthand, since his wife and children had chosen to assert their whiteness. His daughter, Belle da Costa Greene, was librarian and art expert for James P. Morgan, a position that would have been impossible if she did not identify as white and had not been able to convince others she was. [471]

Two of Bulkley's daughters asserted their whiteness. His wife and another daughter and his son moved in a white world. It is only his eldest daughter, Maude, who chose to identify as Black. She married John C.

Dancy Jr., director of the NUL in Detroit, and they both served the Black community there. Passing as white had direct advantages—career advancements and the white privileges of everyday life in such areas as transportation and public accommodations. However, choosing a white identity usually meant cutting off ties with family and community. John C. Dancy, in his autobiography, gave a small insight into how this affected the Bulkley family.

> The marriages of the sisters gave rise to a situation that is far more common than most people realize. Direct communication was broken off. The mother [Mary Bulkley], who was light complexioned, would visit the sisters and relay information about them to my wife. But she could never relay information about my wife to them, unless she was talking on a closed circuit. For, you see their husbands did not know these girls were Negroes. They don't know to this day [1966].

Dancy also related a poignant event in his own life. He had been given a huge bouquet of roses at a conference:

> I thought, I should give these to some of the people who are attending these sessions with me. So I took 35 or 40 roses and went around giving them to a number of the women. ... In the group was . . . my sister-in law; I knew all about her but she didn't know anything about me. When I got to her I gave her about ten of the American Beauty roses. "Oh," she exclaimed, "how do I rate these?" "You'll never know," I replied.[472]

The division traveled through the generations. Descendants of William Bulkley Jr. and Ethel Bulkley Ross did not know about their Black ancestors or about each other until the twenty-first century, when the family had been divided for almost 100 years.

Race and color are fundamental issues that affect life in the United States. During slavery African Americans who were of mixed European and African racial heritage, as the Bulkleys were, were often given favor over their darker-skinned brothers and sisters. They might have been assigned easier jobs, given education and religious training, had permission to earn some income on the side, or even granted their freedom. They were also resented for those privileges and for abandoning their darker brothers and sisters. This hierarchy carried over into the economic and social life of free Black communities as well.

Although Bulkley did not choose to identify as a white person or deny his Black family roots, he undoubtedly also benefited from his light complexion and ambiguous racial appearance. He was described as "nearly white but plainly a negro."[473] When walking on the street, sitting in a rail car, applying for a mortgage, ordering a meal in a restaurant, did others perceive him as white? Did he take advantage of this incidental passing? It clearly did not happen all the time. In 1906 he "told of some recent experience of his of a not encouraging nature, emphasizing the fact that refusal of accommodations to Afro-Americans in this city and vicinity is becoming quite common."[474] Identifying as white and slipping into white society and culture presented a real option to him. But "after emancipation, to pass as white was considered by many African Americans ... to be 'sell[ing] one's birthright for a mess of pottage.'"[475] Bulkley identified very strongly with being a "Negro." He was dedicated to "his people" and missed them when he was in the North or abroad. He felt an obligation to use his considerable talents to challenge injustice and give people skills to create opportunities for themselves. But he abandoned that fight.

In 1940 Ralph Ellison wrote a one-page biography of Bulkley as part of his work for the WPA Writer's Program. Almost every "fact" in this sketch has errors, given the limited sources to which Ellison had access. Most importantly, however, he wrote, "As a reward for his work at P.S. 80, Dr Bukley [*sic*] was given a school downtown on the lower East Side [1909]. But here Dr Bukley seems to have lost his identity as a Negro and little is known of him from that point on."[476] What did it mean for Bulkley to lose his identity as a Negro? Did it imply taking on a white identity? Or did it mean he "lost" his commitment to his race? The source Ellison cited for this comment was an "Interview with Miss Gertrude Ayers [*sic*], New York school principal." Ayer was a teacher, principal, author, and feminist. She had known Bulkley since she was a child and was in a position to make an assessment of the man and his career. Her words were not quotes and were filtered through Ellison's eyes, but the statement should be considered carefully. At a minimum it confirms that Bulkley ceased being an activist at some point after 1909. It also conveys a sense of betrayal. Ayer was a lifelong advocate for civil rights, as were Du Bois and many others Bulkley worked with. He continued to identify as a "Negro" and made no effort to pass as a white person. He continued to speak at forums such as St. Mark's Lyceum and to associate socially with African Americans. However, he gave up the fight, as others would not do. He was very bitter about the racial situation in the United States. John Dancy wrote, "Dr. Bulkely [*sic*] did not intend that his daughters should marry Americans, either Negro or white. He had planned it so they would remain in Europe, but the coming of World War I upset this plan, and he brought them back to the U.S."[477] In Bulkley's mind the caste system here tainted both races. He wanted his family to be rid of it.

Race was very important to Bulkley. He loved the South, the land, his people, and their religion. "But when our yearning [for those things] seizes us, there appears before us the spectral hand of blighting prejudice, inviting uninvitingly."[478] The lure was always there, but reality was as well. He talked of the economic and social loss to the race "because of the loss of a host of mixed-bloods who cross the line. . . . There is scarcely a colored man who could not tell of some friend or relative who has crossed the line North or South, now prominent in business, professors in institutions of learning, married into good society, and rearing families that have no dream of the depths that their parent has escaped."[479] These two things, the loss of his homeland in the South and the temptations of "crossing the line," had to be very personal to him. He missed the balmy air, comradeship, and revivals. He also was surely tempted to cross the line and claim the life of white privilege rather than remaining an elementary principal in New York schools, fighting hard against racism. He didn't.

Class

Class, as well as race, has always been a part of the fabric of society in the United States. Although the boundaries here are more fluid than in Europe, class informs many of our institutions and individual actions. Bulkley's father grew up near Charleston in a free family but not one of the free African American elite. The elite free people of color were wealthy merchants and entrepreneurs who often owned slaves. They formed a class between the white planters and the slaves. On the margins were poor free Black people and lower-class whites. Living on Sullivan's Island, the Bulkleys would have been somewhat isolated from this stratified society. Although not part of the elite, they were privileged to be free, to be carpenters, a skilled profession, and to be able to provide an education for their children. In the next generation, all of V. H. Bulkley's children were able to attend Claflin University, getting degrees that allowed them to pursue middle-class careers—William was a teacher, Charles was a carpenter and a college teacher, Maggie Bulkley Young was a teacher and school administrator, Joseph was a carpenter and a teacher at Claflin, and Edward was a dentist.

Bulkley was also part of the talented tenth. Early in the twentieth century, W.E. B. Du Bois described the talented tenth (a phrase first used by Henry Lyman Morehouse[480]).

> The Negro race, like all races, is going to be saved by its exceptional men. The problem of education, then, among Negroes must first of all deal with the Talented Tenth; it is the problem of developing the Best of this race that they may guide the Mass away from the contamination and death of the Worst, in their own and other races.[481]

This approach was not only effective but also elitist. Bulkley was part of this elite. He endeavored not only to guide but also to provide pathways for the "Mass" away from "the Worst, in their own and other races."

When Bulkley went to New York, his profession, education, and economic status enabled him to become part of the Black bourgeoisie.[482] These were professionals and entrepreneurs who had the wealth and education to live a comfortable middle-class life, own property, and have time for clubs, social life, and service. He felt a deep commitment to his fellow African Americans who did not share that status; he strove to give them the tools to pursue a path into the middle class. He remembered his roots, but he embraced his middle-class status and the privileges it afforded him.

> In the late nineteenth century the light-skinned colored aristocrats exhibited a self-conscious elitism: on some occasions it led to condescension and even arrogance toward other Blacks, especially the poor, uneducated masses at the bottom of the class structure, who were sometimes referred to as 'vicious' and 'degraded'; on others this same elitism produced a sense of awesome responsibility that translated itself into a commitment to improve the lot of the race in general.[483]

Bulkley's patron in Brooklyn was Samuel R. Scottron. His was the class Bulkley joined.

> Scottron typified the elite people of color, who reacted to the advent of two-tier democracy by trying to define themselves as a distinct social group worthy of greater liberties. They were loyal Republicans, conscious of their past in the city, anti-immigrant, and careful stewards of colored institutions. They championed the cause of a people who were stripped of political power; paradoxically, doing so while seeking social distance from that group.[484]

In 1902 Bulkley was treasurer of a committee formed to arrange an evening to honor Samuel R. Scottron for his eight years' service on the board of education. Bulkley and the rest of the committee were accused of being "high-toned" and ignoring the people that got Scottron onto the Board of Education. [485] Bulkley saw some lower-class Black people as degraded but redeemable by education and religion. He commented on the "alarming influx" of the dregs of society from the South.[486] However, in all his projects he included a grassroots component—the parent meetings at PS 80, the community meetings to encourage attendance at the evening school, and the continuation of community meetings as part of his plan for the CIICNNY.

Progressive Movement

Progressivism was a social and political movement of the 1890s to 1920s that addressed the social and economic effects of unfettered capitalism that had dominated the United States after the Civil War. Underlying the movement was a belief that there is a common good or a public interest, that study and analysis could define that interest, and that both government and private organizations could improve society's ills. Teachers, social workers, and other professionals were critical in this process. Progressives exposed corruption in industry and government and addressed child labor, prostitution, and urban poverty. They supported government regulation of food, drugs, workers, and factories as well as organized labor and good education. Reforms such as regulation of railroads, immigration reform, paved roads, settlement houses, and investigative journalism were products of progressivism. Churches became involved in the progressive movement by embracing the social gospel as Christianity in action. Both government and philanthropy supported these reforms.[487]

However, progressivism was also racist. Disfranchisement and segregation of Black people were a part of progressive reforms to "purify the vote" and the rest of society. Most progressives viewed Black people as "racially inferior, morally deficient, and politically unqualified."[488] This had the effect of focusing legislation, fundraising, and volunteer energy into projects that benefited whites and in reforms that discriminated against

Black people. The spirit of reform was not being used to tackle the problems of racism and of African Americans.

Du Bois, Bulkley, Ovington, and other leaders of racial uplift embraced the spirit of progressivism and used its tools in their work. They believed in the value of study and analysis, the creation of new institutions and organizations, the importance of the role of professionals, and the necessity of challenging legal issues in the courts. Many of the movements and people in the early civil rights movement were firmly rooted in progressive ideals. Kirby believed "William Lewis Bulkley was probably the most important southern Black progressive."[489] Bulkley used facts and statistics to illustrate his points and organizational action to fight racism and offer educational and economic options to impoverished African Americans. Home visits and school meetings were part of the progressive movement in using social institutions to educate and improve the lives of the neediest people. He fit the model in many respects but retained a faith in people to know what was best for themselves.

Orator

Bulkley's role as orator intertwined with his role as educator and activist. He used his speaking platform to educate, promote his ideas, and motivate, sharing practical advice, encouragement, and instruction. He used statistics, classical allusions, and history, especially African American history, to illustrate his points. He had a command of ancient and modern languages that allowed him to address the most erudite crowd. He also had an ear for the vernacular and could speak in words for the average person. He was a popular speaker, giving presentations before audiences at the lyceum, the YMCA, and churches and before civil rights and educational organizations. His speeches were described as practical, interesting, and logical. As with his 1890 Emancipation Day speech, they could also be passionate. He spoke on religion: "Science and the Bible," "Faith in the Church and in Claflin."[490] He lectured on African American history and civil rights: "Some Results of Emancipation," "Race Prejudice as Viewed from an Economic

Standpoint."[491] Education was a popular topic: "The Industrial Training of Men and Women in New York," "More Work; Less Talk," "Open Door in Trades."[492] He spoke about values and personal development: "Sober Mindedness," "Struggle of Life," "Sterling Worth vs. Sham."[493]

The fiftieth anniversary of Emancipation Day was celebrated on January 2, 1913, at Young's Casino in Harlem, a Black-owned 2,500-seat auditorium.[494] Speeches on the occasion included one on the progress of women, a review of "the progress of the race" and "a practical talk along racial lines." William L. Bulkley read the Emancipation Proclamation and a poem by James Weldon Johnson.[495] The poem, "Fifty Years, 1863–1913," was written for the occasion. Bulkley spoke the lines that reflected his life, study of history, and passion for freedom:

> This land is ours by right of birth,
> This land is ours by right of toil;
> We helped to turn its virgin earth,
> Our sweat is in its fruitful soil.
>
> . . .
>
> Courage! Look out, beyond, and see
> The far horizon's beckoning span!
> Faith in your God-known destiny!
> We are a part of some great plan.[496]

Legacy

William L. Bulkley's grace and gumption took him from South Carolina to New York and Europe. They took him from poverty to the middle class to a PhD to a life of service. Has he left any footprints on the "adamantine hills of eternity"? Did he tread too lightly to make a mark on that hard and unforgiving stone? Others who worked longer and whose agenda was more radical have left their names in the history books and in our pantheon of heroes. Bulkley was part of their story, too. Bulkley was committed to working with both white and Black people, had a belief in the overriding power of education, and was reluctant to admit the intractability of racism in the North and South. His faith in people and in the right was sorely tested, and his integrationist views were far too naive and too soon to have any hope of reality. But he has a legacy.

From 1903 to 1916 there is no doubt his creative insight, drive to improve conditions, and participation on committees and in speaking aided all the early civil rights movements, particularly the CIICNNY, NLPCW, NLUCAN, and NAACP. Bulkley was the prime mover in the conception and founding of the CIICNNY. The NUL and the NAACP are still leading civil rights and social justice organizations a century later. He was a man of both vision and action. Bulkley could see what needed to be done and make plans to implement the steps to get there. He believed in the power of people to change their own lives and in the power of the organization to change society. He put the problems of underemployment and employment discrimination on the table for reform along with housing, health, and social welfare. His view of education was broad, including all ages and all subjects. He recognized the need for job training as well as for general and advanced education. He offered the gift of hope. He recognized the effect of the student's life at home on performance in the classroom and involved parents in the school for the benefit of the child. He helped raise the next generation of men and women who in turn were the people who pushed the agenda forward in the next decades.

He had high ideals that propelled him to a life of action and service. He came to age during the optimism of Reconstruction and made his way through the repressive segregation that followed. William Lewis Bulkley was one of the African Americans who forged a path through the nadir, on which the next generation could build in the fight for civil rights and economic justice. He used his lamp's oil to light paths of education and activism, and when it was used up found a place for himself in France, an exile from the country he loved. It is all part of our American story.

APPENDIX I

BULKLEY'S FAMILY

Clio Gordon Bulkley, September 27, 1889–June 24, 1890

Clio, the Bulkleys' first child, died at nine months old and is buried in Columbia, South Carolina's Randolph Cemetery, which was founded by her grandfather, C. J. Carroll.

Ethel Catharine Bulkley, July 26, 1894–January, 1978

When Ethel returned to the United States in August 1915, she found a job as a governess in Williamsville, not far from Buffalo, New York. While in Williamsville, she met William R. Ross, an Irish engineer, born in Dublin in 1880 and educated at Trinity College, Dublin. He received a bachelor of arts and a bachelor of engineering in 1901. He came to the United States in 1907 and worked at the Susquehanna Smelting Company in Pennsylvania. Later in life he said, "The United States remains the land of opportunity for the individual. Under our free enterprise system, the opportunity for advancement is far greater than in any other part of the world."[497] In 1910 he transferred to the Niagara Electro Chemical Company in Niagara Falls, New York, where he was appointed works manager in 1917. On December 15, 1917, William and Ethel married in Spartanburg, South Carolina, where a friend was stationed at Camp Wadsworth. Despite this being near the places where she still had family, the only people at the wedding were friends of the bride and groom, mostly associated with the chemical industry. In South Carolina a marriage license could be had at a county probate court for one dollar and could be presented to the officiant with no waiting period. By South Carolina's state law, it was illegal for a white person to marry a person with "one-eighth or more negro blood."[498] Did Ethel know she was flouting the law? Was she so thoroughly identified with being white that it never occurred to her that the Jim Crow South was not a friendly place for someone with African American roots to marry an Irishman?

Ethel and William lived in Niagara Falls until 1939, when William, then working for DuPont, was transferred to Baton Rouge, Louisiana. In the course of his career, he managed engineering departments and managed and designed sodium plants in Niagara Falls, New Jersey, England, and Louisiana. He retired in 1945 but remained a consultant to the industry. He died January 17, 1956, at the age of seventy-five. Ethel died in East Baton Rouge, Louisiana, in January 1978 at eighty-three. Ethel and William had two children: Betty, who died when she was nineteen, and William Bulkley Ross, who followed in his father's footsteps as an engineer.

In 1916 Ethel, along with sister Maude and cousin Inez Williams, attended a candy pull at the New York home of Anna L. Holbrook, a young African American socialite.[499] This was the last time Ethel was mentioned at a social occasion in the African American community. She identified as a white person for the remainder of her life. Her origins and her father's achievements were her secrets, and she never shared them with her son. Small photographs of William and Mary hung in her bedroom, but no one talked about who they were or their race. The family story was lost.

Lillian Ernestine Bulkley, November 26, 1897 – December, 1982

Lillian[xi] was the other sister who identified as white as an adult. In April 1918 Lillian, Wilhelmina, and Maude attended a dance and reception at the home of Dr. and Mrs. Charles Roberts for the lieutenants of the 367th Infantry, an African American unit.[500] Lillian was also in social circles where she met white men, and this is the last time she was mentioned in the social pages of the newspaper participating in the African American community.

[xi] As an adult Lillian usually spelled her name Lilian.

On June 8, 1920, in New York, Lillian Bulkley of Ridgefield Park, New Jersey, married Edward Leeds Gulick Jr. of New York City. Gulick was born in 1891 in Groton, Massachusetts. In 1913 he graduated from the Tuck School of Business and Finance at Dartmouth College. He joined the American Ambulance Hospital as a driver and sailed for France December 30, 1916. He was wounded and returned to the United States in May 1917. In July he returned to Europe as a lieutenant in the American Expeditionary Force, where he served in the air service and was discharged March 1919 and appointed member of the Commission for Relief in the Near East for the Red Cross. He served this organization in Italy, Greece, Serbia, Romania, Bulgaria, and Constantinople. Lillian and Leeds may have met in Lausanne or Paris in early 1917 or in New York in early 1920. The marriage was not successful. On June 18, 1923, Lillian divorced Leeds in Nevada and resumed her maiden name.[501]

On August 15, 1923, two months after her divorce, Lillian married Albert Younglove Meriam at Niagara Falls, New York, where her sister Ethel was living. Meriam was a Yale graduate and real estate investor from Cleveland, Ohio. He was also a veteran of World War I. Almost immediately the Meriams sailed for Europe for an extended honeymoon, returning to Cleveland in April 1924. By 1928 they were separated. Both marriages had been childless.

Sometime in the 1930s[502] Lillian met Jean Michel Guérin du Boscq de Beaumont, a lawyer and diplomat born in Airel, France, in 1896. His home in Airel in the Normandy region of France was the fifteenth-century manor of Mesnil-Vitey. Lillian had a long-term, and apparently happy, relationship with Guerin. In 1943 he was named general agent in New York City of the French Committee of National Liberation. In 1954 he became secretary of state for France and then minister of justice, keeper of the seals, and minister of state, before dying in Nice on October 13, 1955. Lillian lived in Paris throughout the 1930s, returning to the United States only in January 1941 as war raged in Europe. Photographs in Lillian's albums show a young woman who enjoyed other people, parties, the beach, sailing on large ships, and gatherings in restaurants or at home.

Lillian and Ethel remained close. Lillian visited her sister in Niagara Falls and then in Baton Rouge, and Ethel traveled to France with Lillian. After Guerin's death, they bought a historic country house, Chant Oiseaux, in St. Desir-de-Lisieux in the Normandy region of France. They restored the house and visited often. Lillian spent her last years living with Ethel and William in East Baton Rouge, Louisiana, and died there in December 1982.

Mary Fisher Carroll Bulkley, March 22, 1866–November 5, 1949

Mary Fisher Carroll was born to Captain James (C. J.) Carroll and Catharine Rebecca Bryan in Columbia, South Carolina, in 1866. C. J. was the son of James Parsons Carroll and Sarah McMillan, a woman enslaved by James's mother, Mary Carroll, in Edgefield County, South Carolina.[xii] After Mary Carroll's death in 1851, C. J. moved to Columbia, South Carolina, as the property of his cousin, Oscar LaBorde. He accompanied LaBorde throughout the Civil War. After the war, C.J. became a barber and a land investor and was able to provide well for his six children, who all went to Claflin University. Mary graduated from the normal course at Claflin in 1885 and was an associate teacher at Claflin. She and William L. Bulkley married March 8, 1888. She lived in Lausanne, Switzerland, from 1911 to 1917, providing a home and education for the Bulkley children. After William's death in 1933, Mary continued to live in Nice until 1939, when she returned to the United States. With the end of World War II she returned to France in 1946. She remained there until her death on the train as she travelled through Joigny, France, in 1949.

Maude Lucile Bulkley, June 1, 1891–April 1, 1931

Maude returned to the states from Lausanne in 1913 and taught literature and French at Claflin University for a year. The textbooks for her French

---

[xii] The Bryan surname is inferred. McMillan was Sarah's surname at death.

classes were those used by students at École Vinet.[503] After another year in Europe, Maude returned to New York and took a job as secretary of girls' work at the Lexington Avenue YWCA[504] and participated in Brooklyn social life.

About 1905 fourteen-year-old Maude met her future husband, John C. Dancy Jr. (then a young man of seventeen), at a seaside resort in New Jersey. William would not allow the couple to correspond by letter but permitted postcards, which they sent five or six at a time. Maude went to Europe in 1910 to continue her education, but the romance didn't die. When she returned to the United States, they resumed their relationship. Dancy proposed on January 1, 1917, and they married in Brooklyn on October 27 of that year. Dancy was involved in the Big Brother movement in New York but had been keeping an eye on opportunities in Detroit. In 1918 Dancy was appointed director of the NUL branch in Detroit. He and Maude moved to Detroit. Maude was an active associate with Dancy in the work of the Detroit Urban League—running clubs, athletic teams, groups, and aiding the new arrivals to the city.[505]

Dancy wrote:

> We had a very happy life together until her death a dozen years later. She was very talented, very helpful to me in my work. She enjoyed life in Detroit . . . Except for the fact that she was with me, however, there was little to identify her as Negro. I have always felt honored that she chose to cast her lot with me rather than to marry white as did two of her sisters.[506]

Maude had a stroke in 1925, which left her partially paralyzed. Her father came from France to visit her in May of that year. Maude died of her illness, April 1, 1931. She and Dancy had no children.

Wilhelmina Madora Bulkley, February 7, 1896–February 1, 1960

Wilhelmina returned to the United States with her family in 1917 and took up charitable causes. She was on the Women's Liberty Loan Committee (chaired by the indefatigable Mrs. E. F. Horne[507]), which raised $3,950 in Liberty Bonds.[508] She and her mother both became involved with the NUL. About 1922 Wilhelmina returned to France, the place where race did not matter, and lived in Nice the rest of her life. She never married. As World War II engulfed Europe, Lillian and her mother returned to the United States, but Wilhelmina stayed in Nice at 37 rue Maréchal Joffre. She died there February 1, 1960.

William Lewis Bulkley, Jr., December 25, 1903–November 1967

A year after his return to New York, William Jr. graduated from grammar school (eighth grade) at PS 35 in New York City in June 1918. In 1921 he took a job as a clerk for the Hard and Rand Coffee Company and moved to Brazil. He later lived in France and did not return to the United States for many years. He identified as a Frenchman and, like his father and sisters, spoke multiple languages. His daughter, Denise de Murcie, reported he usually spoke French with his European friends and Spanish at home. Sometime before his short-lived first marriage in 1931, he added de Murcie to his name and was known that way for the remainder of his life. William was in Buenos Aires, Argentina, through the forties and fifties and had business interests there. He stayed in Argentina through dictatorships, military coups, and hyperinflation.

Although we can find no records of his education after his eighth-grade graduation, Denise believed he must have earned a university degree. It not only would have contributed to the knowledge and culture he evidenced but also would have allowed him to participate in the social circles in Argentina, where he met Maria Teresa Conde. She was born in 1915 in Montevideo, Uruguay, and raised in Buenos Aires. She and William married in Argentina. In addition to his business ventures, William worked at sea at various times in his life, beginning in 1927 as a messman. In 1945 he was a ship's purser, the officer who handles the ship's accounts, has administrative responsibilities, and takes care of the needs of any passengers. William's fluency in six languages undoubtedly contributed to his success in international shipping and travel. In 1956 William and Maria Teresa's daughter, Denise, was born in Buenos Aires. When William lost his business there, he returned to jobs at sea. The family moved to New Jersey in 1959 to be near his home base. They lived not far from William's childhood home in Ridgefield Park, coming full circle after traveling and living around the world. His daughter remembers him as a caring, loving husband and father and remembers the excitement when he returned from his voyages. She never learned the story of her grandfather or that she had aunts and a cousin in the United States until much later. Denise wrote,

> Learning about the history of slavery and suffering in my family story is very sad, of course. But meeting some of my cousins who are descendants of William Lewis Bulkley and his grandparents has been wonderful. I've also been researching my ancestry on my mother's side of the family. While it's impossible to meet them all, I love knowing I have hundreds of cousins from diverse racial, geographic, cultural, religious and political backgrounds. More people should research their roots to learn how mixed we really are. We are all truly one family.[509]

William died in 1967 in New York and is buried in Hackensack, New Jersey.

APPENDIX II
ACTIVIST NEW YORK
EDUCATORS

Gertrude Elise Ayer, 1884–1971

Gertrude Elise Ayer was born Gertrude Elise Johnson in 1885 in New York City.[xiii] She was married twice—first to Cornelius W. McDougald in 1911 (a wedding Bulkley and his wife attended[510]) and then to Vernon A. Ayer in 1928.[511] She became a teacher in 1905 and also served as a vocational counselor and assistant principal. In 1935 Ayer was appointed principal of PS 24 in Harlem, the first African American principal in New York City since Bulkley's appointment in 1901 and the first female principal of an integrated school. And yet again it was a job no one else wanted. Twenty-one teachers on the list waived their right to the job before she was appointed.[512]

She was active in civic organizations and had personal and professional contacts with Bulkley.[513] Her father, Peter Johnson, was one of the founders of the NLUCAN. She sang at St. Mark's Lyceum when Bulkley gave his

---

[xiii] Gertrude Elise Johnson McDougald Ayer was known as Gertrude Elise Ayer (professional name and name of her collection of papers at New York Public Library) and Elise J. McDougald (author of "The Task of Negro Womanhood" in *The New Negro*, 1925 and title of a portrait by Winold Reiss). For more information start with "Gertrude Elise Johnson McDougald Ayer" in Laila Haidarali, *Brown Beauty: Color, Sex, and Race from the Harlem Renaissance to World War II* (New York: NYU Press, 2018).

address "The Way Out."[514] In 1909 she participated in closing exercises at Bulkley's evening school. Gertrude E. Ayer died in 1971.

Sarah J. Smith Tompkins Garnet, 1831–1911

Sarah J. S. Garnet was born in Brooklyn in 1831. She had two marriages: to Samuel Tompkins and then to abolitionist and minister Henry Highland Garnet. She began teaching at the age of fourteen and remained a teacher and principal in the "colored school system" until 1900, when she retired as principal of PS 80. She owned a seamstress shop in Brooklyn. She founded the Equal Suffrage Club in Brooklyn for Black women and was active in civil rights. She, along with Imogen Howard, was a member of the National Vigilance Committee (promoting awareness of Black history and Black rights) and the Women's Loyal Union (Black women's rights).[515] Garnet and her sister attended the Universal Races Congress in London shortly before Sarah died in 1911.[516]

Susan Elizabeth Frazier, 1863–1924

Susan Frazier was born in 1863 in New York City. She graduated in 1887 from the normal college and was named a substitute teacher but after eight years did not yet have a permanent appointment. Opportunities for training had improved for African Americans, but the jobs were harder to attain. Frazier forced the issue in the courts, and in fall 1895, she became the first African American to teach at a New York City School with white faculty and students.[517] She won a contest for a trip to France to visit World War battlefields, especially graves of the 369th AEF, New York's famous African American regiment. In 1917 she organized the Woman's Auxiliary of the 369th and served as president until she died, supporting soldiers in France and afterward the 369th Infantry National Guard. Even though Frazier was descended from a Revolutionary War soldier, she was denied entrance to the Daughters of the American Revolution.[518] She died in 1924.

William H. Johnson, 1833–1918

William H. Johnson was an African American who had been fighting for racial equality since before the Civil War. He was a delegate to the 1864 National Convention of Colored Men and helped to form the New York Equal Rights League. He was chair of the New York State Equal Rights Committee from 1866 to 1873. Johnson drafted the 1873 New York State general civil rights law that provided that no person be excluded by race or color from accommodations and facilities, including public schools.[519]

J. Imogen Howard, 1851–1937

Imogen[xiv] Howard was born in 1851 in Boston, Massachusetts, to Black abolitionists Edwin Frederick Howard and Joan Louise Turpin. Her first teaching job was in New York City at an African American grammar school under principal Sarah J. S. Garnet. She earned a master of arts in pedagogy at University of the City of New York. She was appointed to the Committee on Education of the Board of Women Managers of the State of New York for the World's Fair in Chicago in 1893. In 1900 she won a trip to Europe in a contest sponsored by *New York Telegram*. After her retirement from New York City schools (about 1901 or 1902), she moved to Philadelphia, cared for elderly relatives, and became active in the community, particularly as a benefactor of Mercy Hospital in Philadelphia. She died in 1937 in Philadelphia.[520]

Charles L. Reason, 1818–1893

Charles Reason attended the African Free School in New York City and became an instructor there at the age of fourteen. He was involved in early civil rights activism, being secretary of the Political Improvement Association, which was fighting to abolish restrictions on the African American right to vote in 1821 in New York. In 1847, with Charles B. Ray and a number of other leading Black citizens, he founded the Society for the Promotion of Education among Colored Children in a continuing effort

[xiv] The correct spelling of her name is Imogen.

to provide buildings and teachers for Black students. He was secretary of the Citizen's Civil Rights Commission that promoted the passage of the 1873 New York State civil rights act. He created a normal school to train Black teachers and committed his own life to teaching. After pursuing opportunities teaching in colleges in Cortland County, New York, and Philadelphia, Reason returned to New York City schools in 1855. He was a teacher and administrator for the next thirty-seven years.[521]

BIBLIOGRAPHIC AND RESEARCH NOTE

I am indebted to the historians who incorporated Bulkley into their writings in the 1960s and 1970s. They pointed the way to the sources that began to illuminate his life and contributions: *NAACP: A History of the National Association for the Advancement of Colored People* by Charles Kellogg (1967), *Blacks in the City: A History of the National Urban League* by Guichard Parris and Lester Brooks (1971), *Harlem: The Making of a Ghetto* by Gilbert Osofsky (1971), "William L. Bulkley and the New York Negro, 1890-1910," by George Psychas (1972), and *The National Urban League, 1910–1940* by Nancy Weiss (1974). Their analyses of Bulkley's role are an important starting point for future research on his work as educator and activist.

There may be more of Bulkley's letters in the collections of people he worked with. The list is long. Finding aids do not always list all correspondents. In addition, early communications about the CIICNNY, NLUCAN, and NAACP may include information that would further elucidate his role in these organizations and perhaps the reasons for his withdrawal from them.

This biography should be only the beginning of incorporating Bulkley into stories in which he had a voice. He has a place in not only the early civil rights movement but also the history of education in New York City and the history of Claflin University. He needs careful study of his ability to work both sides of the Washington–Du Bois division. His life can also contribute to the study of racial identity in the early twentieth century and the Black European exiles. I hope those with broader understanding of these topics will be able to build on my research as they tell our American story.

This research project stretched over twenty years. During that time the nature of research and the access to sources changed dramatically. In particular, searchable access to magazines and periodicals became available and was important in fleshing out the details of Bulkley's life. Where possible guidance has been given to sources for newspapers. No attempt has been made to update URLs. Some sites such as the Historical Census Browser and free digital access to *Booker T. Washington Papers* are no longer available. Digital access to the late nineteenth century *Charleston News and Courier* has changed over the years of this research. It was available on Google News, then GenealogyBank, and is now available through ProQuest Early American Newspapers.

NOTES

Introduction

[1] W. E. B. Du Bois to Mary White Ovington, June 7, 1906, Box 1, Series II. Correspondence, Mary White Ovington Collection, Archives of Labor and Urban Affairs, Wayne State University.

[2] Guichard Parris and Lester Brooks, *Blacks in the City: A History of the National Urban League* (Boston: Little Brown, 1971), 11.

[3] David Levering Lewis, *W. E. B. Du Bois, 1919-1963: The Fight for Equality and the American Century* (New York: Henry Holt and Company, 2001), 239.

[4] Susan D. Carle, *Defining the Struggle: National Racial Justice Organizing, 1880-1915* (New York: Oxford University Press, 2013), 30.

I. The Triumph of Perseverance

[5] "A Slave-Boy; Now a Professor," *Success*, April 8, 1899, 33.

[6] "Prof. Wm. Lewis Bulkley," in *Progress of a Race: The Remarkable Advancement of the Afro-American Negro*, by H. F. Kletzing and W. H. Crogman (Atlanta: J. L. Nichols & Co., 1897), 491–94.

[7] Johnson, 169.

[8] Bernard Powers, *Black Charlestonians: A Social History, 1822-1885* (Fayetteville: University of Arkansas Press, 1994), 269.

[9] University of Virginia Library, "Historical Census Browser," University of Virginia, Geospatial and Statistical Data Center, accessed March 16, 2015, http://mapserver.lib.virginia.edu.

[10] Warren Eugene Milteer Jr. *Beyond Slavery's Shadow: Free People of Color in the South* (Chapel Hill: University of North Carolina Press, 2021), 4-7.

[11] Michael P. Johnson, *Black Masters: A Free Family of Color in the Old South* (New York: W. W. Norton & Company, 1986).

[12] T. C. Fay, *Charleston Directory, and Strangers' Guide, for 1840 and 1841* (Charleston, S. C.: [T. C. Fay], 1840); Larry Koger, *Black Slaveowners: Free Black Slave Masters in South Carolina, 1790-1860* (Columbia: University of South Carolina Press, 1985), 150–51.

[13] Koger, 148.

[14] Sarah Bartlett, "Brown Fellowship Society (1790—1945)," BlackPast.org, entry posted September 14, 2010, www.blackpast.org/aah/brown-fellowship-society-1790-1945 (accessed February 21, 2022); Douglas R. Egerton, "Brown Fellowship Society," in *Encyclopedia of African American History, 1619-1895: From the Colonial Period to the Age of Frederick Douglass* (New York: Oxford University Press, 2006), 214–15, https://www.google.com/books/edition/Encyclopedia_of_African_American_History/cCMbE4KKlX4C.

[15] Marina Wikramanayake, *A World in Shadow: The Free Black in Antebellum South Carolina*, Tricentennial Studies 7 (Columbia: University of South Carolina Press, 1973), 65.

[16] Johnson, *Black Masters*, 175–76.

[17] Johnson, *Black Masters*, 187.

[18] Archie Vernon Huff Jr., *Greenville: The History of the City and County in the South Carolina Piedmont* (Columbia: University of South Carolina Press, 1995), 121.

[19] University of Virginia Library, "Historical Census Browser;" United States Bureau of the Census, *Population of The United States in 1860* (Government Printing Office, 1864), 452, http://archive.org/details/usa_statistics-1860.

[20] J. B. Middleton, "Memoir [Rev. Vincent Henry Bulkley]," in *Minutes of the Eightieth Session of the South Carolina Annual Conference of the Methodist Episcopal Church for 1886* (Florence, SC: Methodist Episcopal Church, 1887), 20–21.

[21] Greenville County, South Carolina, "Register of Deeds—Digital Archive: Deeds," Headen to Walker, 21 January, 1848. Book V, page 336-338, accessed July 27, 2015, http://www.greenvillecounty.org/apps/DirectoryListings/ROD_DirectoryListing/.

[22] Wm. L. Bulkley, passport application, issued May 3, 1893, No. 1264; National Archives and Records Administration, *U.S. Passport Applications, 1795-1925,* Roll 405, Ancestry.com; "From a Missionary's Diary in Dixie," *Zion's Herald*, February 13, 1867, ProQuest American Periodicals.

[23] Huff, *Greenville*, 137.

[24] E. Renee Ingram, *In View of the Great Want of Labor: A Legislative History of African American Conscription in the Confederacy* (Westminster, MD: Willow Bend Books, 2002); Middleton, "Memoir [Rev. Vincent Henry Bulkley]."

[25] Middleton, "Memoir [Rev. Vincent Henry Bulkley]."

[26] Middleton.

[27] Methodist Episcopal Church. General Conference, *Journals of the General Conference of the Methodist Episcopal Church.* Volume I. 1796-1836. (New

York: Carlton & Phillips, 1855), 22,
http://archive.org/details/journalsofgenera01meth.

[28] L. M. [Lewis M.] Hagood, *The Colored Man in the Methodist Episcopal Church* (Cincinnati: Cranston & Stowe, 1890), 68,
https://archive.org/details/coloredmaninmeth00hagoiala.

[29] Vivian Glover, *Men of Vision: Claflin College and Her Presidents* (Orangeburg, SC: Claflin College, 1995), 6.

[30] Glover, 5–6.

[31] Vincent Peter, "Will," written August 10, 1823, proved January 15, 1842, *South Carolina, Wills and Probate Records, 1670-1980, Charleston Wills, 1834-1845,* Will Book H: 180, image 367 of 517, Ancestry.com.

[32] Horace Mann Bond, *The Education of the Negro in the American Social Order* (New York: Octagon Books, 1966), 23.

[33] John William De Forest, *A Union Officer in the Reconstruction*, ed. James H. Croushore and David Morris Potter (Baton Rouge: Louisiana State University Press, 1997), 118.

[34] "Prof. Wm. Lewis Bulkley," in Crogman, *Progress of a Race*, 491.

[35] Bond, *The Education of the Negro in the American Social Order*, 29, citing J. W. Alvord, *Semi-annual Report on Schools for Freedmen*, No. 10 (1866-1870).

[36] De Forest, *A Union Officer in the Reconstruction*, xxix.

[37] William L. Bulkley, "Our Foreign Letter," *Southwestern Christian Advocate* 28, no. 41 (October 12, 1893): 5, Gale Nineteenth Century U.S. Newspapers.

[38] William L. Bulkley "Our Foreign Letter," *Southwestern Christian Advocate*, 28, no. 43 (October 26, 1893): 5, Gale Nineteenth Century U.S. Newspapers.

[39] "Term Examination Ending March 1877," University of South Carolina Reconstruction Records, University of South Carolina Archives, Digital Collections,
http://digital.tcl.sc.edu/cdm/ref/collection/reconstruct/id/24.

[40] Colyer Meriwether and Edward McCrady, *History of Higher Education in South Carolina: With a Sketch of the Free School System* (Washington, DC: Government Printing Office, 1889), 185,
https://www.google.com/books/edition/History_of_Higher_Education_in_South_Car/XK2gAAAAMAAJ.

[41] William L. Bulkley, "Our Foreign Letter," *Southwestern Christian Advocate* 28, no. 41 (October 12, 1893): 5, Gale Nineteenth Century U.S. Newspapers.

[42] Roger L. Geiger, *The History of American Higher Education: Learning and Culture from the Founding to World War II* (Princeton: Princeton University Press, 2015), 221, 270–77, 281–87, 544.

[43] Michael Brem Bonner and Fritz Hamer, eds., *South Carolina in the Civil War and Reconstruction Eras: Essays from the Proceedings of the South Carolina Historical Association* (Columbia: University of South Carolina Press,

2016), 185.

[44] *Catalogue of Claflin University, College of Agriculture, and Mechanics Institute, Orangeburg, S. C., 1888-1889*, 48.

[45] Alexander Crummell, *Civilization the Primal Need of the Race, and The Attitude of the American Mind Toward the Negro Intellect*, The American Negro Academy Occasional Paper No. 3 (Washington, DC: The American Negro Academy, 1898), https://www.gutenberg.org/ebooks/31268.

[46] Michele Valerie Ronnick, *Twelve African American Members of the Society for Classical Studies: The First Five Decades, 1875-1925* (New York: Society for Classical Studies, 2018).

[47] Lawson Bush, "William H. Crogman (1841-1931)," BlackPast.org, entry posted January 23, 2007, https://www.blackpast.org/african-american-history/crogman-william-h-1841-1931/ (accessed February 21, 2022).

[48] Katherine Reynolds Chaddock, *Uncompromising Activist: Richard Greener, First Black Graduate of Harvard College* (Baltimore: Johns Hopkins University Press, 2017); Michael Robert Mounter, "Richard Theodore Greener : The Idealist, Statesman, Scholar and South Carolinian" (PhD diss., Columbia, University of South Carolina, 2002).

[49] William Sanders Scarborough, *Autobiography of William Sanders Scarborough: An American Journey from Slavery to Scholarship* (Detroit: Wayne State University Press, 2005); William Sanders Scarborough and Michele Valerie Ronnick, *The Works of William Sanders Scarborough: Black Classicist and Race Leader* (New York: Oxford University Press, 2006).

[50] David Levering Lewis, *W. E. B. Du Bois, 1868-1919: Biography of a Race* (New York: Henry Holt and Company, 1994).

[51] W. E. B Du Bois, "Education and Work," *The Journal of Negro Education* 1, no. 1 (1932): 62, https://doi.org/10.2307/2292016.

[52] Allen Ballard, *One More Day's Journey: The Story of a Family and a People* (New York: McGraw-Hill, 1984), 125.

[53] Blinzy L. Gore, *On a Hilltop High: The Origin and History of Claflin College to 1984* (Spartanburg, SC: The Reprint Company, 1993), 43.

[54] Gore, 50; *Catalogue of Claflin University: 1885-1886*, 1886.

[55] Glover, *Men of Vision*, 15.

[56] Gore, *On a Hilltop High*, 58.

[57] Geiger, *The History of American Higher Education*, 281–87.

[58] United States Office of Education, *Annual Report of the Commissioner of Education* (Government Printing Office, 1880); *Catalogue of Claflin University, 1888-1889*.

[59] Geiger, *The History of American Higher Education*, 468.

[60] E. Horace Fitchett, "The Free Negro in Charleston, South Carolina" (PhD diss., Chicago, University of Chicago, 1950), 281–82.

[61] E. Horace Fitchett, "The Role of Claflin College in Negro Life in South Carolina," *Journal of Negro Education* 12 (Winter 1943): 42.

[62] *Catalogue of Claflin University and College of Agriculture, Orangeburg, S. C., 1883-'84* (Charleston, SC: Walker, Evans, and Cogswell, 1884), http://archive.org/details/catalogueofclafl00claf.

[63] *Catalogue of Claflin University, 1883-'84*, 31.

[64] *Charleston News and Courier*, June 14, 1882, GenealogyBank; *Catalogue of Claflin University, 1883-'84*.

[65] "The Colored University," *Charleston News and Courier*, June 8, 1882, 1, GenealogyBank .

[66] "The Colored University."

[67] United States Office of Education, *Annual Report of the Commissioner of Education*, xxxvi.

[68] "The Colored University."

[69] "Claflin University;" *Charleston News and Courier*, June 14, 1882, GenealogyBank.

[70] *Times and Democrat* (Orangeburg, SC), June 8, 1882, microfilm, South Caroliniana Library, University of South Carolina.

[71] *Catalogue of Claflin University, 1883-'84*.

[72] Wesleyan University, "Wesleyan University: A Brief History," accessed July 23, 2013, http://www.wesleyan.edu/about/uhistory.html.

[73] "Prof. Wm. Lewis Bulkley," 492.

[74] David B. Potts, *Wesleyan University, 1831–1910: Collegiate Enterprise in New England* (Middletown, CT: Wesleyan University Press, 1999), 106, quoting Cyrus D. Foss.

[75] *The Wesleyan Argus*, October 28, 1885, https://digitalcollections.wesleyan.edu/object/argus-5438.

[76] "A Slave-Boy; Now a Professor."

[77] Stuart G. Svonkin, "The Pluralistic Ideal at Wesleyan: Wesleyan's Orientation toward Race, Class, Gender, and Religion within the Student Body, 1870-1970" (BA Honors Thesis, Wesleyan University, 1989), Special Collections, Olin Library, Wesleyan University.

[78] Wesleyan University (Middletown, CT), *Catalogue*, 1884–1885 and 1885–1886, http://hdl.handle.net/2027/mdp.39015064435228; *The Wesleyan Argus*, March 31,1885 and March 31, 1886, https://digitalcollections.wesleyan.edu/object/argus-5045 and https://digitalcollections.wesleyan.edu/object/argus-7024.

[79] *North Adams Transcript* (MA), April 27, 1898, 5, AccessNewspaperARCHIVE.

[80] "Prof. Wm. Lewis Bulkley," 493; Alumni Association of Syracuse University, *Alumni Record and General Catalogue of Syracuse University 1872-99 Including Genesee College, 1852-71 and Geneva Medical College, 1835-72*, 1899, 649, http://surface.syr.edu/annals/2.

[81] *Catalogue of Claflin University: 1885-1886*, 23; Fitchett, "The Role of Claflin College in Negro Life in South Carolina," 258.

[82] Bobb Hane, "African-American History Clashes with Library's Parking," *Star Reporter*, (Columbia, SC), November 17, 1994, Walker Local and Family History Center, Richland Library (Columbia, SC).

[83] "How It Looks to a Negro," *Charleston News and Courier*, December 5, 1888, 5, microfilm, University of South Carolina.

[84] World's Sunday-School Convention, *The World's Sunday-School Convention, Held in the Congregational Memorial Hall and City Temple, London: A Complete Record of Its Proceedings Day by Day, July 1 to 6, 1889* (New York: F. H. Revell, 1889), 19, http://www.archive.org/details/worldssundaysch00worl.

[85] City of London, "The Mansion House," accessed July 23, 2013, http://www.cityoflondon.gov.uk/about-the-city/history-and-heritage/mansion-house/Pages/default.aspx.

[86] William L. Bulkley, *Our Race as We See It: An Address Delivered at Orangeburg, S.C., January 1st, 1890, in Claflin University Chapel* (Orangeburg, SC: Berry & Howell, 1890), 17; Frank Smalley and Lewis M. Dunton, "Dr. W. L. Bulkley," *Southwestern Christian Advocate* 28, no. 34 (August 24, 1893): 4, *Gale Nineteenth Century U.S. Newspapers*.

[87] "Exposition Universelle (1889)," Wikipedia, the free encyclopedia, accessed July 23, 2013, http://en.wikipedia.org/wiki/Exposition_Universelle_(1889).

II. Troublous Times

[88] William L. Bulkley, "A Voice from the South," *The Wesleyan Argus*, February 15, 1890, 95–96, https://digitalcollections.wesleyan.edu/object/argus-6760.

[89] Michael Trinkley, "South Carolina African Americans - Major Events in Reconstruction Politics," South Carolina's Information Highway, accessed August 21, 2014, http://www.sciway.net/afam/reconstruction/majorevents.html.

[90] "Emancipation Day," *Orangeburg Times and Democrat* (SC), January 8, 1890, microfilm, South Caroliniana Library, University of South Carolina; "Emancipation Day," *Charleston News and Courier*, January 3, 1890, Google News.

[91] Bulkley, *Our Race as We See It*, 1, 4.

[92] Bulkley, 8.

[93] Bulkley, *Our Race as We See It*, 5.

[94] Bulkley, 6.

[95] Bulkley, 21.

[96] Bulkley, 21.

[97] Bulkley, 21.

[98] Benjamin William Arnett, *The Annual Address Delivered before the Faculty, Students and Friends of Claflin University and the Claflin College of Agriculture and Mechanical Institute, May 22nd, 1889, Orangeburg, S.C.* (Columbia, SC: William Sloane, 1889), 32, http://hdl.loc.gov/loc.rbc/lcrbmrp.t0d08.

[99] Bulkley, *Our Race as We See It*, 22.

[100] Bulkley, 26.

[101] Bulkley, 29.

[102] Bulkley, 30.

[103] Bulkley, 31.

[104] Bulkley, 34.

[105] Bulkley, unpaginated following p. 34

[106] Bulkley, unpaginated facing p. 35

[107] Isabel Wilkerson, *The Warmth of Other Suns: The Epic Story of America's Great Migration* (New York: Random House, 2010), 6.

[108] Bulkley, *Our Race as We See It*, 35–36.

[109] Bulkley, 36–37.

[110] Bulkley, 37–38.

[111] Bulkley, 39.

[112] Bulkley, 36.

[113] James Loewen, Exposing All-White Towns: A Civil Rights Book Club Interview with James Loewen, transcription, 2006, http://www.civilrights.org/resources/bookclub/loewen-interview.html.

[114] Bulkley, *Our Race as We See It*, 2.

[115] "Emancipation Day," *Charleston News and Courier*; "Emancipation Day," *Orangeburg Times and Democrat*.

[116] William L. Bulkley, "A Voice from the South."

[117] Quoted in Kerry Segrave, *Lynchings of Women in the United States: The Recorded Cases, 1851-1946* (Jefferson, NC: McFarland, 2010), 18.

[118] Account based on "Shot Down in Cold Blood," *Charleston News and Courier*, December 29, 1889, 1, and "The Butchery in Barnwell," *Charleston News and Courier*, December 30, 1889, 1, GenealogyBank.

[119] "Eight Colored Men Shot," *Richmond Planet*, January 4, 1890, 4, Chronicling America; "Blemished Barnwell," *Watchman and Southron* (Sumter, SC), January 15, 1890, 1, Chronicling America.

[120] "From Danville," *Richmond Planet*, May 3, 1890, 4, Chronicling America.

[121] W. E. Chandler, letter to the editor of the *New York Tribune*, published in *Appeal* (St. Paul, MN), March 15, 1890, Chronicling America.

[122] "Barnwell Lynching," *St. Paul Appeal* (MN), March 15, 1890, Chronicling America.

[123] "Project HAL," Historical American Lynching Data Collection Project, accessed August 22, 2014, http://people.uncw.edu/hinese/HAL/HAL%20Web%20Page.htm.

[124] "Shot Down in Cold Blood."

[125] "The Barnwell Lynching," *Manning Times* (SC), January 1, 1890, Chronicling America.

[126] *New York Tribune*, January 5, 1890, quoted in *Public Opinion: A Comprehensive Summary of the Press Throughout the World on All Important Current Topics* 8, no. 14 (January 11, 1890), 330, www.google.com/books/edition/Public_Opinion/KGo9AQAAIAAJ.

[127] "Shot Down in Cold Blood."

[128] "Eight Colored Men Shot."

[129] "Colored Men Aroused," *Richmond Planet*, January 4, 1890, 3, Chronicling America.

[130] "The Colored Conference," *Charleston News and Courier*, January 3, 1890, 1, Google News; "Eighteen Colored Men Lynched," *Richmond Planet*, January 4, 1890, Chronicling America; Bulkley, "A Voice from the South.".

[131] "Negroes in Council," *Abbeville Press and Banner* (SC), January 8, 1890, Chronicling America.

[132] "The Colored Conference."

[133] "Eighteen Colored Men Lynched;" "Shot Down in Cold Blood;" and "The Butchery in Barnwell."

[134] "Barnwell Lynching," *St. Paul Appeal* (MN), March 15, 1890, Chronicling America.

[135] "The Butchery in Barnwell," *Keowee Courier* (SC), March 27, 1890, Chronicling America.

[136] *Chicago Tribune* editorial as reported in "The Barnwell Horror," *Cleveland Gazette*, January 18, 1890, http://dbs.ohiohistory.org/africanam/nwspaper/gazette.cfm.

[137] "Negroes Leaving Barnwell County," *New York Tribune*, January 23, 1890, Chronicling America.

[138] Story Matkin-Rawn, "'The Great Negro State of the Country': Arkansas's Reconstruction and the Other Great Migration," *The Arkansas Historical Quarterly* 72, no. 1 (Spring 2013): 1–41, EBSCO Academic Search Elite.

[139] Quoted in George Brown Tindall, *South Carolina Negroes: 1877-1900*, Southern Classics Series (Columbia: University of South Carolina Press, 2003), 177.

[140] V. H. Bulkley, *The Truth about Arkansas* (Sumter, SC: Watchman and Southron Print, 1883).

[141] "Negro on the Stand," *Charleston News and Courier*, February 2, 1890, 2, microfilm.

[142] Thomas Adams Upchurch, *Legislating Racism: The Billion Dollar Congress and*

the Birth of Jim Crow (Lexington: University Press of Kentucky, 2004), 36.

[143] Carlyle McKinley, *An Appeal to Pharaoh; the Negro Problem, and Its Radical Solution* (New York: Fords, Howard & Hulbert, 1889), http://archive.org/details/anappealtophara01mckigoog.

[144] "Negro on the Stand."

III. Crisis at Claflin

[145] J. W. Cardozo [I. N. Cardozo], "Prof. DeTreville's Murderous Assault on Prof. Cardozo at Claflin University, Orangeburg, S. C.," *Southwestern Christian Advocate* 25, no. 14 (April 3, 1890): 4, Gale Nineteenth Century U.S. Newspapers.

[146] Bulkley, Our Race as We See It, 36.

[147] "The Claflin Rebellion," Charleston News and Courier, March 10, 1890, 8, GenealogyBank.

[148] "The Claflin Rebellion."

[149] "A Row at Claflin," Charleston News and Courier, March 5, 1890, GenealogyBank.

[150] Gore, On a Hilltop High, 108; Fitchett, "The Role of Claflin College in Negro Life in South Carolina," 262.

[151] Samuel Hart Wright and Archibald Edward Miller, Miller's Planters' & Merchants' State Rights Almanac, for the Year of Our Lord 1862 (A.E. Miller, 1861), 19, http://archive.org/details/460659992.3827.emory.edu.

[152] Alexia Jones Helsley, Beaufort: A History (Charleston, SC: The History Press, 2005), 120.

[153] Union University, Catalogue of the Living Alumni of Union College (Schenectady, N.Y., C. Burrows, 1887), 69, http://archive.org/details/catalogueoflivin00unio; "A Row at Claflin."

[154] South Carolina General Assembly, *Reports and Resolutions of the General Assembly of the State of South Carolina* (Columbia: Charles A. Calvo, Jr., 1884), 667, http://books.google.com/books?id=wmwbAQAAIAAJ&dq; Fitchett, "The Role of Claflin College in Negro Life in South Carolina," 262.

[155] "Schools and Colleges," *Southwestern Christian Advocate* 25, no. 11 (March 13, 1890): 5, Gale Nineteenth Century U.S. Newspapers.

[156] "An Insult and a Cane," *Orangeburg Times and Democrat* (SC), March 5, 1890, microfilm, South Caroliniana Library, University of South Carolina.

[157] Cardozo, "Prof. DeTreville's Murderous Assault"

[158] *Rockford Morning Star* (IL), March 11, 1890, GenealogyBank.

[159] *Independent—Devoted to the Consideration of Politics, Social and Economic Tendencies, History, Literature, and the Arts* [cited as *Independent* below], May 8, 1890, ProQuest American Periodicals.

[160] Account based on "A Row at Claflin;" "The Claflin Commotion," *Charleston News and Courier*, March 8, 1890, 1; and "The City on the Edisto," March 12, 1890, GenealogyBank.

[161] J. C. Hartzell to L. M. Dunton, March 15, 1890. Freedmen's Aid Society, Methodist Episcopal Church. *Freedmen's Aid Society Records, Series I,* microfilm, United Methodist Archives and History Center, Drew University, Madison, NJ.

[162] J. C. Hartzell to L. M. Dunton, March 17, 1890; J. C. Hartzell to L. M. Dunton, March 18, 1890. *Freedmen's Aid Society Records, Series I.*

[163] J. C. Hartzell to Gov. John P. Richardson, April 14, 1890. *Freedmen's Aid Society Records, Series I.* The second page of the letter is not on the microfilm and was copied by the Robert W. Woodruff Library, Atlanta University, from Letterpress Book 6, 413.

[164] "Claflin University," *Northern Christian Advocate*, May 8, 1890, 1, GenealogyBank.

[165] "Claflin University."

[166] *Independent,* May 15, 1890, ProQuest American Periodicals.

[167] "The Claflin Commotion."

[168] *Boston Journal*, April 12, 1890, GenealogyBank.

[169] *Independent,* June 5, 1890, ProQuest American Periodicals.

[170] J. C. Hartzell to A. G. Haygood, March 8, 1890. *Freedmen's Aid Society Records: Series I.*

[171] J. C. Hartzell to Rev. L. Arthur, March 22, 1890. *Freedmen's Aid Society Records: Series I.*

[172] Gore, *On a Hilltop High*, 110.

[173] Dunton to William B. Claflin, March 24, 1890, Claflin Papers. Hayes Memorial Library, quoted in James M. McPherson, *The Abolitionist Legacy: From Reconstruction to the NAACP* (Princeton University Press, 1995), 281.

[174] "The Claflin Rebellion," *Charleston News and Courier*, March 10, 1890, GenealogyBank.

[175] Glover, *Men of Vision*, 66-7.

[176] Gore, *On a Hilltop High*, 92.

[177] *Zion's Herald*, September 23, 1891, ProQuest American Periodicals.

[178] "Funeral of Prof Cardozo," *Charleston News and Courier*, April 5, 1898, GenealogyBank.

[179] Reid, Richard, "USC Alumni Snubbed Townsend Despite His Many Accomplishments," *The Times and Democrat*, posted July 31, 2011, www.thetandd.com, accessed August 14, 2011; "Orangeburg Cemetery," folder in vertical file, Walker Local and Family History Center, Richland Library, Columbia, SC.

[180] *Charleston News and Courier*, November 12, 1890, GenealogyBank.

[181] "A Model Colored College," *Charleston News and Courier*, December 5, 1890, 3, GenealogyBank.

[182] "The Claflin Rebellion."

[183] "The Claflin Commotion," *Charleston News and Courier*, March 8, 1890, GenealogyBank.

[184] *Cleveland Gazette*, April 26, 1890, GenealogyBank.

[185] *Southwestern Christian Advocate* 25, no. 13, (March 27, 1890): 1, Gale 19th Century U.S. Newspapers.

[186] "Doings of the Methodists at Boston—The Claflin University Trouble," *Springfield Republican*, April 13, 1890, NewsBank.

[187] "A Model Colored College."

IV. Loyalty to the Southland

[188] William L. Bulkley, "Economic Analysis of American Prejudice," *Colored American Magazine* 17, no. 1 (July 1909): 17–22.

[189] William L. Bulkley, "Our Foreign Letter," *Southwestern Christian Advocate* 28, no. 41 (October 12, 1893): 5, Gale Nineteenth Century U.S. Newspapers.

[190] "Claflin University, Orangeburg . . .," *Southwestern Christian Advocate* 26, no. 23 (June 4, 1891): 5

[191] "An Annual Address." *The State* (Columbia, SC), June 13, 1891, 8, GenealogyBank.

[192] *Southwestern Christian Advocate* 26, no. 35 (August 27, 1891): 2; and *Southwestern Christian Advocate* 25, no. 35 (August 28, 1890): 4, Gale Nineteenth Century U.S. Newspapers.

[193] "Colored Teachers' Institute of Anderson County Convened, " *Anderson Intelligencer* (SC), October 3, 1889, 3, Chronicling America; "Colored Teachers' Institute," *Anderson Intelligencer* (SC), October 17, 1889, 1, Chronicling America.

[194] "A Colored State Teachers' Institute," *The State* (Columbia, SC), July 18, 1898, GenealogyBank; "Colored Teachers," *Charleston News and Courier*, August 13, 1898, 2, GenealogyBank; "Colored Teachers," *Weekly News and Courier* (Charleston, SC), August 17, 1898, 6, Gale Nineteenth Century US Newspapers.

[195] "The Work of the Y.M.C.A.," *Charleston News and Courier*, November 2, 1891, GenealogyBank.

[196] Frank Smalley and L. M. Dunton, "Dr. W. L. Bulkley," *Southwestern Christian Advocate* 28, no. 34 (August 24, 1893): 4, Gale Nineteenth Century U.S. Newspapers; "Personal," *Southwestern Christian Advocate* 25, no. 35 (August 28, 1890): 4, Gale Nineteenth Century U.S. Newspapers.

[197] "The International Epworth Convention," *Southwestern Christian Advocate* 30, no. 32 (August 8, 1895): 2, Gale Nineteenth Century U.S. Newspapers.

[198] *Weekly News and Courier* (Charleston, SC), February 4, 1896, 8, Gale Nineteenth Century U.S. Newspapers.

[199] Lewis Curts, *The General Conferences of the Methodist Episcopal Church, from 1792 to 1896* (Cincinnati: Curts & Jennings, 1900), 348 ff., https://www.google.com/books/edition/The_General_Conferences_of_t he_Methodist/3GZKAAAAMAAJ.

[200] Rev. David S. Monroe, ed., *Journal of the General Conference of the Methodist Episcopal Church Held in Cleveland, Ohio, May 1-28, 1896* (New York: Eaton & Mains, 1896), 369, 374, https://www.google.com/books/edition/Journal_of_the_General_Confer ence_of_the/ad4pAAAAYAAJ.

[201] W. Freeman Galpin, *Syracuse University: The Pioneer Days* (Syracuse: Syracuse University Press, 1952), 212.

[202] Galpin, 206 ff.

[203] W. Freeman Galpin, *Syracuse University: The Growing Years* (Syracuse: Syracuse University Press, 1960), 20.

[204] Smalley and Dunton, "Dr. W. L. Bulkley."

[205] "Dr. W. L. Bulkley."

[206] *Catalogue of Claflin University, 1888-1889*, 48.

[207] William L. Bulkley, "Our Foreign Letter," *Southwestern Christian Advocate* 28, no. 30 (July 27, 1893): 4, Gale Nineteenth Century U.S. Newspapers.

[208] William L. Bulkley, "Our Foreign Letter," *Southwestern Christian Advocate* 29, no. 24 (June 14, 1894): 4, Gale Nineteenth Century U.S. Newspapers.

[209] William L. Bulkley, "Our Foreign Letter," *Southwestern Christian Advocate* 28. no. 39 (September 28, 1893): 5, Gale 19th Century U.S. Newspapers.

[210] William L. Bulkley, "Our Foreign Letter," *Southwestern Christian Advocate* 28, no. 42 (October 19, 1893): 5, Gale Nineteenth Century U.S. Newspapers.

[211] Lewis, *W. E. B. Du Bois, 1868-1919*, 147.

[212] William L. Bulkley, "Our Foreign Letter," (June 14, 1894).

[213] Wm. L. Bulkley, "Our Foreign Letter," *Southwestern Christian Advocate* 29, no. 31 (August 2, 1894): 4, Gale Nineteenth Century U.S. Newspapers.

[214] William L. Bulkley, "Education Extension in a Southern Town," *The University Extension Bulletin: A Record of Current University Extension Work* 2, no. 5 (January 31, 1895): 56, https://books.google.com/books?id=FzTnAAAAMAAJ.

[215] Glover, *Men of Vision*, 72.

[216] Brian Duignan, "Plessy v. Ferguson, Law Case," Encyclopedia Britannica, accessed August 7, 2015, http://www.britannica.com/event/Plessy-v-Ferguson.

[217] "Claflin University," *Southwestern Christian Advocate* 31, no. 44 (October 29, 1896): 2, Gale Nineteenth Century U.S. Newspapers.

[218] Blair L. M. Kelley, *Right to Ride: Streetcar Boycotts and African American*

Citizenship in the Era of Plessy v. Ferguson (Chapel Hill: University of North Carolina Press, 2010).

219 "Louisiana's Jim Crow Car Law," *The State* (Columbia, SC), May 19, 1896, GenealogyBank.

220 William L. Bulkley, "A Question of Chivalry," letter to the editor, *The State* (Columbia, SC), February 13, 1897, GenealogyBank.

221 William L. Buckley [*sic*] et. al. "Claflin Leaders Want No Jim Crow," letter to the editor, *The State* (Columbia, SC), January 17, 1898, 5, GenealogyBank.

222 William L. Bulkley, "A Quarter Century Well Spent," *Christian Advocate*, 74 (March 9, 1899): 384, https://www.google.com/books/edition/Christian_Advocate/PzQxAQA AMAAJ.

223 W. H. Lawrence, "Our Trip South," *Christian Advocate*, 74, (February 16, 1899): 252, https://www.google.com/books/edition/Christian_Advocate/PzQxAQA AMAAJ.

224 "Plantation Melodies," *Brooklyn Daily Star* (NY), May 13, 1899, fultonhistory.com.

225 "The Worship of Booker T. Washington," *The Independent*, December 8, 1898, 1708, ProQuest American Periodicals.

226 Michele Valerie Ronnick, "Black Classicism: 'Tell Them We Are Rising,'" *Classical Journal* 106 (2011): 359–70.

227 William L. Bulkley, "The School as a Social Center," in *The Negro in the Cities of the North* (New York: The Charity Organization Society, 1905), 70.

228 "Color Question in Schools," *Brooklyn Daily Eagle*, December 27, 1899, 3, Brooklyn Newsstand, New York Public Library.

V. Giving His Most Sympathetic Attention

229 Carleton Mabee, *Black Education in New York State: From Colonial to Modern Times* (Syracuse, N.Y.: Syracuse University Press, 1979), 35.

230 Theophilus Gould Steward, *The Colored Regulars in the United States Army* (Philadelphia: A. M. E. Book Concern, 1904), 52–56, http://archive.org/details/coloredregularsi02stew.

231 Mabee, *Black Education in New York State*, 189.

232 William Henry Johnson, *Autobiography of Dr. William Henry Johnson* (Albany: Argus Company, 1900), 18, http://archive.org/details/tohisadoptedhome00johnrich.

233 New York, *Laws of the State of New York Passed at the One Hundred and Seventh Session of the Legislature.* (Albany: Banks & Brothers, 1884), 307, https://books.google.com/books?id=D3M4AAAAIAAJ.

234 *New York Press*, September 10, 1893, 22, fultonhistory.com; *New York Press*, October 14, 1894, 5, fultonhistory.com.

[235] Seth M Scheiner, *Negro Mecca: A History of the Negro in New York City, 1865-1920* (New York: New York University Press, 1965), 176–77; Claude J Mangum, "Afro-American Thought on the New York City Public School System, 1905-1954: An Analysis of New York City Afro-American Newspaper Editorials" (PhD diss., Teachers College, Columbia University, 1976), 24–26, 43–56.

[236] "That School Color Line," *New York Sun*, October 31, 1895, 8, fultonhistory.com.

[237] Diane Ravitch, *The Great School Wars: New York City, 1805-1973; A History of the Public Schools as Battlefield of Social Change.* (New York: Basic Books, 1974), 157–68.

[238] Ravitch, 167.

[239] "Public-School Education," *New York Evening Post*, January 12, 1899, 4, fultonhistory.com.

[240] "Colored Man is Ousted," *Brooklyn Daily Eagle*, March 4, 1900, Newspapers.com.

[241] *Brooklyn Daily Eagle Almanac* (New York: Brooklyn Daily Eagle, 1900).

[242] "Training School for Teachers," *Brooklyn Daily Eagle*, November 12, 1899, 17, Brooklyn Newsstand, New York Public Library.

[243] "Color Question in Schools," *Brooklyn Daily Eagle*, December 27, 1899, Brooklyn Newsstand, New York Public Library.

[244] "Northerners Don't Want Colored Teachers," *Free Lance* (Fredericksburg, VA), January 2, 1899 [1900], 1, Chronicling America.

[245] "Employment of Colored Teachers," *New York Tribune*, December 28, 1899, 3, GenealogyBank.

[246] "Who's Who and What's What: Negro Public School Teachers in New York," *Chicago Daily Tribune*, December 29, 1899, 6, ProQuest Historical Newspapers.

[247] "Short School Board Session," *Brooklyn Daily Eagle*, January 3, 1900, 5, Brooklyn Newsstand, New York Public Library.

[248] "Demands an Investigation," *Washington Evening Times*, March 5, 1900, 5, Chronicling America.

[249] "Colored Man is Ousted," *Brooklyn Daily Eagle*, March 4, 1900, Newspapers.com.

[250] "Demands an Investigation,"

[251] Gore, *On a Hilltop High*, 132.

[252] "Demands an Investigation;" "Northerners Don't Want Colored Teachers."

[253] Gilbert Osofsky, *Harlem: The Making of a Ghetto; Negro New York, 1890-1930*, 2nd ed. (Chicago: Ivan R. Dee, 1996), 48.

[254] "The Borough School Board," *New York Times*, March 7, 1901, 9, ProQuest Historical Newspapers.

255 Meg Meneghel MacDonald, "Sarah J. Smith Tompkins Garnet (1831-1911)," BlackPast.org, entry posted November 19, 2008, www.blackpast.org/african-american-history/garnet-sarah-j-smith-tompkins-1831-1911/ (accessed February 21, 2022).

256 "Colored School Principal," *New York Times,* February 18, 1901, 2, ProQuest Historical Newspapers.

257 Bulkley, "The School as a Social Center," 78

258 "Praises Professor Bulkley," *New York Age,* April 6, 1905, 2, fultonhistory.com.

259 Bulkley, "The School as a Social Center," 76.

260 William L. Bulkley, "The Industrial Condition of the Negro in New York City," in *The Industrial Condition of the Negro in the North,* Publications of the American Academy of Political and Social Science 498 (Philadelphia: American Academy of Political and Social Science, 1906), 130-131.

261 William L. Bulkley, "Handicap in City Schools: Noises and Other Distractions Reduce Degree of Mental Application," *New York Times,* March 25, 1906, 8, ProQuest Historical Newspapers.

262 Bulkley, "The Industrial Condition of the Negro in New York City," 128-134.

263 Bulkley, 128.

264 Bulkley, 128.

265 Bulkley, 131.

266 Bulkley, 133.

267 Bulkley, 134.

268 Mary Van Kleeck, *Working Girls in Evening Schools: A Statistical Study.* Russel Sage Foundation Study (New York: Survey Associates, 1914), 10-12, http://archive.org/details/workinggirlsinev00vank.

269 Selma C. Berrol, "From Compensatory Education to Adult Education: The New York City Evening Schools, 1825-1935," *Adult Education* 26, no. 4 (1976): 208–25.

270 William L. Bulkley, "An Evening Industrial School for Adults," *Southern Workman,* October 1906, 543.

271 Bulkley, "An Evening Industrial School for Adults, " 543

272 "The Evening Trade School No. 67 . . .," *New York Age,* September 8, 1910, 7, fultonhistory.com; "Industrial Campaign: Bulkley's Committee to Hold Series of Meetings," *New York Age,* July 12, 1906, 3, fultonhistory.com.

273 Evening Schools, Manhattan, 1905, Payroll Ledgers, 1893-1920, Bureau of Finance. Series 806, Records of the New York City Board of Education, New York City Department of Records, Municipal Archives.

274 "A Night Industrial School," *New York Age,* October 31, 1907, fultonhistory.org.

275 "Gift from Negro Children," *New York Times,* February 15, 1906, 2, ProQuest Historical Newspapers.

276 Bulkley, "The Industrial Condition of the Negro in New York City," 133.

277 William L. Bulkley, "Future of Colored Race: Object Lesson in School Next Door to Where 'The Clansman' Is Playing," *New York Times*, January 11, 1906, ProQuest Historical Newspapers.

278 New York Board of Education, *Journal of the Board of Education of the City of New York* (New York: Wm. C. Bryant & Company, 1906).

279 W. L. Bulkley to L. Hollingsworth Wood, 18 April 1913, L. Hollingsworth Wood Papers, 1903-1953, Ms. Coll. 1175, Special Collections, Haverford College Libraries.

280 William L. Bulkley to W. E. B. Du Bois, December 22, 1923, W. E. B. Du Bois Papers (MS 312). Special Collections and University Archives, University of Massachusetts Amherst Libraries, http://oubliette.library.umass.edu/view/full/mums312-b020-i331.

281 "Public Evening Industrial Schools," *Charities and the Commons* 18 (1907): 199–200.

282 "Closing Exercises of the Evening Industrial School," program, April 1, 1909 (digital image, collection of the author).

283 Matilda Vann. *1915 New York State Census*, New York, New York, A.D. 17, E.D. 22, p. 46, Ancestry.com; Frances E. Hebbens. *1910 U.S. Federal Census*, Manhattan, New York, New York, ward 20, E.D. 1202, p. 3B, household 122, Ancestry.com.

284 James A. Norwood, *1910 US Federal Census*, Manhattan, New York, New York, ward 12, E.D. 535, p. 1A, household 7, Ancestry.com; James Norwood, in household of Alice Haynes, *1920 US Federal Census*, Manhattan, New York, New York, A.D. 21, E.D. 1439, p. 55A, household 1119, Ancestry.com.

285 *New York World*, September 19, 1900, 13, fultonhistory.com.

286 Kevin L. Borg, *Auto Mechanics: Technology and Expertise in Twentieth-Century America* (Baltimore: Johns Hopkins University Press, 2007), 13, https://www.google.com/books/edition/Auto_Mechanics/pudAWmB7dxwC.

287 "Cosmopolitan Automobile School," [advertisement] *The Crisis* 1, no. 1 (November, 1910): 19, Modernist Journals Project.

288 Borg, *Auto Mechanics*, 59; Susan Kerr Chandler, "'Almost a Partnership': African Americans, Segregation, and the Young Men's Christian Association," *Journal of Sociology & Social Welfare* 21, no. 1 (March 1994): 97, ScholarWorks, Western Michigan University.

289 "Hudspeth-Hill," [marriage] *New York Age*, August 14, 1913, 8, fultonhistory.com.

290 Louise Fleming, *1910 U.S. Federal Census*, Manhattan, New York, New York, Ward 20, E.D. 1202, p. 3A, household 120, Ancestry.com.

291 "73 Years Old; Goes to School," *New York Age*, January 2, 1913, 1,

fultonhistory.com.

292 George Edmund Haynes Collection, 1909-1953, Box 6, f. 7, Special Collections and Archives, Fisk University Library.

293 Marguerite Randall to Dr. Bulkley, April 2, 1908, George Edmund Haynes Collection, 1909-1953; Margaret Randall, *1910 U.S. Federal Census,* Manhattan, New York, New York, ward 20, E.D. 318, p. 11B, household 294, Ancestry.com.

294 Martin V. Washington to Dr. W. M. [*sic*] Bulkley, March 30, 1909, George Edmund Haynes Collection, 1909-1953; Martin V. Washington, *World War II Draft Registration Cards, 1942,* New York City, National Archives and Records Administration Record Group 147, Ancestry.com.

295 Samuel Harris, *1900 U.S. Federal Census.* Manhattan, New York, New York, ward 26, E.D. 456, p. 22A, household 71, Ancestry.com.

296 Saml. Harris to Dr. Bulkley, March 30, 1909, George Edmund Haynes Collection, 1909-1953.

297 Walter H. Johnson, March 16, 1909, George Edmund Haynes Collection, 1909-1953."

VI. Not Alms, But Opportunity

298 William L. Bulkley, "Race Prejudice as Viewed from an Economic Standpoint," in *Proceedings of the National Negro Conference 1909, New York, May 31 and June 1* ([New York], 1909), 97, http://archive.org/details/proceedingsof00nati.

299 Mabee, *Black Education in New York State,* 127.

300 "Say It Plain: A Century of Great African American Speeches: Booker T. Washington," American RadioWorks, accessed February 7, 2016, http://americanradioworks.publicradio.org/features/sayitplain/btwashingt on.html.

301 George Mason University, "Booker T. Washington Delivers the 1895 Atlanta Compromise Speech," History Matters, accessed February 15, 2022, http://historymatters.gmu.edu/d/39/.

302 Nathan Huggins, ed., *W. E. B. Du Bois: Writings* (New York: Library of America, 1986), 398–99, https://www.loa.org/books/39-writings.

303 Lewis, *W. E. B. Du Bois, 1868-1919*; Robert J. Norrell, *Up from History: The Life of Booker T. Washington* (Cambridge: Harvard University Press, 2011).

304 Parris and Brooks, *Blacks in the City,* 11.

305 N. Barnett Dodson, "Carlton Avenue Branch of the Brooklyn, N. Y., Young Men's Christian Association," *The Colored American Magazine* 7 (1904): 117.

306 Young Men's Christian Associations of Brooklyn and Queens, *Fifty Years in Brooklyn, 1853-1903* (Brooklyn Young Men's Christian Association, 1903), 93.

[307] Cheryl Bullock Hannah, "Charles H. Bullock, Sr. (1875-1950)," BlackPast.org, entry posted February 26, 2011, www.blackpast.org/african-american-history/bullock-charles-h-sr-1875-1950/ (accessed February 21, 2022)

[308] Young Men's Christian Associations of Brooklyn and Queens, *Fifty Years in Brooklyn,* 108.

[309] "Carlton Ave. Branch Y. M. C. A." *Brooklyn Daily Eagle,* May 16, 1904, Brooklyn Newsstand, New York Public Library.

[310] Dodson, "Carlton Avenue Branch."

[311] "Y.M.C.A. Officers Resign," *New York Age,* January 18, 1905, 1, Newspapers.com.

[312] "New Carlton Y. M. C. A. To Be Ready in a Year," *New York Age,* November 25, 1915, 1, fultonhistory.com.

[313] Nancy Weiss, *The National Urban League, 1910-1940* (New York: Oxford University Press, 1974), 21.

[314] W. E. B. Du Bois, *The Philadelphia Negro: A Social Study,* Publications of the University of Pennsylvania. Series in Political Economy and Public Law 14 (Philadelphia: University of Pennsylvania, 1899).

[315] "First Meeting of Persons Interested in the Welfare of the Negroes of New York City (1903)" in W. E. B. Du Bois, *Against Racism: Unpublished Essays, Papers, Addresses, 1887-1961* (Amherst: University of Massachusetts Press, 1985), 72–74.

[316] William Henry Baldwin, Jr. to Booker T. Washington, January 23, 1903, *Booker T. Washington Papers* 7: 9.

[317] "Constitutional Convention, Virginia (1901–1902)," Encyclopedia of Virginia, accessed January 19, 2016, http://www.encyclopediavirginia.org/Constitutional_Convention_Virginia_1901-1902.

[318] Shawn Leigh Alexander, *An Army of Lions: The Civil Rights Struggle Before the NAACP* (Philadelphia: University of Pennsylvania Press, 2013), 203.

[319] "Gotham Notes: The Louisville Convention," *Colored American* [newspaper] (Washington, DC), July 11, 1903, 6, GenealogyBank; "Negro Mass Meeting," *Journal* (Lockport, NY), February 20, 1903, fultonhistory.com; "Negroes Indorse President Roosevelt," *New York Times,* February 20, 1903, 6, ProQuest Historical Newspapers.

[320] Charity Organization Society, "Report of the Committee on the Prevention of Tuberculosis of the Charity Organization Society for the Year 1903-1904," in *A Handbook on the Prevention of Tuberculosis* (New York: Charity Organization Society, 1903), 9 (after the index), https://books.google.com/books?id=VRk1AQAAMAAJ.

[321] Frances A. Kellor, *Out of Work: A Study of Unemployment* (New York: Putnam, 1915), http://archive.org/details/outofworkstudyof00kelluoft.

[322] Parris and Brooks, *Blacks in the City*, 4–5.

[323] "Negro Women in the North," *Evening Post* (New York), June 7, 1905, 7, fultonhistory.com.

[324] E. M. Rhodes, "A New Opportunity for Women," *Colored American Magazine* 10, no. 1 (January 1906): 25.

[325] "We Need Your Help," *Brooklyn Daily Eagle*, October 2, 1905, 2, fultonhistory.com.

[326] Frances A. Kellor, "Associations for Protection of Colored Women," *Colored American Magazine* 9, no. 6 (December 1905): 695–99.

[327] Parris and Brooks, *Blacks in the City*, 8.

[328] "Associations for the Protection of Negro Women," African-American History Online, Facts On File History Online, accessed August 8, 2013, http://www.fofweb.com.proxy.mcpl.lib.mo.us/NuHistory/default.asp?ItemID=WE01.

[329] "A Useful Citizen," *New York Age*, June 7, 1906, fultonhistory.com.

[330] Benjamin Ray Justesen, "The National Afro-American Council: Towards a New Interpretation" (PhD diss., Cincinnati, Union Institute and University, 2011).

[331] "Council Ends Best Session," *New York Age*, October 18, 1906, 2, fultonhistory.com.

[332] "Council Ends Best Session."

[333] "Council Ends Best Session."

[334] "Council Ends Best Session."

[335] Angela Jones, *African American Civil Rights: Early Activism and the Niagara Movement* (Santa Barbara: Praeger, 2011), 19.

[336] Secretaries and Committees of the Niagara Movement, April 1, 1907, W. E. B. Du Bois Papers (MS 312), Special Collections and University Archives, University of Massachusetts Amherst Libraries, http://credo.library.umass.edu/view/full/mums312-b004-i138.

[337] Jones, *African American Civil Rights*, 87; Minutes of the 3rd Annual Niagara Movement Meeting, August 26, 1907, W. E. B. Du Bois Papers, MS 312, Special Collections and University Archives, University of Massachusetts Amherst Libraries, http://credo.library.umass.edu/view/full/mums312-b004-i151.

[338] "Committee for Improving Industrial Condition of the Negro in New York" pamphlet (n.d.) Box 18, folder "Misc. Negro Schools, etc.," James Graham Phelps Stokes Papers, 1779-1960, (Bulk 1884-1960), MS#1207, Columbia University Libraries.

[339] "Permanent Organization Formed at Dr. Bulkly's [sic] School," *New York Age*, April, 26, 1906, 3, Newspapers.com.

[340] "The 1900 William Jay Schieffelin House—No. 5 East 66th Street," Daytonian in

Manhattan, accessed August 3, 2013,
http://daytoninmanhattan.blogspot.com/2011/12/1900-william-jay-
schieffelin-house-no-5.html.

[341] "To Win Industrial Chances," *New York Age*, May 17, 1906, 1, fultonhistory.com.

[342] Parris and Brooks, *Blacks in the City*, 10, 12, 15.

[343] "To Win Industrial Chances."

[344] "'Square Deal' for Negroes," *Brooklyn Daily Eagle*, June 19, 1906, 3,
fultonhistory.com.

[345] "'Square Deal' for the Negro," *New York Tribune*, June 20, 1906, 8, Chronicling
America; "Industrial Comm. at Work," *New York Age*, June 21, 1906, 1,
Newspapers.com.

[346] Mary White Ovington to W. E. B. Du Bois, May 20, 1906, W. E. B. Du Bois
Papers, MS 312, Special Collections and University Archives, University of
Massachusetts Amherst Libraries,
http://credo.library.umass.edu/view/full/mums312-b004-i269.

[347] "For Economic Regeneration," *Colored American Magazine* 11, no. 1 (July
1906): 10.

[348] *Springfield Republican* (MA), June 21, 1906, 8, GenealogyBank.

[349] Parris and Brooks, *Blacks in the City*, 15.

[350] "Urge Industrial Classes," *New York Age*, May 24, 1906, fultonhistory.com.

[351] "Industrial Campaign: Bulkley's Committee to Hold Series of Meetings," *New
York Age*, July 12, 1906, 3, fultonhistory.com.

[352] "Negroes in the North," *New York Times*, September 21, 1906, 5, ProQuest
Historical Newspapers; "Washington Advises Negroes," *New York Sun*,
September 21, 1906, Chronicling America; *New York Age*, September 27,
1906, 1, fultonhistory.com; *New York Tribune*, September 22, 1906, 12,
Chronicling America.

[353] "Open Door in Trades," *New York Age*, September 27, 1906, 1,
fultonhistory.com.

[354] *Montana Plaindealer*, October 5, 1906, 1, Chronicling America.

[355] "For the Negroes in New York," *Charities and the Commons* 17, no. 2 (October
13, 1906): 109.

[356] "Meeting for Negro Improvement," *Colored American Magazine* 11, no. 5
(November 1906): 286.

[357] "Wetmore Combats Charge of Political Corruption in South," *New York Age*,
November 1, 1906, 1, fulthonhistory.com.

[358] Carle, *Defining the Struggle*, 173.

[359] "Work of the Committee for Improving the Industrial Condition of Negroes in
New York," *Colored American Magazine* 12 (June 1907): 459–64.

[360] "Improving Industrial Conditions Here in New York City," *New York Age*,
March 7, 1907, 4, fultonhistory.com.

361 Mary White Ovington, "The Negro in the Trades Unions in New York," *Annals of the American Academy of Political and Social Science* 27 (May 1, 1906): 551–58.

362 Scheiner, *Negro Mecca*, 59.

363 Scheiner, 154.

364 "Conditions Are Improved," *New York Age*, November 25, 1909, 1, fultonhistory.com.

365 "Negroes in New York," *The Survey: Social, Charitable, Civic; a Journal of Constructive Philanthropy* 23 (October 2, 1909): 5.

VIII. His Own Efforts

366 Frank M. Lander, letter to the editor, quoting William L. Bulkley, *Southwestern Christian Advocate* 27, no. 34 (August 25, 1892): 5, Gale Nineteenth Century U.S. Newspapers.

367 Landmarks Preservation Commission, "High School of the Performing Arts (Designation List 162)," 1982, *Neighborhood Preservation Center*, accessed March 26, 2016, http://neighborhoodpreservationcenter.org/db/bb_files/1982HighSchool PerformingArts.pdf.

368 *Brooklyn Daily Eagle Almanac* (New York: Brooklyn Daily Eagle, 1900).

369 *Brooklyn Daily Eagle Almanac* (New York: Brooklyn Daily Eagle, 1909).

370 "Object to Negro Principal," *The Sun* (New York, NY), July 2, 1909, 1, Chronicling America.

371 "Principal Wm. Bulkley Wins Over the Protests of White Teachers at School 125," *New York Age*, July 22, 1909, 1, fultonhistory.com.

372 "Schoolma'ams Rebel Against Negro Chief," *New York Times*, July 3, 1909, 16, ProQuest Historical Newspapers.

373 "Race Prejudice in the Public Schools," *Hebrew Standard* as reprinted in *New York Age*, July 22, 1909, 1, fultonhistory.com.

374 "Rebellion of the Teachers," *New York Age*, July 8, 1909, fultonhistory.com.

375 "Principal Wm. Bulkley Wins Over the Protests of White Teachers."

376 "Mrs. Gertrude Ayers [sic] Appointed Principal," *Chicago Defender*, February 2, 1935, 13, ProQuest Historical Newspapers.

377 *New York City, v. 1, revised* (G. W. Bromley & Co., 1915), plate 22, Historic Map Works.

378 *New York City, v. 1, revised*, plate 24.

379 *Brooklyn Daily Eagle Almanac*, 1911, 1919

380 "St. Mark's Lyceum," *New York Age*, May 7, 1908, 1, fultonhistory.com.

381 William English Walling, "The Race War in the North," *The Independent*, 65, no. 3118 (September 3, 1908): 529, ProQuest American Periodicals.

[382] Mary White Ovington, *Black and White Sat Down Together: The Reminiscences of an NAACP Founder* (New York: Feminist Press at the City University of New York, 1995), 56–57.

[383] Committee on the Negro 'Call' for a National Conference, February, 1909, Ray Stannard Baker Papers, Library of Congress, Manuscript Division, Digital ID # na0018p3, http://www.loc.gov/exhibits/naacp/founding-and-early-years.html.

[384] Adam Fairclough, *Better Day Coming: Blacks and Equality, 1890-2000* (New York: Viking, 2001), 70.

[385] National Negro Conference, *Proceedings of the National Negro Conference 1909, New York, May 31 and June 1* (New York, 1909), http://archive.org/details/proceedingsof00nati; Charles Kellogg, *NAACP: A History of the National Association for the Advancement of Colored People* (Baltimore: Johns Hopkins Press, 1967), 19.

[386] "First NAACP Group Met 50 Years Ago," *California Eagle* (Los Angeles), June 4, 1959, Newspapers.com.

[387] Bulkley, "Race Prejudice as Viewed from an Economic Standpoint," 1909, 97.

[388] Mary White Ovington, "How the National Association for the Advancement of Colored People Began," *Crisis*, 8, no. 4 (August 1914): 184.

[389] Charles William Anderson to Booker T. Washington, May 31, 1909, *Booker T. Washington Papers* 10: 127.

[390] Kellogg, *NAACP*, 18–19.

[391] Board Minutes, NAACP, as quoted in Kellogg, *NAACP*, 41.

[392] Ovington, "How the National Association for the Advancement of Colored People Began;" "The N. A. A. C. P." *The Crisis*, 1, no. 1 (November 1910): 12, The Modernist Journals Project.

[393] Kellogg, *NAACP*, 32; National Negro Committee, Minutes of the 1909 National Negro Conference, W. E. B. Du Bois Papers, MS 312, Special Collections and University Archives, University of Massachusetts Amherst Libraries, http://credo.library.umass.edu/view/full/mums312-b004-i066.

[394] "The N. A. A. C. P." *The Crisis*, 1, no. 1 (November 1910): 12, The Modernist Journals Project.

[395] National Association for the Advancement of Colored People, *Annual Reports, 1910-1916* (New York: The Association), http://catalog.hathitrust.org/Record/006784887.

[396] "Conditions in the North," *New York Age*, January 27, 1910, 1, fultonhistory.com.

[397] George Edmund Haynes, *The Negro at Work in New York City: A Study in Economic Progress* (New York: Columbia University, 1912), http://www.gutenberg.org/ebooks/24712.

[398] Weiss, *The National Urban League, 1910-1940*, 31, 41.

399 George Edmund Haynes, "The Birth and Childhood of the National Urban League" (typescript, 1960), 7, National Urban League records, Box I:E29, Manuscript Division, Library of Congress.

400 Booker T. Washington to Charles W. Anderson, October 1, 1907, Washington Papers, Library of Congress, Box 37, quoted in Gilbert Osofsky, *Harlem: The Making of a Ghetto*, note 51, 234.

401 Booker T. Washington to Charles W. Anderson, October 1, 1907 and Charles W. Anderson to Booker T. Washington, May 25, 1906, cited in Weiss, *The National Urban League, 1910-1940*. 24.

402 Parris and Brooks, *Blacks in the City*, 34.

403 Haynes, "The Birth and Childhood of the National Urban League," 8.

404 National League on Urban Conditions Among Negroes, "Report 1912-1913; Announcement 1913-1914," https://catalog.hathitrust.org/Record/100569911.

405 Weiss, *The National Urban League, 1910-1940*, 74–75.

406 "Organizations Consolidate," *Cleveland Gazette*, November 18, 1911, 1, GenealogyBank.

407 Weiss, *The National Urban League, 1910-1940*, 65, citing Haynes Papers, Fisk University.

408 Weiss, 45.

409 Parris and Brooks, *Blacks in the City*, 32–36; Weiss, *The National Urban League, 1910-1940*, 40–46.

410 "Social Work in New York," *Baltimore Afro-American*, December 16, 1911, 7, ProQuest Historical Newspapers.

411 E. E. Pratt to George E. Haynes, March 20, 1912, Series I: Correspondence, 1912-1916, Box 1, folder 3, *National Urban League Records, 1911-1916*, MS#1466, Columbia University Libraries, Rare Book & Manuscript Library.

412 Bulkley, "Race Prejudice as Viewed from an Economic Standpoint," 1909, 97.

413 "E. E. Pratt to members of NLUCAN, November 2, 1912, Series I: Correspondence, 1912-1916, Box 1, folder 3, *National Urban League Records, 1911-1916*, MS#1466, Columbia University Libraries, Rare Book & Manuscript Library.

414 L. Hollingsworth Wood to George E. Haynes, January 13, 1913, Series I: Correspondence, 1912-1916, Box 1, folder 4, *National Urban League Records, 1911-1916*.

415 George E. Haynes to Mrs. William H. Baldwin, Jr., May 5, 1913, box 55, folder 12, National Urban League "Correspondence," *L. Hollingsworth Wood Papers, 1903-1953*, Ms. Coll. 1175, Special Collections, Haverford College Libraries, Haverford, PA.

416 George E. Haynes to L. Hollingsworth Wood, May 5, 1913, box 55, folder 12,

National Urban League "Correspondence," *L. Hollingsworth Wood Papers, 1903-1953.*

[417] E. E. Pratt to George E. Haynes, March 10, 1913, Series I: Correspondence, 1912-1916, Box 1, folder 3, *National Urban League Records, 1911-1916.*

[418] E. E. Pratt to George E. Haynes, March 18, 1913, Series I: Correspondence, 1912-1916, Box 1, folder 3, *National Urban League Records, 1911-1916.*

[419] Cheryl D. Hicks, *Talk with You Like a Woman: African American Women, Justice, and Reform in New York, 1890-1935* (Chapel Hill: University of North Carolina Press, 2010), 166–69.

[420] L. Hollingsworth Wood to George E. Haynes, October 16, 1913 and George E. Haynes to L. Hollingsworth Wood, November 10, 1913, Series I: Correspondence, 1912-1916, Box 1, folder 4, *National Urban League Records, 1911-1916.*

[421] Parris and Brooks, *Blacks in the City,* 62.

[422] National League on Urban Conditions Among Negroes, "Report 1912-1913; Announcement 1913-1914."

[423] W. E. B. Du Bois, *The Amenia Conference: An Historic Negro Gathering,* Troutbeck Leaflets 8 (Amenia, NY: Troutbeck Press, 1925), 9 and 12, http://www.loc.gov/exhibits/naacp/founding-and-early-years.html#obj25.

[424] Johnson Weldon James, *Along This Way: The Autobiography of James Weldon Johnson* (New York: Penguin Books, 1990), 308–9.

[425] "The Struggle of Life," *Baltimore Afro-American,* March 12, 1910, 6, ProQuest Historical Newspapers.

[426] William L. Bulkley to W. E. B. Du Bois, August 8, 1921, W. E. B. Du Bois Papers, MS 312, Special Collections and University Archives, University of Massachusetts Amherst Libraries, http://credo.library.umass.edu/view/full/mums312-b166-i062.

[427] William L. Bulkley, "As the Candle Burns," letter to the editor, *New York Times,* February 21, 1906, 8, ProQuest Historical Newspapers.

[428] William L. Bulkley to W. E. B. Du Bois, December 22, 1923, W. E. B. Du Bois Papers, MS 312, Special Collections and University Archives, University of Massachusetts Amherst Libraries, http://credo.library.umass.edu/view/full/mums312-b020-i331.

[429] "William L. Bulkley to W. E. B. Du Bois, December 22, 1923."

[430] "Only Negro School Principal Resigns," *Amsterdam News,* August 29, 1923, 7, ProQuest Historical Newspapers.

[431] E. Horace Fitchett, "The Influence of Claflin College on Negro Family Life," *Journal of Negro History* 29, no. 4 (October 1944): 429.

[432] William Bulkley arriving on the *Providence* from Monaco, May 29, 1925, *Providence,* p. 170, line 5, *New York Arriving Passenger and Crew Lists, 1820-1957,* Ancestry.com.

433 William L. Bulkley, death, August 5, 1933, filed August 11, 1933. *Reports of Deaths of American Citizens Abroad, 1835-1974*; General Records of the Department of State; Record Group 59, Entry 205, Box 1460: 1930-1939 France, Bi-Ch., Ancestry.com.

434 "Dr. William L. Bulkley, Retired New York School Principal, Dies in Paris," *New York Age*, September 2, 1933, 1; "W. L. Bulkley, Retired Principal, Dead," *New York Sun*, September 6, 1933, fultonhistory.com.

435 Eben Miller, *Born along the Color Line: The 1933 Amenia Conference and the Rise of a National Civil Rights Movement* (Oxford University Press, 2012).

436 "The Students' Club of Brooklyn Reviewed," *The Broad Ax* (Chicago), December 3, 1904, GenealogyBank.

437 "Future of the Colored Man" *Brooklyn Daily Eagle*, January 25, 1901, Brooklyn Newsstand, New York Public Library.

438 "Future of the Colored Man."

439 "O. G. Villard a Guest of the Students' Club," *Daily Standard Union* (New York, NY), April 29, 1905, 3, fultonhistory.com.

440 Kellogg, *NAACP*, 71.

441 Craig Steven Wilder, *A Covenant with Color: Race and Social Power in Brooklyn 1636-1990* (New York: Columbia University Press, 2000), 148.

442 "Whites to Marry with Negroes," *Rockford Daily Republic* (IL), April 28, 1908, 1, fultonhistory.com.

443 "Police Expect Trouble Over Dinner Given by the Cosmoplitan [*sic*] Club," *Wilkes-Barre Times* (PA), April 29, 1908, 1, GenealogyBank.

444 "Cosmopolitan Society Dinner," *New York Age*, April 30, 1908, fultonhistory.com.

445 "Mixed Dinner Stirs Great Indignations," *Evening News* (Tonawanda, NY), May 22, 1908, fultonhistory.com; "Mixed Dinner Stirs Great Indignations," *Utica Herald Dispatch* (NY), April 29, 1908, fultonhistory.com; Louis R. Harlan, *Booker T. Washington: Volume 2; The Wizard of Tuskegee, 1901-1915* (New York: Oxford University Press, 1983), 376–77.

446 "Dr. and Mrs. William L. Bulkley . . .," *New York Age*, November 28, 1907, fultonhistory.com.

447 William Buckley [*sic*], *1900 US Census*, Brooklyn, Kings County, New York, 7th ward, E.D. 83, sheet 3, household 57, Ancestry.com.

448 William L. Bulkley, *1905 New York State Census*, Brooklyn, Kings, New York, E.D. 18, block A, A.D. 17, p. 5, Ancestry.com.

449 "Ridgefield Park," classified ad, *New York Times*, May 18, 1924, ProQuest Historical Newspapers.

450 George Fosdick, ed., *Ridgefield Park, 1685-1985* (Ridgefield Park, NJ: History Book Committee, 1985), 72, www.ridgefieldpark.org/fil/150C.pdf.

451 *New York Age*, June 21, 1906, fultonhistory.com.

[452] "Sunrise Park. Exceptional Advantages Offered Home Seekers in Englewood, N. J.," *New York Age*, April 30, 1908, 5, fultonhistory.com.

[453] "Lightfoot Mixed Up with Color Line," *Jersey Journal*, March 1, 1910, under "Englewood," ProQuest.

[454] Weldon, *Along This Way: The Autobiography of James Weldon Johnson*, 209.

[455] *New York Age*, July 6, 1911, 7, fultonhistory.com; *New York Age*, September 8, 1910, 7, fultonhistory.com.

[456] William L. Bulkley, April 10, 1917, letter appended to passport application of William L. Bulkley, Jr., certificate 50549, March 2, 1917, National Archives and Records Administration, *U.S. Passport Applications, 1795-1925* Roll 356, Ancestry.com.

[457] E. P. Roberts. *New York State Census.* 1915. New York, New York, A.D. 27, E.D. 5, p. 4, Ancestry.com.

[458] Isabel L. Rhys, *The Education of Girls in Switzerland and Bavaria* (London: Blackie & Son, 1905), 22, http://archive.org/details/educationofgirls00rhysuoft.

[459] "Hélène Monastier," *Wikipédia*, accessed March 12, 2016, https://fr.wikipedia.org/w/index.php?title=H%C3%A9l%C3%A8ne_Monastier&oldid=124268935.

[460] "Bulkley Marooned in Switzerland by War," *New York Age*, September 3, 1914, 1, fultonhistory.com.

[461] *Brooklyn Daily Eagle*, July 24, 1917, 17, fultonhistory.com.

[462] "Give Dance for Lieutenants," *New York Age*, April 27, 1918, 8, fultonhistory.com; "Brooklyn Y. W. C. A.," *New York Age*, November 2, 1918, 2, fultonhistory.com.

[463] "Mrs. King Entertained at Breakfast," *New York Age*, October 4, 1919, 7, fultonhistory.com.

[464] "The Afro-American Investment and Building Company," *The Colored American Magazine* 7, no. 9 (September 1904) classified advertisements preceding title page; "The Afro-American Investment Company," *Colored American Magazine* 9, no. 1 (July 1905): 390.

IX. The Quiet Legacy

[465] A verse from a poem by Henry Wadsworth Longfellow, with edits by William L. Bulkley, *Southwestern Christian Advocate* 28, no. 43 (October 26, 1893): 5, Gale Nineteenth Century U.S. Newspapers.

[466] "St. Mark's Lyceum," *New York Age*, May 7, 1908, 1, fultonhistory.com.

[467] Reginald F. Hildebrand, *The Times Were Strange and Stirring: Methodist Preachers and the Crisis of Emancipation* (Durham: Duke University Press, 1995).

[468] "How it Looks to a Negro," *Charleston News and Courier*, Dec 5, 1888, 5, microfilm, South Caroliniana Library, University of South Carolina.

[469] Bond, *The Education of the Negro in the American Social Order*, 25–26.

[470] "More Trouble over the Color Question," *Indianapolis Recorder*, April 23, 1910, IUPUI University Library, http://ulib.iupui.edu/digitalscholarship/collections/IRecorder.

[471] Heidi Ardizzone, *An Illuminated Life: Belle Da Costa Greene's Journey from Prejudice to Privilege* (New York: W. W. Norton, 2007).

[472] John C. Dancy, *Sand against the Wind: The Memoirs of John C. Dancy.* (Detroit: Wayne State University Press, 1966), 84.

[473] "Schoolma'ams Rebel," *New York Times*, July 3, 1909, 16, ProQuest Historical Newspapers.

[474] "To Protect Civil Rights," *New York Age*, July 26, 1906, 3, fultonhistory.com.

[475] Allyson Hobbs, *A Chosen Exile: A History of Racial Passing in American Life* (Cambridge: Harvard University Press, 2014), 5–6.

[476] Ralph Ellison, "William Bulkley," 1940, Writers' Program, New York City: Negroes of New York Collection, 1936-1941, Roll 5, Schomburg Center, New York Public Library.

[477] Dancy, *Sand against the Wind*, 82.

[478] William L. Bulkley, "Race Prejudice as Viewed from an Economic Standpoint," 92.

[479] Bulkley, 93.

[480] Henry Louis Gates, "'The Talented Tenth' Origins," The African Americans: Many Rivers to Cross, entry posted January 10, 2013, https://www.pbs.org/wnet/african-americans-many-rivers-to-cross/history/who-really-invented-the-talented-tenth/ (accessed January 8, 2022).

[481] W. E. B. Du Bois, "The Talented Tenth," in *The Negro Problem: A Series of Articles by Representative American Negroes of Today* (New York: J. Pott & Company, 1903), 33, http://archive.org/details/negroproblemseri00washrich.

[482] Franklin Frazier, *Black Bourgeoisie* (New York: Collier Books, 1962).

[483] Willard B. Gatewood, *Aristocrats of Color: The Black Elite, 1880-1920* (Fayetteville: University of Arkansas Press, 1990), 203.

[484] Wilder, *A Covenant with Color*, 114.

[485] "Silk Sock Politics Rouses Colored People," *Daily Standard Union* (New York City, NY), May 8, 1902, 2, fultonhistory.com.

[486] Bulkley, "An Evening Industrial School for Adults."

[487] Jack Temple Kirby, *Darkness at the Dawning: Race and Reform in the Progressive South* (Philadelphia: J. B. Lippincott Company, 1972); David W. Southern, *The Progressive Era and Race: Reaction and Reform, 1900 - 1917* (Wiley,

2005); Walter Nugent, *Progressivism: A Very Short Introduction* (New York: Oxford University Press, 2010).

[488] Fairclough, *Better Day Coming*, 70.

[489] Kirby, *Darkness at the Dawning*, 156.

[490] "Claflin University—Report of Committee," *Christian Advocate*, July 7, 1881, 5, ProQuest American Periodicals; "The M. E. Conference," *Columbia State* (SC), Feb 5, 1897, GenealogyBank.

[491] "Lincoln Day Observances," *New York Tribune*, Feb 13, 1899, America's GenealogyBank; Bulkley, "Race Prejudice as Viewed from an Economic Standpoint," 1972.

[492] *Annual Report of the Supervisor of Lectures to the Board of Education.* (New York: Board of Education, 1906), 51, https://catalog.hathitrust.org/Record/000060182; "More Work; Less Talk," *Brooklyn Daily Eagle*, Apr 24, 1903, 6, Brooklyn Newsstand, New York Public Library; "Program Out for Council," *New York Age*, Sep 27, 1906, 6, fultonhistory.com.

[493] "The Struggle of Life," *Baltimore Afro-American*, Mar 12, 1910, 6, ProQuest Historical Newspapers; "Manhattan and Bronx," *New York Age*, July 19, 1906, 6, fultonhistory.com.

[494] "Young's Casino Opens in a Blaze of Glory," *New York Age*, July 25, 1912, Newspapers.com.

[495] "Nation Celebrates 50th Anniversary of the Emancipation Proclamation," *New York Age*, January 9, 1913, 1, fultonhistory.com.

[496] James Weldon Johnson, "Fifty Years (1863-1913)," in *The Book of American Negro Poetry* (New York: Harcourt, Brace and company, 1922), 89, http://archive.org/details/bookofamericanne1922john.

Appendix I: Bulkley's Family

[497] "William Ross Was Recognized Sodium Authority," *The Antiknock* (Baton Rouge, LA)18, no. 2 (February 1956): 2.

[498] Code Commissioner of South Carolina, *Code of Laws of South Carolina, 1912* (Charlottesville, VA: Michie Company, 1912), §3757, v. 1, 1042, http://archive.org/details/codeoflawsofsout01andr.

[499] "Brooklyn Notes," *New York Age*, February 10, 1916, 8, Newspapers.com..

[500] "Give Dance for Lieutenants." *New York Age*, April 27, 1918, fultonhistory.com.

[501] Lillian B. Gulick vs. E. Leeds Gulick, Jr. No. 19479, Washoe County, June 28, 1923, Judgment Roll of the Second Judicial District Court of the State of Nevada.

[502] Lillian Bulkley, photograph albums, private collection. Photographs from the early 1930's show her with Guerin.

[503] Catalogs of Claflin University for 1913-1914 and 1914-1915.

[504] "New Movement for Education," *Indianapolis Recorder*, June 17, 1916, 1, IUPUI University Library, http://ulib.iupui.edu/digitalscholarship/collections/IRecorder .

[505] Dancy, *Sand against the Wind*.

[506] Dancy, 84.

[507] Nancy Page Fernandez, "Biographical Sketch of Cora Catherine Calhoun Horne (Horn), 1865-1932" *Women and Social Movements in the United States, 1600-2000* (Alexander Street, a ProQuest Company, 2018).

[508] "Brooklyn Y. W. C. A.," *New York Age*, November 2, 1918, 2, fultonhistory.com.

[509] Denise de Murcie, email to Peggy W. Norris, "Re: Bulkley," March 11, 2017.

Appendix II. Activist New York Educators

[510] "McDougald-Johnson Wedding," *New York Age*, January 26, 1911, 7, fultonhistory.com.

[511] "Elise Johnson McDougald," in *Wikipedia*, accessed November 10, 2016, https://en.wikipedia.org/wiki/Elise_Johnson_McDougald.

[512] "Name Mrs. Ayer Head of School," *New York Amsterdam News*, January 18, 1936, 1, ProQuest Historical Newspapers.

[513] *Baltimore Afro-American*, February 2, 1935 in scrapbook, Gertrude Elise Ayer Papers, 1931-1966, Schomburg Library, New York Public Library," SC M87-42, microfilm.

[514] "St. Mark's Lyceum," *New York Age*, May 7, 1908, p 1, fultonhistory.com.

[515] Mabee, *Black Education in New York State*, 127.

[516] MacDonald, "Garnet, Sarah J. Smith Tompkins (1831-1911);" Jessie Carney Smith, "Sarah Garnet (1831-1911)," in *Notable Black American Women*, ed. Jessie Carney Smith and Shirelle Phelps (Detroit: Gale Research, 1992), 388–91.

[517] Hallie Q. Brown, *Homespun Heroines and Other Women of Distinction* (New York: Oxford University Press, 1988), 222.

[518] [Susan Elizabeth Frazier] obituary, *New York Age*, February 9, 1924, 1-2, fultonhistory.com; "Women's Auxiliary at Work for Soldiers," *New York Age*, May 17, 1917, 1, fultonhistory.com.

[519] *Proceedings of the National Convention of Colored Men: Held in the City of Syracuse, N.Y.; October 4, 5, 6, and 7, 1864* (Boston: J. S. Rock and Geo. L. Ruffin, 1864) http://coloredconventions.org/items/show/282; Donald Yacovone, *Freedom's Journey: African American Voices of the Civil War* (Chicago Review Press, 2004), 92, books.google.com; Johnson, *Autobiography of Dr. William Henry Johnson*.

520 Jessie Carney Smith, "J. Imogene [*sic*] Howard (1851-19??)," in *Notable Black American Women, Book II*, ed. Jessie Carney Smith (Detroit: Gale Research, 1996), 307–9.

521 "Memorialize Chas. Reason's Death," *New York Age*, August 21, 1943, 12, fultonhistory.com; Scott W. Williams, "Charles L. Reason, African American Mathematician 1818-1893," Mathematicians of the African Diaspora, 2001,
http://www.math.buffalo.edu/mad/special/reason_charles_l.html.

BIBLIOGRAPHY

"A Slave-Boy; Now a Professor." *Success*, April 8, 1899, 33.

"The Afro-American Investment Company." *Colored American Magazine* 9, no. 1 (July 1905): 390.

Alexander, Shawn Leigh. *An Army of Lions: The Civil Rights Struggle Before the NAACP*. Philadelphia: University of Pennsylvania Press, 2013.

Alumni Association of Syracuse University. *Alumni Record and General Catalogue of Syracuse University 1872-99 Including Genesee College, 1852-71 and Geneva Medical College, 1835-72*. Syracuse, NY: Alumni Association of Syracuse University, 1899. http://surface.syr.edu/annals/2.

Annual Report of the Supervisor of Lectures to the Board of Education. New York: Board of Education, 1906. https//catalog.hathitrust.org/Record/000060182.

Ardizzone, Heidi. *An Illuminated Life: Belle Da Costa Greene's Journey from Prejudice to Privilege*. New York: W. W. Norton, 2007.

Arnett, Benjamin William. *The Annual Address Delivered before the Faculty, Students and Friends of Claflin University and the Claflin College of Agriculture and Mechanical Institute, May 22nd, 1889, Orangeburg, S.C.* Columbia, SC: William Sloane, 1889. http://hdl.loc.gov/loc.rbc/lcrbmrp.t0d08.

Ballard, Allen. *One More Day's Journey: The Story of a Family and a People*. New York: McGraw-Hill, 1984.

Berrol, Selma C. "From Compensatory Education to Adult Education: The New York City Evening Schools, 1825-1935." *Adult Education* 26, no. 4 (1976): 208–25.

Bond, Horace Mann. *The Education of the Negro in the American Social Order*. New York: Octagon Books, 1966.

Bonner, Michael Brem, and Fritz Hamer, eds. *South Carolina in the Civil War and Reconstruction Eras: Essays from the Proceedings of the South*

Carolina Historical Association. Columbia: University of South Carolina Press, 2016.

Borg, Kevin L. *Auto Mechanics: Technology and Expertise in Twentieth-Century America*. Baltimore: Johns Hopkins University Press, 2007. https://www.google.com/books/edition/Auto_Mechanics/pudAW mB7dxwC.

Brooklyn Daily Eagle Almanac. New York: Brooklyn Daily Eagle, 1900-1919

Brown, Hallie Q. *Homespun Heroines and Other Women of Distinction*. New York: Oxford University Press, 1988.

Bulkley, V. H. *The Truth about Arkansas*. Sumter, SC: Watchman and Southron Print, 1883.

Bulkley, William L. "As the Candle Burns." *New York Times*, February 21, 1906.

———. [W. L. Buckley], et. al. "Claflin Leadebs [Leaders] Want No Jim Crow." *The State* (Columbia, SC), January 17, 1898, 5.

———. "Economic Analysis of American Prejudice." *Colored American Magazine* 17, no. 1 (July 1909): 17–22.

———. "Education Extension in a Southern Town." *The University Extension Bulletin: A Record of Current University Extension Work* 2, no. 5 (January 31, 1895): 56.

———. "An Evening Industrial School for Adults." *Southern Workman*, October 1906, 540–44.

———. "Fighting Ridicule." *New York Age*, May 31, 1917.

———. "Future of Colored Race: Object Lesson in School Next Door to Where 'The Clansman' Is Playing." *New York Times*, January 11, 1906, 8.

———. "Handicap in City Schools: Noises and Other Distractions Reduce Degree of Mental Application." *New York Times*, March 25, 1906, 8.

———. "How It Looks to a Negro" *Charleston News and Courier*, December 5, 1888, 5.

———. "The Industrial Condition of the Negro in New York City." In *The Industrial Condition of the Negro in the North*, 128–34. Publications of the American Academy of Political and Social Science 498. Philadelphia: American Academy of Political and Social Science, 1906.

———. "The Negro and the Future." *The Colored American Magazine* 10, no. 5 (1906): 313.

———. "Our Foreign Letter." *Southwestern Christian Advocate* 28, nos. 31, 33-44, 47 (1893) and *Southwestern Christian Advocate* 29, nos. 24 and 31 (1894).

———. *Our Race as We See It: An Address Delivered at Orangeburg, S.C., January 1st, 1890, in Claflin University Chapel*. Orangeburg, SC: Berry & Howell, 1890.

———. "Prof W. L. Bulkley, of Claflin University." In "The Negro on the Stand: Testimony from Colored Men about the Exodus." *Charleston News and Courier*, February 2, 1890, 2.

———. "A Quarter Century Well Spent." *Christian Advocate* 74 (March 9, 1899): 348.

———. "A Question of Chivalry." *State* (Columbia, SC). February 13, 1897.

———. "Race Prejudice as Viewed from an Economic Standpoint." In *Proceedings of the National Negro Conference 1909, New York, May 31 and June 1*, 89–97. [New York], 1909. http://archive.org/details/proceedingsof00nati.

———. "The School as a Social Center." In *The Negro in the Cities of the North*, 76–78. New York: The Charity Organization Society, 1905.

———. "Some Results of Emancipation: Address by Professor William L. Bulkley." *New York Tribune*, February 13, 1899.

———. "Training the Voters of Tomorrow." *The A.M.E. Church Review*, August 30, 1913, 35.

———. "A Voice from the South." *The Wesleyan Argus*, February 15, 1890, 95–96.

Cardozo, J. W. [I.N.]. "Prof. De Treville's Murderous Assault on Prof. Cardozo at Claflin University, Orangeburg, S. C." *Southwestern Christian Advocate* 25, no. 14 (April 3, 1890): 4.

Carle, Susan D. *Defining the Struggle: National Racial Justice Organizing, 1880-1915*. New York: Oxford University Press, 2013.

Catalogue of Claflin University, 1881-1900.

Chaddock, Katherine Reynolds. *Uncompromising Activist: Richard Greener, First Black Graduate of Harvard College*. Baltimore: Johns Hopkins University Press, 2017.

Chandler, Susan Kerr. "'Almost a Partnership': African Americans, Segregation, and the Young Men's Christian Association." *Journal of Sociology & Social Welfare* 21, no. 1 (March 1994): 97.

Charity Organization Society. "Report of the Committee on the Prevention of Tuberculosis of the Charity Organization Society for the Year 1903-1904." In *A Handbook on the Prevention of Tuberculosis*, 9. New York: Charity Organization Society, 1903. https://www.google.com/books/edition/A_Handbook_on_the_Prevention_of_Tubercul/VRk1AQAAMAAJ.

Code Commissioner of South Carolina. *Code of Laws of South Carolina, 1912*. Charlottesville, VA: Michie Company, 1912. http://archive.org/details/codeoflawsofsout01andr.

Crummell, Alexander. *Civilization the Primal Need of the Race, and The Attitude of the American Mind Toward the Negro Intellect*. The American Negro Academy Occasional Paper No. 3. Washington, DC: The American Negro Academy, 1898. https://www.gutenberg.org/ebooks/31268.

Curts, Lewis. *The General Conferences of the Methodist Episcopal Church, from 1792 to 1896*. Cincinnati: Curts & Jennings, 1900. https://www.google.com/books/edition/The_General_Conferences_of_the_Methodist/3GZKAAAAMAAJ.

Dancy, John C. *Sand against the Wind: The Memoirs of John C. Dancy*. Detroit: Wayne State University Press, 1966.

De Forest, John William. *A Union Officer in the Reconstruction*. Edited by James H. Croushore and David Morris Potter. Baton Rouge: Louisiana State University Press, 1997.

Dixon, Robert S. "Education of the Negro in the City of New York, 1853 to 1900." MS thesis, City College of New York, 1935. Schomburg Center, New York Public Library.

Dodson, N. Barnett. "Carlton Avenue Branch of the Brooklyn, N. Y., Young Men's Christian Association." *The Colored American Magazine* 7 (1904): 117.

Du Bois, W. E. B. *Against Racism: Unpublished Essays, Papers, Addresses, 1887-1961*. Amherst: University of Massachusetts Press, 1985.

———. "Education and Work." *The Journal of Negro Education* 1, no. 1 (1932): 60–74. https://doi.org/10.2307/2292016.

———. *The Amenia Conference: An Historic Negro Gathering*. Troutbeck Leaflets 8. Amenia, NY: Troutbeck Press, 1925. https://www.loc.gov/exhibits/naacp/founding-and-early-years.html.

———. *The Philadelphia Negro: A Social Study*. Publications of the University of Pennsylvania. Series in Political Economy and Public Law 14. Philadelphia: University of Pennsylvania, 1899.

———. "The Talented Tenth." In *The Negro Problem: A Series of Articles by Representative American Negroes of Today*, 31–75. New York: J. Pott & Company, 1903. http://archive.org/details/negroproblemseri00washrich.

Ellison, Ralph. "William Bulkley," 1940. Writers' Program, New York City: Negroes of New York Collection, 1936-1941, Roll 5. Schomburg Center, New York Public Library.

Fairclough, Adam. *Better Day Coming: Blacks and Equality, 1890-2000*. New York: Viking, 2001.

Fay, T. C. *Charleston Directory, and Strangers' Guide, for 1840 and 1841*. Charleston, S. C.: T. C. Fay, 1840.

Fitchett, E. Horace. "The Free Negro in Charleston, South Carolina." PhD diss., University of Chicago, 1950.

———. "The Influence of Claflin College on Negro Family Life." *Journal of Negro History* 29, no. 4 (October 1944): 429.

———. "The Role of Claflin College in Negro Life in South Carolina." *Journal of Negro Education* 12 (Winter 1943): 42–68.

"For Economic Regeneration." *Colored American Magazine* 11, no. 1 (July 1906): 10–11.

"For the Negroes in New York." *Charities and the Commons* 17, no. 2 (October 13, 1906): 109.

Fosdick, George, ed. *Ridgefield Park, 1685-1985*. Ridgefield Park, NJ: History Book Committee, 1985. www.ridgefieldpark.org/fil/150C.pdf.

Frazier, Franklin. *Black Bourgeoisie*. New York: Collier Books, 1962.

Freedmen's Aid Society Records, 1866-1932. United Methodist Archives and History Center, Drew University, Madison, NJ.

Galpin, W. Freeman. *Syracuse University: The Growing Years*. Syracuse: Syracuse University Press, 1960.

———. *Syracuse University: The Pioneer Days*. Syracuse: Syracuse University Press, 1952.

Gatewood, Willard B. *Aristocrats of Color: The Black Elite, 1880-1920*. Fayetteville: University of Arkansas Press, 1990.

Geiger, Roger L. *The History of American Higher Education: Learning and Culture from the Founding to World War II*. Princeton: Princeton University Press, 2015.

George Edmund Haynes Collection. Special Collections and Archives, Fisk University Library.

Gertrude Elise Ayer Papers, 1931-1966. SC M87-42. New York Public Library.

Glover, Vivian. *Men of Vision: Claflin College and Her Presidents*. Orangeburg, SC: Claflin College, 1995.

Gore, Blinzy L. *On a Hilltop High: The Origin and History of Claflin College to 1984*. Spartanburg, SC: The Reprint Company, 1993.

Hagood, L. M. [Lewis M.]. *The Colored Man in the Methodist Episcopal Church*. Cincinnati: Cranston & Stowe, 1890. https://archive.org/details/coloredmaninmeth00hagoiala.

Hane, Bobb. "African-American History Clashes with Library's Parking." *Star Reporter*. November 17, 1994. Walker Local and Family History Center, Richland (SC) Library.

Harlan, Louis R. *Booker T. Washington: Volume 2; The Wizard of Tuskegee, 1901-1915*. New York: Oxford University Press, 1983.

Haynes, George Edmund. "The Birth and Childhood of the National Urban League." Typescript, 1960. National Urban League records. Box I:E29. Manuscript Division, Library of Congress.

———. *The Negro at Work in New York City: A Study in Economic Progress*. New York: Columbia University, 1912. http://www.gutenberg.org/ebooks/24712.

Helsley, Alexia Jones. *Beaufort: A History*. Charleston, SC: The History Press, 2005.

Hicks, Cheryl D. *Talk with You Like a Woman: African American Women, Justice, and Reform in New York, 1890-1935*. Chapel Hill: University of North Carolina Press, 2010.

Hildebrand, Reginald F. *The Times Were Strange and Stirring: Methodist Preachers and the Crisis of Emancipation*. Durham: Duke University Press, 1995.

Hobbs, Allyson. *A Chosen Exile: A History of Racial Passing in American Life*. Cambridge: Harvard University Press, 2014.

Huff, Archie Vernon, Jr. *Greenville: The History of the City and County in the South Carolina Piedmont*. Columbia: University of South Carolina Press, 1995.

Huggins, Nathan, ed. *W. E. B. Du Bois: Writings*. New York: Library of America, 1986. https://www.loa.org/books/39-writings.

Ingram, E. Renee. *In View of the Great Want of Labor: A Legislative History of African American Conscription in the Confederacy*. Westminster, MD: Willow Bend Books, 2002.

James Graham Phelps Stokes Papers, 1779-1960. MS#1207. Rare Book and Manuscript Library, Columbia University Libraries.

Johnson, James Weldon. *Along This Way: The Autobiography of James Weldon Johnson*. New York: Penguin Books, 1990.

———. "Fifty Years (1863-1913)." In *The Book of American Negro Poetry*. New York: Harcourt, Brace and Company, 1922. http://archive.org/details/bookofamericanne1922john.

Johnson, Michael P. *Black Masters: A Free Family of Color in the Old South*. New York: W. W. Norton & Company, 1986.

Johnson, William Henry. *Autobiography of Dr. William Henry Johnson*. Albany: Argus Company, 1900. http://archive.org/details/tohisadoptedhome00johnrich.

Jones, Angela. *African American Civil Rights: Early Activism and the Niagara Movement*. Santa Barbara: Praeger, 2011.

Justesen, Benjamin Ray. "The National Afro-American Council: Towards a New Interpretation." PhD diss., Union Institute and University, 2011.

Kelley, Blair L. M. *Right to Ride: Streetcar Boycotts and African American Citizenship in the Era of Plessy v. Ferguson*. Chapel Hill: University of North Carolina Press, 2010.

Kellogg, Charles. *NAACP: A History of the National Association for the Advancement of Colored People*. Baltimore: Johns Hopkins Press, 1967.

Kellor, Frances A. "Associations for Protection of Colored Women." *Colored American Magazine* 9, no. 6 (December 1905): 695–99.

———. *Out of Work: A Study of Unemployment*. New York: Putnam, 1915. http://archive.org/details/outofworkstudyof00kelluoft.

Kirby, Jack Temple. *Darkness at the Dawning: Race and Reform in the Progressive South*. Philadelphia: J. B. Lippincott Company, 1972.

Koger, Larry. *Black Slaveowners: Free Black Slave Masters in South Carolina, 1790-1860*. Columbia: University of South Carolina Press, 1985.

L. Hollingsworth Wood Papers, 1903-1953, Ms. Coll. 1175. Special Collections, Haverford College Libraries.

Lewis, David Levering. *W. E. B. Du Bois, 1868-1919: Biography of a Race*. New York: Henry Holt and Company, 1994.

———. *W. E. B. Du Bois, 1919-1963: The Fight for Equality and the American Century*. New York: Henry Holt and Company, 2001.

Mabee, Carleton. *Black Education in New York State: From Colonial to Modern Times*. Syracuse, NY: Syracuse University Press, 1979.

Mangum, Claude J. "Afro-American Thought on the New York City Public School System, 1905-1954: An Analysis of New York City Afro-American Newspaper Editorials." PhD diss., Teachers College, Columbia University, 1976.

Mary White Ovington Collection. Archives of Labor and Urban Affairs. Wayne State University.

Matkin-Rawn, Story. "'The Great Negro State of the Country': Arkansas's Reconstruction and the Other Great Migration." *The Arkansas Historical Quarterly* 72, no. 1 (Spring 2013): 1–41.

McKinley, Carlyle. *An Appeal to Pharaoh; the Negro Problem, and Its Radical Solution*. New York: Fords, Howard & Hulbert, 1889. http://archive.org/details/anappealtophara01mckigoog.

McPherson, James M. *The Abolitionist Legacy: From Reconstruction to the NAACP*. Princeton University Press, 1995.

"Meeting for Negro Improvement." *Colored American Magazine* 11, no. 5 (November 1906): 286.

Meriwether, Colyer and Edward McCrady. *History of Higher Education in South Carolina: With a Sketch of the Free School System*. Washington, DC: Government Printing Office, 1889. https://www.google.com/books/edition/History_of_Higher_Education_in_South_Car/XK2gAAAAMAAJ.

Methodist Episcopal Church. General Conference. *Journals of the General Conference of the Methodist Episcopal Church. Volume I. 1796-1836*. New York: Carlton & Phillips, 1855. http://archive.org/details/journalsofgenera01meth.

Middleton, J. B. "Memoir [Rev. Vincent Henry Bulkley]." In *Minutes of the Eightieth Session of the South Carolina Annual Conference of the Methodist Episcopal Church for 1886*, 20–21. Florence, SC: Methodist Episcopal Church, 1887.

Miller, Eben. *Born along the Color Line: The 1933 Amenia Conference and the Rise of a National Civil Rights Movement.* New York: Oxford University Press, 2012.

Milteer, Warren Eugene Jr. *Beyond Slavery's Shadow: Free People of Color in the South.* Chapel Hill: University of North Carolina Press, 2021.

Monroe, Rev. David S., ed. *Journal of the General Conference of the Methodist Episcopal Church Held in Cleveland, Ohio, May 1-28, 1896.* New York: Eaton & Mains, 1896. https://www.google.com/books/edition/Journal_of_the_General_Conference_of_the/ad4pAAAAYAAJ.

Moore, Jesse Thomas, Jr. *A Search for Equality: The National Urban League, 1910-1961.* University Park: Pennsylvania State University Press, 1981.

Mounter, Michael Robert. "Richard Theodore Greener : The Idealist, Statesman, Scholar and South Carolinian." PhD diss., University of South Carolina, 2002.

NAACP: A Century in the Fight for Freedom; Founding and Early Years. Library of Congress. https://www.loc.gov/exhibits/naacp/founding-and-early-years.html

National Association for the Advancement of Colored People. *Annual Reports, 1910-1916.* New York: The Association. http://catalog.hathitrust.org/Record/006784887.

National League on Urban Conditions Among Negroes. "Report 1912-1913; Announcement 1913-1914." http://catalog.hathitrust.org/Record/100569911.

National Negro Conference. *Proceedings of the National Negro Conference 1909, New York, May 31 and June 1.* New York, 1909. http://archive.org/details/proceedingsof00nati.

National Urban League: 40th Anniversary Year Book, 1950. [New York?]: National Urban League, 1950.

National Urban League Records, 1911-1916. Rare Book and Manuscript Library, Columbia University Libraries.

"Negroes in New York." *The Survey: Social, Charitable, Civic; a Journal of Constructive Philanthropy* 23 (October 2, 1909): 5.

New York. *Laws of the State of New York Passed at the One Hundred and Seventh Session of the Legislature.* Albany: Banks & Brothers, 1884. https://books.google.com/books?id=D3M4AAAAIAAJ.

New York City Board of Education. *Journal of the Board of Education of the City of New York*. New York: Wm. C. Bryant & Company, 1906.

New York City Board of Education, Bureau of Finance. *Annual Financial and Statistical Report, 1906-1908: Appendix, Real Estate Data*. Identifier: boe_1908_report, Collection: BOE: Board of Education. https://nycma.lunaimaging.com/luna/servlet/detail/RECORDSPH OTOUNITARC~33~33~1243157~1210814:boe_1908_report.

Norrell, Robert J. *Up from History: The Life of Booker T. Washington*. Cambridge: Harvard University Press, 2011.

Nugent, Walter. *Progressivism: A Very Short Introduction*. New York: Oxford University Press, 2010.

Osofsky, Gilbert. *Harlem: The Making of a Ghetto; Negro New York, 1890-1930*. 2nd ed. Chicago: Ivan R. Dee, 1996.

Ovington, Mary White. *Black and White Sat Down Together: The Reminiscences of an NAACP Founder*. New York: Feminist Press at the City University of New York, 1995.

———. "How the National Association for the Advancement of Colored People Began." *Crisis* 8, no. 4 (August 1914): 184.

———. "The Negro in the Trades Unions in New York." *Annals of the American Academy of Political and Social Science* 27 (May 1, 1906): 551–58.

Parris, Guichard, and Lester Brooks. *Blacks in the City: A History of the National Urban League*. Boston: Little Brown, 1971.

Potts, David B. *Wesleyan University, 1831–1910: Collegiate Enterprise in New England*. Middletown, CT: Wesleyan University Press, 1999.

Powers, Bernard. *Black Charlestonians: A Social History, 1822-1885*. Fayetteville: University of Arkansas Press, 1994.

Proceedings of the National Convention of Colored Men: Held in the City of Syracuse, N.Y.; October 4, 5, 6, and 7, 1864. Boston: J. S. Rock and Geo. L. Ruffin, 1864. http://coloredconventions.org/items/show/282.

"Prof. Wm. Lewis Bulkley." In *Progress of a Race: The Remarkable Advancement of the Afro-American Negro*, 491–94. Atlanta: J. L. Nichols & Co., 1897.

Psychas, George. "William L. Bulkley and the New York Negro, 1890-1910." *Historical Journal of Western Massachusetts* 1, no. 1 (Spring, 1972): 5-18.

"Public Evening Industrial Schools." *Charities and the Commons* 18 (1907): 199–200.

Ravitch, Diane. *The Great School Wars: New York City, 1805-1973; A History of the Public Schools as Battlefield of Social Change.* New York: Basic Books, 1974.

Records of the New York City Board of Education. New York City Department of Records, Municipal Archives.

Rhodes, E. M. "A New Opportunity for Women." *Colored American Magazine* 10, no. 1 (January 1906): 25.

Rhys, Isabel L. *The Education of Girls in Switzerland and Bavaria.* London: Blackie & Son, 1905
http://archive.org/details/educationofgirls00rhysuoft.

Ronnick, Michele Valerie. "Black Classicism: 'Tell Them We Are Rising.'" *Classical Journal* 106 (2011): 359–70.

———. *Twelve African American Members of the Society for Classical Studies: The First Five Decades, 1875-1925.* New York: Society for Classical Studies, 2018.

Scarborough, William Sanders. *Autobiography of William Sanders Scarborough: An American Journey from Slavery to Scholarship.* Edited by Michele Valerie Ronnick. Detroit: Wayne State University Press, 2005.

Scarborough, William Sanders, and Michele Valerie Ronnick. *The Works of William Sanders Scarborough: Black Classicist and Race Leader.* New York: Oxford University Press, 2006.

Scheiner, Seth M. *Negro Mecca: A History of the Negro in New York City, 1865-1920.* New York: New York University Press, 1965.

Segrave, Kerry. *Lynchings of Women in the United States: The Recorded Cases, 1851-1946.* Jefferson, NC: McFarland, 2010.

Smalley, Frank, and Lewis M. Dunton. "Dr. W. L. Bulkley." *Southwestern Christian Advocate* 28, no. 34 (August 24, 1893): 4.

South Carolina General Assembly. *Reports and Resolutions of the General Assembly of the State of South Carolina.* Columbia: Charles A. Calvo, Jr., 1884.
http://books.google.com/books?id=wmwbAQAAIAAJ&dq.

Southern, David W. *The Progressive Era and Race: Reaction and Reform, 1900 - 1917.* Wheeling, IL: H. Davidson, 2005.

Steward, Theophilus Gould. *The Colored Regulars in the United States Army.* Philadelphia: A. M. E. Book Concern, 1904. http://archive.org/details/coloredregularsi02stew.

Svonkin, Stuart G. "The Pluralistic Ideal at Wesleyan: Wesleyan's Orientation toward Race, Class, Gender, and Religion within the Student Body, 1870-1970." BA Honors Thesis, Wesleyan University, 1989. Special Collections, Olin Library, Wesleyan University.

"Term Examination Ending March 1877." University of South Carolina Reconstruction Records, University of South Carolina Archives, Digital Collections. http://digital.tcl.sc.edu/cdm/ref/collection/reconstruct/id/24.

Tindall, George Brown. *South Carolina Negroes: 1877-1900.* Southern Classics Series. Columbia: University of South Carolina Press, 2003.

Union University. *Catalogue of the Living Alumni of Union College.* Schenectady: C. Burrows, 1887. http://archive.org/details/catalogueoflivin00unio.

United States Office of Education. *Annual Report of the Commissioner of Education.* Washington, DC: Government Printing Office, 1880.

Upchurch, Thomas Adams. *Legislating Racism: The Billion Dollar Congress and the Birth of Jim Crow.* Lexington: University Press of Kentucky, 2004.

Van Kleeck, Mary. *Working Girls in Evening Schools: A Statistical Study.* Russel Sage Foundation Study. New York: Survey Associates, 1914. http://archive.org/details/workinggirlsinev00vank.

W. E. B. Du Bois Papers, MS 312. Special Collections and University Archives, University of Massachusetts Amherst Libraries.

Walling, William English. "The Race War in the North." *The Independent* 65, no. 3118 (September 3, 1908): 529.

Washington, Booker T. *Booker T. Washington Papers.* Edited by Louis R. Harlan. Urbana: University of Illinois Press, 1979.

Weiss, Nancy. *The National Urban League, 1910-1940.* New York: Oxford University Press, 1974.

Wesleyan University (Middletown, CT). *Catalogue.* http://hdl.handle.net/2027/mdp.39015064435228.

———. "Wesleyan University: A Brief History." Accessed July 23, 2013. http://www.wesleyan.edu/about/uhistory.html.

Wikramanayake, Marina. *A World in Shadow: The Free Black in Antebellum South Carolina*. Tricentennial Studies 7. Columbia: University of South Carolina Press, 1973.

Wilder, Craig Steven. *A Covenant with Color: Race and Social Power in Brooklyn 1636-1990*. New York: Columbia University Press, 2000.

Wilkerson, Isabel. *The Warmth of Other Suns: The Epic Story of America's Great Migration*. New York: Random House, 2010.

"Work of the Committee for Improving the Industrial Condition of Negroes in New York." *Colored American Magazine* 12 (June 1907): 459–64.

World's Sunday-School Convention. *The World's Sunday-School Convention, Held in the Congregational Memorial Hall and City Temple, London: A Complete Record of Its Proceedings Day by Day, July 1 to 6, 1889*. New York: F. H. Revell, 1889. http://www.archive.org/details/worldssundayscho00worl.

Wright, Samuel Hart, and Archibald Edward Miller. *Miller's Planters' & Merchants' State Rights Almanac, for the Year of Our Lord 1862*. A.E. Miller, 1861. http://archive.org/details/460659992.3827.emory.edu.

Yacovone, Donald. *Freedom's Journey: African American Voices of the Civil War*. Chicago: Chicago Review Press, 2004. https://www.google.com/books/edition/Freedom_s_Journey/QwK MLC3_blkC.

Young Men's Christian Associations of Brooklyn and Queens. *Fifty Years in Brooklyn, 1853-1903*. Brooklyn Young Men's Christian Association, 1903

ILLUSTRATION CREDITS

Page

viii *National Urban League: 40ᵗʰ Anniversary Year Book, 1950.* [New York?]: National Urban League, 1950, p. 10.

xviii Upper: *Fifty Years in Brooklyn, 1853-1903.* Brooklyn Young Men's Christian Association, 1903, p. 63. Courtesy of HathiTrust. https://catalog.hathitrust.org/Record/008924884.

xviii Lower: private collection.

23 Upper: "Wesleyan University." *Scribner's Monthly,* 12 (1876): 649.

23 Lower: "Wesleyan University." *Scribner's Monthly,* 12 (1876): 654.

24 Upper: "London. Mansion House" London: E. B. Horwood & Co., postcard.

24 Lower: "Le Palais de[s] Beaux-Arts, Exposition Universelle, Paris France." Paris, 1889. Photograph, Library of Congress Prints and Photographs Division. www.loc.gov/item/2001698574/.

44 Upper: *Catalogue of Claflin University, Orangeburg, S. C., 1897-1898.* Orangeburg: R. Lewis Berry, 1898, 78, *Internet Archive.* https://archive.org/details/annualcatalog8998claf.

44 Lower: Claflin University Chapel, interior, *Catalogue of Claflin University College of Agriculture and Mechanics' Institute, 1892-1893.* Orangeburg: Berry & Howell, 1893, 47. *Internet Archive.* https://archive.org/details/annualcatalog8998claf.

62 *Proceedings of the Convention of Southern Governors, Held in the City of Richmond, Virginia, on April 12th and 13th, 1893.* Richmond, VA: C. N. Williams, 1893, following p. 60. https://www.google.com/books/edition/Proceedings_of_the_Convention _of_Souther/NragFQLQgWIC.

76 Upper: "Hall of Languages, Syracuse University, Syracuse N. Y." New York: Illustrated Postal Card Co.

76 Lower: "W.L. Bulkley. A Noble Example of the Triumph of Perserverance [sic]" Digital Collections. General Research Division, The New York Public Library. From "A Slave-boy; Now a Professor." *Success* (April 8, 1899): 33. https://digitalcollections.nypl.org/items/88c63f33-0840-e37b-e040-e00a18067a92.

77 Upper: "Delftsche Poort, Groeten uit Rotterdam." J. G. Vileger, Rotterdam, briefkaart.

77 Lower: Heidelberg, seen from the Hirschgasse, Baden, Germany, ca. 1890. Photograph, Library of Congress Prints and Photographs Division. www.loc.gov/item/2002713583/.

78 Upper: Strasbourg University main building around 1900, digital image. Snapshots of the Past. Creative Commons Attribution-Share Alike 2.0 Generic license. https://commons.wikimedia.org/wiki/File:Strasbourg_University_main_building_around_1900.jpg.

78 Lower: "Cour de la Sorbonne, à Paris" from V. A. Malte-Brun. La France illustrée. Paris: Rouff et Cie, 1881.

100 Upper: PS 80, New York City Board of Education, Bureau of Finance, *Annual Financial and Statistical Report, 1906-1908: Appendix, Real Estate Data*, New York City Board of Education (Identifier: boe_1908_report, Collection: BOE: Board of Education), p. 37. https://nycma.lunaimaging.com/luna/servlet/detail/RECORDSPHOTOUNITARC~33~33~1243157~1210814:boe_1908_report.

100 Lower: PS 125, New York City Board of Education, Bureau of Finance, *Annual Financial and Statistical Report, 1906-1908: Appendix, Real Estate Data*, p. 54.

101 Upper: PS 67, New York City Board of Education, Bureau of Finance, *Annual Financial and Statistical Report, 1906-1908: Appendix, Real Estate Data*, p.31.

101 Lower: Cooking Class, PS 67 Evening School, Board of Education Collection, Courtesy of the Municipal Archives, City of New York.

102 Upper: Tailoring Class, PS 67 Evening School, Board of Education Collection, Courtesy of the Municipal Archives, City of New York.

102 Lower: Steamfitting and Boilermaking Class, PS 67 Evening School, Board of Education Collection, Courtesy of the Municipal Archives, City of New York.

123 Upper: E. Chickerings [Elmer Chickering] (photographer), *Niagara Movement delegates, Boston, Mass., 1907.* W. E. B. Du Bois Papers (MS 312), Special Collections and University Archives, UMass Amherst Libraries. http://credo.library.umass.edu/view/full/mums312-i0402.

123 Lower: "Group portrait of men and women attending the NAACP sponsored Amenia Conference in Amenia, N.Y., Aug. 24-26, 1916." Library of Congress, Prints and Photographs Division, Visual Materials from the NAACP Records, LC-DIG-ds-13564.

153 Upper: "Directors of the Afro-American Investment and Building Co., Brooklyn, N. Y." in *The Negro in Business* (Boston: Hertel, Jenkins & Co., 1907) facing p. 201. Schomburg Center for Research in Black Culture, Jean Blackwell Hutson Research and Reference Division, The New York Public Library Digital Collections. https://digitalcollections.nypl.org/items/7f31d42a-6082-f1a9-e040-e00a18064e97.

153 Lower: 826 Lafayette Avenue, Brooklyn (Block 1792, Lot 40). *DOF: Brooklyn 1940s Tax Photo*s, nynyma_rec0040_3_01792_0040, Municipal Archives, City of New York.

154 Upper: private collection.

154 Lower: "Frank White Park, Ridgefield Park, N. J." Germany: Mergler & Stephens, postcard.

155 Upper: Promenade des Anglais, "Nice — Le Casino de la Jettée et la Promenade des Anglais." From *Nice 20 Photographies*, Editions A. Noyer, Paris.

155 Lower: private collection.

GENERAL INDEX

233

NAME INDEX

ABOUT THE AUTHOR

Peggy W. Norris, a retired reference librarian, has a BA degree in English from the College of Wooster and an MS and MLS from Rutgers University. During her career as a reference librarian, she became interested in history told through genealogical records, newspapers, and archives. These tell stories about ordinary men and women, as well as that of extraordinary men like Bulkley. Her liberal arts education, professional experience, and life-long interest in American history prepared her for finding and telling William L. Bulkley's story. Her other research projects include the multiracial community at Huyler's Landing in Bergen County, NJ, the origins of freedom for the Bulkley family, and study of quilts to illuminate the history of women in the nineteenth and twentieth centuries.

www.ingramcontent.com/pod-product-compliance
Lightning Source LLC
Chambersburg PA
CBHW020226130626
46549CB00005B/1764

* 9 7 9 8 9 8 5 8 4 2 4 0 1 *